Beginning Analysis

How does a psychoanalysis begin? What goes on when analyst and prospective analysand meet for the first time, and what processes are activated to make the project for an analysis possible?

This unique contribution to the surprisingly sparse literature on this most essential aspect of the psychoanalytical practitioner's work, is the clinical companion to *Initiating Psychoanalysis: Perspectives*, also part of the 'Teaching' Series of the New Library of Psychoanalysis. Replete with clinical illustrations, this book is based on the findings of an ambitious research project on first interviews carried out from 2004 to 2016 by an international group of psychoanalysts, the Working Party on Initiating Psychoanalysis (WPIP) of the European Psychoanalytic Federation. The authors, all members of the Investigative Team, are senior psychoanalysts from member societies of the European Psychoanalytic Federation, all with extensive experience in the practice and teaching of psychoanalytic consultation.

Psychoanalysts and analytic therapists, in particular those in training or setting up their practice, will find *Beginning Analysis* to be essential reading in deepening their understanding of how analysand and analyst arrive at the decision to begin analysis.

Authors: Bernard Reith, Mette Møller, John Boots, Penelope Crick, Alain Gibeault, Ronny Jaffè, Sven Lagerlöf, and Rudi Vermote.

THE NEW LIBRARY OF PSYCHOANALYSIS TEACHING SERIES

General Editor: Alessandra Lemma

The New Library of Psychoanalysis was launched in 1987 in association with the Institute of Psychoanalysis, London. It took over from the International Psychoanalytical Library which published many of the early translations of the works of Freud and the writings of most of the leading British and Continental psychoanalysts. The purpose of the New Library of Psychoanalysis is to facilitate a greater and more widespread appreciation of psychoanalysis and to provide a forum for increasing mutual understanding between psychoanalysts and those working in other disciplines such as the social sciences, medicine, philosophy, history, linguistics, literature and the arts. It aims to represent different trends both in British psychoanalysis and in psychoanalysis generally. The New Library of Psychoanalysis is well placed to make available to the English-speaking world psychoanalytic writings from other European countries and to increase the interchange of ideas between British and American psychoanalysts.

Through the *Teaching* subseries, the New Library of Psychoanalysis publishes books that provide comprehensive, yet accessible, overviews of selected subject areas aimed at those studying psychoanalysis and related fields such as the social sciences, philosophy, literature and the arts.

For a full list of all the titles in the New Library of Psychoanalysis main series and the New Library of Psychoanalysis 'Beyond the Couch' subseries, please visit the Routledge website.

TITLES IN THE NEW LIBRARY OF PSYCHOANALYSIS TEACHING SERIES

Reading Freud: A Chronological Exploration of Freud's Writings Jean-Michel Quinodoz
Listening to Hanna Segal: Her Contribution to Psychoanalysis Jean-Michel Quinodoz
Reading French Psychoanalysis Edited by Dana Birksted-Breen, Sara Flanders and Alain Gibeault
Reading Winnicott Lesley Caldwell and Angela Joyce
Initiating Psychoanalysis: Perspectives Bernard Reith, Sven Lagerlöf, Penelope Crick, Mette Møller and Elisabeth Skale
Infant Observation Frances Salo
Reading Anna Freud Nick Midgley
Reading Italian Psychoanalysis Edited by Franco Borgogno, Alberto Luchetti and Luisa Marino Coe
Reading Klein Margaret Rustin and Michael Rustin
Beginning Analysis: On the Processes of Initiating Psychoanalysis Bernard Reith, Mette Møller, John Boots, Penelope Crick, Alain Gibeault, Ronny Jaffè, Sven Lagerlöf, and Rudi Vermote

THE NEW LIBRARY OF PSYCHOANALYSIS:
TEACHING SERIES

General Editor: Alessandra Lemma

Beginning Analysis

On the Processes of Initiating Psychoanalysis

Bernard Reith, Mette Møller, John Boots,
Penelope Crick, Alain Gibeault, Ronny Jaffè,
Sven Lagerlöf, and Rudi Vermote

Routledge
Taylor & Francis Group
LONDON AND NEW YORK

First published 2018
by Routledge
2 Park Square, Milton Park, Abingdon, Oxon OX14 4RN

and by Routledge
711 Third Avenue, New York, NY 10017

Routledge is an imprint of the Taylor & Francis Group, an informa business

British Library Cataloguing in Publication Data
A catalogue record for this book is available from the British Library

Library of Congress Cataloging in Publication Data
A catalog record has been requested for this book

ISBN: 978-1-138-57927-9 (hbk)
ISBN: 978-1-138-57928-6 (pbk)
ISBN: 978-1-351-26236-1 (ebk)

Typeset in Bembo
by Swales & Willis Ltd, Exeter, Devon, UK

CONTENTS

Notes on the authors vi

Foreword viii
David Tuckett

Acknowledgements xiii

1 Introduction: how and why do people enter psychoanalysis? 1

2 Are you an analyst, Ma'am? Overview of the clinical issues with an example of a case study 9

3 The lens we looked through: exploring a method for qualitative clinical research in psychoanalysis 22

4 Analysts being analysts: the group exploratory method in action 40

5 Facing the storm and creating psychoanalytic space: the vicissitudes of the analytic couple in first interviews 62

6 The opening scene: from anticipation to initiation 88

7 Different beginnings 104

8 Initiating psychoanalysis in institutional settings 127

9 Countertransference and enactment 150

10 Where are we now? 170

Appendices 183
References 192
Case index 202
General index 203

NOTES ON THE AUTHORS

Bernard Reith is a Psychoanalyst in private practice in Geneva, a Training Analyst and Chair of the Committee for Research in Psychoanalysis of the Swiss Psychoanalytical Society, Co-Chair for Europe of the IPA Working Parties Committee and a Board Member of the Analyst at Work Section of the *International Journal of Psychoanalysis*.

Mette Møller is a Psychoanalyst in private practice in Copenhagen, a Training Analyst and former Chair of the Consultation Service of the Danish Psychoanalytic Society.

John Boots is a Child and Family Psychiatrist and Psychoanalyst in private practice in Sydney, a Training and Supervising Analyst and past President of the Australian Psychoanalytical Society.

Penelope Crick is a Fellow of the British Psychoanalytical Society, Clinical Director and Head of Adult Services, Institute of Psychoanalysis Clinical Services at the London Clinic of Psychoanalysis and a Psychoanalyst in private practice in London.

Alain Gibeault is a Psychoanalyst in private practice in Paris, a Training Analyst of the Paris Psychoanalytical Society and past Director of the E & J Kestemberg Centre for Psychoanalysis and Psychotherapy, past President of the European Psychoanalytical Federation and past Secretary General of the International Psychoanalytical Association.

Ronny Jaffè is a Psychoanalyst in private practice in Milan, a Training Analyst of the Italian Psychoanalytical Society, President of the Milanese Centre for Psychoanalysis, a Co-Chair of the Committee on Ethics of the International Psychoanalytical Association and former Vice-President of the European Psychoanalytical Federation.

Sven Lagerlöf is a Psychoanalyst in private practice in Stockholm, a Training Analyst of the Swedish Psychoanalytical Association and former Chair of the Clinic of the Swedish Psychoanalytical Society.

Rudi Vermote is Head of the Psychoanalytic Psychotherapy Unit for Personality Disorders, University Psychiatric Centre of the University of Leuven, Campus Kortenberg; Associate Professor of the Faculty of Medicine and Faculty of Psychology, University of Leuven and a Psychoanalyst and Training Analyst and past President of the Belgian Society of Psychoanalysis.

FOREWORD

David Tuckett

This book is very, very important, particularly at the present time. It explores crucial questions for psychoanalysts and, indeed, psychoanalytic patients. What has to happen for a meaningful psychoanalytic treatment to take off and to become established as worthwhile? What are the challenges in doing so?

The authors report detail from eight years of discussions of clinical material held in 45 workshops with up to 500 psychoanalysts from all over the world. Facing the challenges for analysts and patients raised in those discussions, the authors describe how they came to extend the diagnostic-type envelope within which questions of first interviews have been hitherto contained and to begin to question the essence of what makes a psychoanalytic encounter 'psychoanalytic'.

The point is that confronting what happened in first interviews, particularly as they were trying to do it while retaining the idea that there are different successful traditions of doing psychoanalysis, forced them to touch on fundamental issues as to what psychoanalysis demands from patient and analyst. Their work and the emphasis they place on the deep emotional challenge the patient–analyst couple must manage in their first interviews, may prove to mark a watershed. Today, in many parts of the world, reports from psychoanalytic societies often state that people are reluctant to undertake psychoanalysis as much as they once did. Most often, in my experience, the 'modern' patient is identified as the problem. The core psychoanalytic method, relying on frequent regular sessions, the couch, free association and interpretation, is indicted, perhaps as an out of date relic in the modern world. Critics, wishing to change the demanding nature of the method and associated training procedures, argue it should be adapted to suit new kinds of patients with new kinds of more disturbed pathologies who, it is supposed, cannot tolerate old-fashioned approaches.

The original questions behind the creation of the WPIP reflected and concerned just these kinds of issues: then called a crisis in psychoanalysis (Tuckett, 2003, 2016).

The authors describe how, early in their work, they undertook a review of the evidence that identifiable patient characteristics, noticeable in first interview, were diagnostic indicators. They found no consensus substantiating that view. In fact, they conclude in these pages that the totality of research trying to isolate patient characteristics which might usefully inform the decision of whether psychoanalysis should be initiated or not, or to predict whether a psychoanalysis with a given patient will succeed, reaches no firm conclusion at all (Chapter 1).

Partly for that reason, and in line with the approach taken by other EPF working parties set up at the same time,[1] the authors found that to understand what was happening they needed to focus less on patients and more on analysts. In this book, they describe how gradually their focus of investigation shifted towards the analyst, to his or her experience and soon to possible resistances that analysts themselves may struggle with when taking on new patients and which may cause them to lose trust in what they are doing.

Tentative conclusions in this direction emerged when they identified a literature describing different aspects of these resistances to offering psychoanalysis and were further confirmed through iterations of discussion of the clinical cases.

They found previous work in the literature had clearly pointed out the anxiety aroused by a new meeting. It had been linked to a more or less unconscious bias against psychoanalysis because of unpredictable and disturbing countertransference reactions or to anxieties from the confrontation with the patient's and the analyst's own 'madness'. Alternatively, doubts present in the analyst's own mind (based on his/her own experience of analysis) were described to emerge suggesting that during first interviews analysts worry if they will be able to contain the strains of the work – perhaps hinting at an implicit lack of trust in psychoanalysis as a treatment or the psychoanalytic method as an approach. These considerations led to the view that perhaps psychoanalytic patients are not 'found' but 'created' by psychoanalysts – who, therefore, need to be armed with specific skills to help their patients to begin the treatment (Chapter 1).

The main chapters, written as a highly readable and clinically exemplified story of genuinely psychoanalytic research, elaborate on what they had found in the literature. We are shown the struggle the authors lived through as they tried to make sense of their discussion data gradually to reach a central conclusion: what happens in an initial interview to a greater or lesser extent is that an inter-psychic dynamic, central to the patient's and analyst's experience of each other and therefore central to the patient's dynamics, is worked through. This awareness emerged although at first obscured by manifest differences in the consultation process related to differences in approach in psychoanalytic subcultures and the specific institutional/social context in which analysis can be offered, as well as the individual patients' pathology. Through their successive iterations and discussions (beautifully represented in the flow charts in Chapter 3) and by challenging and revising their ideas in a disciplined manner, the Team came to the conclusion that the outcome of each consultation could usually be understood as a result of how analyst and patient adapted, often unconsciously, to the emotional situation created by their encounter, including the broader sociocultural and institutional context.

The early chapters lay out the discussion methodology (which others could certainly follow to continue and develop this work) and introduce a series of worked examples and initial thoughts on which the conclusions are built. Chapter 5 draws on three beautifully worked clinical examples presented in those early chapters to describe the process and its evolution: we are introduced to an initial hypothesis and then the reasons why it turned out to be inadequate to account for the observed realities. Their different picture of the unconscious interview dynamics is set out and elaborated further and convincingly with numerous further examples in later chapters. The initial hypothesis was that in some way a psychoanalyst would say something that switched the level from an ordinary interaction to an 'analytic one':

> *The analyst's work would encourage the upwelling of unconscious phantasy, and so help the patient to become aware of something new, which was previously preconscious or unconscious. This discovery would allow the analytic couple to move from an ordinary kind of interview to another, more meaningful, psychoanalytic level of exchange.*
>
> (Chapter 5)

However, although this occurred sometimes it was not always there and it was not always evident that it played as central a role:

> *In what was retrospectively an overly simplistic model of the process we had expected to see such a 'switch' predominantly affecting the patient, whereas it rapidly became clear* ***that it also fundamentally involved the analyst****.*
>
> (Chapter 5)

In a seminal case discussed in depth, it was clearly not correct to say that increased awareness was the main factor in the patient's decision to begin analysis with that analyst. Neither was it that the analyst pointed to some new meaning. Rather, what was conveyed through the meeting was that the analyst was emotionally open to its emergence. The challenge in these interviews was emotional openness, and how the analyst dealt with the emotions that opened up seemed to be the key determinant. 'During successful work in such cases', they write, 'it was the analyst who opened an internal door to become aware of his/her participation in something that was being played out in the interview dynamics' (Chapter 5). 'Sometimes there was a sudden insight', they write, 'but at other times it seemed to be acquired as the result of a struggle in which s/he had to do considerable internal work to reach some understanding of what could be at stake'. Summarizing one case, they write,

> *If we try to summarize what happened, through his unconscious verbal, para-verbal, and non-verbal communications, this apparently self-possessed patient induced strong feelings in the analyst from the moment of their first telephone exchange. After their*

talk on the telephone, she found herself not only in contact with his anxiety about asking for help, but also having to deal with her own feelings of being both seduced and rejected by him. This was intensified during their first contacts in the waiting room and as they settled down for the interview, when she had to deal with additional, powerful feelings of being invaded by him, wanting to push him away, feeling guilty about that, but protective towards him as well.

(Chapter 5)

Many more examples played this out. The intensity of the unconscious dynamics invading the initial encounter and the variety of their modes of communication put considerable pressure on the analyst. This was the case both in the analyst's internal experience, and through the pressure s/he would notice in reacting to various forms of verbal or non-verbal enactment. Far from being only a neutral observer, or a specialist performing a technical function, s/he was also a participant in a human drama. When the analyst did not feel disturbed, it actually emerged, the analyst, or later the Clinical Workshop participants or the WPIP Investigative Team, often had a sense that something was missing – a sense that itself became an emotional indicator. The point is that a solely self-observing position didn't seem to work well without the analyst in some way or other (perhaps temporarily and inadvertently) becoming involved personally. How they dealt with this tendency to participate, to engage in mutual enactment, was crucial.

Being involved and feeling affected provided the impetus and the material for self-reflective work. In other words, analysts found that they must function fully both as participant and as observer (including self-observer), and that they need to sustain the inevitable tension between these poles.

(Chapter 5)

After the 45 workshops and then the in-depth study of 28 cases presented in them over eight years, the core conclusion of this book was now clear:

> *On the basis of our own experience with the WPIP study, we believe that what actually happens is that the patient and analyst work together to co-create an analytic couple, and that the analyst's role as a participating agent in this process is essential. It then becomes interesting to understand the developing dynamics of the analytic couple, and how the analyst functions in this context.*
>
> (Chapter 1)

The working model developed was that while 'switching the level' indicates a successful psychoanalytic process in some first interviews, for this movement to be possible, the analyst–patient pair must somehow manage to 'weather' the 'unconscious storm' of the intense interview dynamics, and use these dynamics as an opportunity to 'open psychoanalytic space', rather than 'hiding away' from the 'storm'. In fact, even when 'switching the level' does not take place, in the sense of becoming conscious of something unconscious, 'opening psychoanalytic space' may be sufficient to initiate the psychoanalytic process.

Why is all this the case? The authors argue it is probably because the interview introduces the patient to a way of working with a psychoanalyst through which something in the patient's experience, that was initially felt to be meaningless, could take on at least some promise of meaning. An analyst's ability to tolerate the 'storm' and to work within it might be what gives a patient some measure of trust and hope in psychoanalysis, even for patients who do not yet think quite symbolically.

I hope I have said enough to show how this book is a wonderful example of psychoanalytical clinical research, pursued rigorously but without the loss of the psychoanalytic level of experience and reaching firm and well-argued conclusions. As such, this book is a milestone, even a watershed, in a field which has so rarely managed to commit itself to research and sometimes has even been frightened of it, perhaps with the consequence that the profession can show signs of lacking confidence and trust even in itself. Reith and his colleagues have amply repaid the trust the European Psychoanalytic Federation put in them.

References

Tuckett, David (2003) Presidential Address: A Ten-Year European Scientific Initiative. *European Psychoanalytical Federation Bulletin* 57: 7–22.

Tuckett, David (2016) 1999–2004. In: Frisch, S., Bleger, L., Burkert, U., Janssen, A., Schmid-Gloor, E., Ylander, F., (Eds.) *50 Years of the European Psychoanalytical Federation*. Bod Third Party Titles.

Note

1 The Comparative Clinical Methods (CCM) working party chose to focus on the function of what the analyst was doing and the End of Training Evaluation Project (ETEP) working party chose to focus on what the candidate was doing.

ACKNOWLEDGEMENTS

The work of hundreds of psychoanalysts went into the making of this book: the presenting analysts who contributed their process notes of first interviews and gave us permission to publish disguised extracts as vignettes to illustrate our findings; their analytic peers, who studied this case material in our Clinical Workshops; and the members of the Investigative Team of the Working Party on Initiating Psychoanalysis (WPIP). For reasons pertaining both to the confidentiality of the case material and to the research process, the presenting analysts must remain anonymous, so that we unfortunately cannot thank them personally here. The workshop participants, without whom nothing could have been done, are not anonymous, but far too numerous to list by name, so we must thank them as a group.

For the WPIP Team the adventure began in 2003, when David Tuckett, then President of the European Psychoanalytical Federation (EPF), brought together a number of psychoanalysts designated by their home Societies to discuss the possibility of setting up a working party to study recommendations and referrals for psychoanalysis. This was in the context of the EPF's Ten-Year European Scientific Initiative which had been launched in 2001. Five of the authors of this book (Ronny Jaffè, Sven Lagerlöf, Mette Møller, Bernard Reith and Rudi Vermote) were present at that first meeting, where the Working Party on Initiating Psychoanalysis got its name, before being formally founded by the EPF in 2004. The other three authors (John Boots, Penelope Crick and Alain Gibeault) joined the WPIP early on in its work. Longstanding WPIP member Elisabeth Skale was an active and indispensable participant throughout the case studies and case reviews, contributing significantly to the findings. We also wish to thank former WPIP members Rainer Dahlbender, Rachael Davenhill, Christine Diercks, Kari Hauge, Janet King, Ursula Walter and Peter Wegner, who have all participated in the development and activities of the Working Party.

We are also grateful to later EPF Presidents Evelyne Séchaud, Peter Wegner, Serge Frisch and Jorge Canestri who, together with the EPF Council and Executive, have unfailingly supported the WPIP, scientifically, financially, and through the infrastructure for the Clinical Workshops and panels. We also thank International Psychoanalytical Association (IPA) Presidents Daniel Widlöcher, Cláudio Laks Eizirik, Charles Hanly and Stefano Bolognini, together with their administrations, for supporting the organization of workshops and panels at IPA conferences; as well as the IPA Developing Psychoanalytic Training and Practice (DPPT) program, which helped to fund the WPIP conjointly with the EPF until 2007.

David Tuckett, as well as chairing the Working Party on Comparative Clinical Methods, was part of the original WPIP Team and chaired it until Bernard Reith could take over in 2005; he has been a major source of support and inspiration ever since. The Chairs of other EPF Working Parties, in particular Jorge Canestri (Working Party on Theoretical Issues), Shmuel Erlich (Working Party on Interface), and Gabrielle Junkers and Mira Erlich-Ginor (Working Party on Education), all provided indispensable scientific and moral support during the first stages of the Working Party process. We also wish to thank the members of the North American Initiating Psychoanalysis Working Party, Nancy Wolf (Chair), Maxine Anderson and Bill Glover, who created opportunities to extend and pursue this kind of work in North America and within the IPA.

Jan Abram and Sverre Varvin, who reviewed our report on Phase 1 of the study for the EPF Bulletin in 2010, both considerably helped us to improve our thinking and reporting. Later Mira Erlich-Ginor, Bill Glover, David Tuckett and Nancy Wolf kindly read early drafts of some of this book's chapters, pointing out problems and shortcomings and very much helping us to improve them. Many thanks too, to Alessandra Lemma, General Editor of The New Library of Psychoanalysis, Anne Patterson, Assistant Editor, and the reviewers of the manuscript for their very helpful comments and advice. We are also grateful to Kate Hawes and Charles Bath of Routledge for their support in the final production stage. As former General Editor of the New Library, we also want to thank Dana Birksted-Breen who has given us supportive encouragement throughout the whole project.

Brigitte Reusch and Birgitta Geber of Geber & Reusch provided indispensable and good-humoured practical assistance for the organization of the Clinical Workshops. A book written by an international team working in several different countries requires the help of a central compiler of the text to ensure consistency and we are very grateful to Era Trieman for his diligent work in preparing the manuscript for us.

We thank John Wiley & Sons, Inc., the publisher of *The International Journal of Psychoanalysis*, for permission to reproduce material from the following papers:

- Møller, M. (2014). The Analyst's Anxieties in the First Interview: Barriers Against Analytic Presence. *International Journal of Psychoanalysis 95*: 485–503, for clinical case material appearing in Chapter 7;

- Reith, B. (2015). The First Interview: Anxieties and Research on Initiating Psychoanalysis. *International Journal of Psychoanalysis 96*: 637–657, for the clinical case material that appears in Chapter 2, as well as theoretical portions of text appearing in Chapters 2 to 5.

We also thank the editors of *Psychoanalysis in Europe: Bulletin of the European Psychoanalytical Federation* for permission to reproduce material from the papers we published there from 2010 to 2012.

The work on the workshops, research and writing process has been supported over the years by our families and we would, last, but by no means least, like to give them our thanks, with particular thanks to Joëlle Reith and Beth McIntyre for their practical help and advice.

1 INTRODUCTION

How and why do people enter psychoanalysis?

Imagine more than 500 psychoanalysts from all over the world participating over a period of eight years in a total of 45 workshops where case material from first interviews was presented and discussed. This gives an idea of what an immense amount of clinical material has been metabolized, and of what an extraordinary wealth of information, details, nuances, different perspectives and first-hand experiences of what actually happens in initial interviews this study draws upon. Then imagine an international team of 12 psychoanalysts working together to pursue an in-depth study of 28 of these cases, looking for common patterns or contrasts, through several rounds of elaboration.

In the following chapters, based on the study of this rich material, the Working Party on Initiating Psychoanalysis (WPIP) of the European Psychoanalytical Federation (EPF) will try to clarify how analysts actually perform the task resulting in recommendation of analysis, and what goes on that makes it possible to initiate an analysis.

We want to thank all the analysts who have participated in these Clinical Workshops. Without their active and engaged involvement and their permission to keep recordings and notes from the workshops, the material would have been much poorer. We are especially indebted to those analysts who offered their own experiences and session material from initial interviews where they explored the possibility of initiating a psychoanalysis, and who were prepared to participate in the workshop process, being not only willing to discuss the material but also, at times, to be open and frank about their own emotional feelings and responses. These presenting analysts also gave permission for the WPIP to continue work on the interview protocols and workshop minutes. It has been a fascinating opportunity to follow these presentations through the initial workshop meetings and subsequent WPIP Investigative Team meetings, where the various dynamic elements were not just objects for static study but generators of further processes within the subsequent research Stages, which sometimes became a secondary line of containment and transformation.

These analysts have also approved the case-material vignettes used in the following chapters. For reasons of confidentiality, we unfortunately cannot recognize the individual analysts nominally for their gracious participation and permission.

The original questions behind the creation of the WPIP were: why don't more people enter psychoanalysis, and how can we help more people to do so? The psychoanalytic community has often worked on the basis of the implicit assumption that it is something about the patient that decides whether psychoanalysis will be suggested or not. But all research that has tried to isolate patient characteristics which could inform the decision of whether psychoanalysis should be initiated or not, or could predict whether a psychoanalysis with a given patient will succeed, has consistently failed to find any (Bachrach and Leaff 1978, Bachrach et al. 1991, Wallerstein 1994, Caligor et al. 2009).

As a result of this another question has arisen, namely why analysts seem to be reluctant to take on analytic patients. The focus of investigation has shifted towards the analyst, in order to examine the possible resistances that analysts themselves may experience about taking on new patients. Several authors (Ogden 1992; Rothstein 1994, 1998a; Caper 1997; Quinodoz 2001; Ehrlich 2004, 2013; Wille 2012; Møller 2014) have described different aspects of these resistances: the anxiety aroused by a new meeting, linked to a bias against psychoanalysis because of unpredictable and disturbing countertransference reactions; the confrontation with the patient's and the analyst's own 'madness'; lack of trust in psychoanalysis and the need for psychoanalysis as a good internal object in order to be able to contain the strains for the analyst. These thoughts have brought much light on the burdens of practising psychoanalysis.

Several authors have already advocated the view that the indication for analysis lies as much in the analyst as in the patient. According to some, psychoanalytic patients are not 'found', they are 'created' by analysts who are able to help patients to begin what could be the best treatment for them (Rothstein 1998a, Levine 2010, Crick 2014). On the basis of our own experience with the WPIP study, we believe that what actually happens is that the patient and analyst work together to co-create an analytic couple, and that the analyst's role as a participating agent in this process is essential. It then becomes interesting to understand the developing dynamics of the analytic couple, and how the analyst functions in this context.

Judy Kantrowitz's work (1986, 1993, 2002) can be considered to be a part of an important shift away from the focus on analyzability, first towards the compatibility of patient and analyst as individuals, and later to their functioning as a unique, working analytic couple. She has described how the analyst is also changed by the interaction, and has done a careful study of the patient's impact on the analyst (Kantrowitz 1996).

Arnold Rothstein (1998b) gave an articulate account of how the impact on the analyst can lead the latter to diagnose instead of entering the psychoanalytic relationship. More recently, Antonio Pérez-Sánchez (2012) described indicators of suitability for psychoanalytic treatment, but which are rooted in the developing relationship, including the examination of the analyst's countertransference. Many other relevant viewpoints that represent the shift in the field are to be found in the collected readings published by the WPIP,

Initiating Psychoanalysis: Perspectives (Reith et al. 2012). We see the present study as another contribution to this debate.

Our study originated as part of the European Psychoanalytical Federation's Ten-Year European Scientific Initiative, launched in 2001 under the presidency of David Tuckett (Tuckett 2002, 2003, 2004; Tuckett et al. 2008; Basile et al. 2010).

The aim of this programme was to do clinical research. By getting psychoanalysts from many different orientations to work together in peer groups, the hope was to turn the diversity of psychoanalytic cultures within the EPF into a resource that might help us to discover more about the clinical realities of psychoanalysis than what can be extracted from the existing psychoanalytic models.

In particular, we wanted to look at how psychoanalysts *really* work – not how we would ideally like to *think* that they work – and attempt to see how we can understand real-life psychoanalytic practice. One of the basic plans was to ask the groups to study process notes of psychoanalytic sessions (or, in our case, process notes of first interviews) to see what goes on there – or not.

In practice, several investigative teams, called Working Parties, were set up, each ideally composed of members from different EPF societies and psychoanalytic cultures. These Working Parties were responsible for setting up investigative programmes addressing specific issues of interest to the analytic community and in which EPF analysts, also from different EPF societies and psychoanalytic cultures, were invited to take part. Many of these programmes involved bringing together the participating analysts in Clinical Workshops, held annually at the EPF conferences (as well as IPA and other conferences), where they could study the case material.

A palette of workshop methods was tried out, ranging from very structured to purely free-associative group work (for a detailed description of the different methods, see Chapter 3). Our own Working Party, WPIP (Reith et al. 2010), chose an intermediate format, with some structure, for example asking the groups to respond to a few basic discussion questions as part of their task but also leaving considerable space for free-associative group work; the reasons for this choice will be described in Chapter 3. The aim of such procedures is to use something psychoanalysts already know how to do well, namely clinical case discussion groups, as a starting point for more disciplined and systematic forms of study, i.e. to turn clinical case discussions into a research tool. We see these procedures as attempts to develop forms of qualitative research in psychoanalysis (see Chapter 3).

This Working Party (WPIP) was formally established in 2004. Its Team members were delegates designated by their EPF societies. The WPIP conducted its Workshops at the EPF Conferences from Vilamoura in 2005 up to and including the Paris conference in 2012; workshops were also held at the IPA congresses in Berlin and Chicago. During this period, a North American Initiating Psychoanalysis Working Party was also set up, and we have collaborated with them to hold similar workshops at the IPA conferences in Mexico, Prague and Boston.

What the WPIP set out to study was based on the original broad mandate of the European Scientific Initiative, which called for:

1) the development of skills for assessing patients for psychoanalysis and determining the conditions for advising psychoanalytic treatment both in private and institutional settings; and
2) finding ways to improve referrals for full analysis and to share them among practitioners.

Implicit in this was also an aim to secure the future training in and practice of psychoanalysis.

The evolution of the WPIP's work is described in its interim report to the EPF in 2010 (Reith et al. 2010). After exploring several options it was decided to concentrate its efforts on a core issue that seemed relevant to all aspects of the mandate, and so the following central research theme was chosen:

> *The specific dynamics of preliminary interviews, how psychoanalysts work with them, and what it is in these dynamics that leads a potential patient to enter full analysis (or not).*

From the outset, our focus was on the dynamics of the *analytic couple* in first interviews. Although these dynamics can of course be expected to be influenced in part by the patients' unconscious structures and dynamics, to focus on the impact of the latter would require another study. We see this couple-oriented perspective as complementary to, rather than opposed to or exclusive of, more patient-oriented perspectives.

Our research on first interviews can be defined as a psychoanalytic study, using psychoanalytic exploration by peer groups of psychoanalysts as its core procedure. It is a hypothesis-generating study, aiming to develop grounded theory based on careful and disciplined observation (see Chapter 3), and not a hypothesis-testing study, designed to test the logical consequences of a pre-existing theory. It is based on clinical work discussed by practising analysts, using their divergent theoretical backgrounds as leverage for more precise, experience-near observation. It is therefore intended to be as independent of specific psychoanalytic theories as possible. Whether or not our findings fit in with existing theories remains an open question warranting further exploration.

It is not, therefore, a controlled experimental or epidemiological study, nor is it a standardized observational study designed to reliably apply and test pre-defined psychoanalytic concepts. What is empiric about the method is that it is a study of many real cases, and that the same specific pre-defined procedures have been followed for all the cases: from the presentation of the clinical material, through the semi-structured discussion in the Clinical Workshops, to WPIP´s subsequent work with the clinical material and the workshop findings. Comparing the cases, deriving explanatory hypotheses from them and checking these against further cases were also done following systematic procedures, as described in Chapter 3.

We are not offering a manual or textbook on how to initiate psychoanalysis, but a psychoanalytic study of the initiation processes as we think they can be seen to take place in the work of practising analysts. The aim is to use the findings of this study to promote reflection on what happens when patient and analyst meet. Our study on how analysts and patients work together in their first meeting has enabled us to develop ideas about the initiating processes along different but interlinked lines, which are all related to the unconscious dynamics of the patient-analyst couple, and which will be described in the successive chapters of the book. Our aims will have been reached if our work promotes further debate, exploration and research in the psychoanalytic community, if it stimulates clinical reflection on our psychoanalytic practice, and most especially if it helps psychoanalysts in training to overcome their fears about beginning analyses.

To describe consultations from these dynamic perspectives provides a kind of evaluation of the possibility for analysis that is more in accordance with psychoanalytic principles and the interactive psychoanalytic process that will eventually be initiated, than with a more assessment-like search for analysable patients, which as mentioned above has proven ineffective. This does not mean that it becomes irrelevant to consider the patient's psychological structure and other characteristics, but it transforms the decision to recommend analysis into a different undertaking. It becomes more complex, but is based on a grasp of the situation that is more in accordance with its nature.

We have seen work involving very different patients, with very different pathologies, and very different analysts, coming from different analytic subcultures, who met and interacted in consultations that led to the initiation of psychoanalysis, or in some cases to other choices of treatment.

While we recognize that differences in the consultation process are related to differences in psychoanalytic subcultures and the specific institutional/social context in which analysis can be offered, as well as to the individual patients' pathologies, we have come to the conclusion that it makes sense to understand these differences from a specifically psychoanalytic, inter-psychic perspective. By this we mean that the outcome of each consultation can be understood as a result of how analyst and patient adapted, often unconsciously, to the situation created by their encounter, including the broader sociocultural and institutional context. In one way or another, this inter-psychic dynamic will be the specific focus of all the following chapters. The chapters follow a developmental line, beginning with a description of the research method, and moving on to the different perspectives that the WPIP came to adopt in order to understand the interview dynamics.

The whole WPIP Team is regarded as author of the book. We have functioned as one research group, and want this to be reflected in the presentation of our findings. Because the work within the WPIP has been so intense that it has become difficult to figure out who first came up with what idea, or who helped to clarify or develop it, it seemed increasingly absurd to put individual names on the chapters. Our way of working has rested on the conviction that it is clinical peer-group co-work between individuals from different psychoanalytic schools that can bring out the essence of psychoanalysis.

Chapter 2, *Are you an analyst, Ma'am?* is a description of one typical case. Besides being a demonstration of the richness and forcefulness of the dynamics in first interviews, it is used to illustrate how the case material was analysed through a research process characterized by three Stages: the interview, the Clinical Workshop and the subsequent work with the material by the WPIP Team.

Chapter 3, *The lens we looked through: exploring a method for qualitative clinical research in psychoanalysis*, goes into the details of the research method that the WPIP came to develop. The method will be described and compared to other kinds of research.

The following Chapter 4, *Analysts being analysts: the group exploratory method in action*, will go further into the psychoanalytic processes at work in the Clinical Workshops and in the WPIP Team when dealing with, exploring and analysing the case material. The parallel processes and the resistances towards the transformational potential imbedded in this kind of research will be demonstrated through a more thorough analysis of one case.

Special accent is placed in these chapters on the power of unconscious and preconscious dynamics and how they seem to penetrate the three 'Stages' of psychoanalytic elaboration (the original interview, the Clinical Workshop, and the Investigative Team). Early on in our work we became aware that the combination of the powerful transmission of unconscious dynamics through the three Stages and the increasing distance from the original meeting was a method whereby aspects of the original dynamics could progressively be seen and conceptualized in ways that were not possible for the analyst in action. The power of transmission of unconscious dynamics and how it could be dealt with through our method of processing the material will be a theme running through all subsequent chapters. It is the *method* which supports insight, elaboration and understanding, not some hypothetical intrinsic quality of individuals or groups.

Chapter 5, *Facing the storm and creating psychoanalytic space: the vicissitudes of the analytic couple in first interviews*, zooms into the interaction between analyst and patient and explores how analysts cope with the pressures of what cannot be conceptualized on the spur of the moment, and how they adapt to the fluctuations in the contact with the patient, creating possibilities for a more analytic dialogue. The notion of 'opening psychoanalytic space' is proposed to describe this kind of work.

The impact of what the patient brings to the first meeting is further investigated in Chapter 6, *The opening scene: from anticipation to initiation*, where the focus is especially on what happens up to and at the threshold of the first meeting, seeing these developments as the first enigmatic manifestation of the unconscious conflicts of the patient and of central issues arising in the transference/countertransference field. The analysts' spontaneous reactions to this demonstrate their immediate participation in a setup, a preview of what cannot be conceptualized until later. In the chapter, this way of thinking is linked to the concept of metaphor.

In Chapter 7, *Different beginnings*, the perspective is zoomed back out in order to look a bit more from a distance on several shorter case vignettes. The aim is partly to give an impression of what might be a surprising variation in how first interviews are conducted, and partly to show different routes to recommending or not recommending psychoanalysis; but it is also to show how far the actual first interviews are from textbook images of first interviews as a slow progressing and deepening of contact and understanding of the patient's problems. We found the first meeting in general to be much more overwhelming than we had expected, for the analyst as much as for the patient; and also far more unpredictable, irregular, and with more unprocessed material implicitly influencing the dialogue.

The question of referrals, meaning that the interviewing analyst will have to refer the patient to someone else, is dealt with in Chapter 8, *Initiating psychoanalysis in institutional settings*. Here the differences and similarities of various routes to psychoanalysis are explored: direct beginnings with an analyst in private practice, referrals in private practice, and referrals in institutional settings with provision of analysis through a psychoanalytic clinic. *Initiating psychoanalysis in institutional settings* highlights the role of the psychoanalytic method, relative to that of the person of the analyst, in the recommendation process. This leads to a deeper examination of the method as a virtual third, as well as of the function of the institution as a more concrete presence of the third. Thus understood, the referral process is shown to elucidate important aspects of the initiation process that are relevant for all three routes to psychoanalysis mentioned above.

How analysts struggle to reach an analytic stance in first interviews is a theme that runs through all chapters and more particularly is elaborated in Chapter 9, *Countertransference and enactment*, where the vicissitudes of an analyst's countertransference reactions are followed through the detailed analysis of one case. The chapter shows how mutual enactments structure the dynamic field and its development.

The final Chapter 10, *Where are we now?* recapitulates the findings of the study. A persistent observation throughout the whole research process is the extent to which the analyst in the first interview is caught up in a forceful field, and to what a high degree analytic functioning is related to the ability to cope with the disturbing pressures of the field. Another thread running through our findings is that, just as there are no patient characteristics that secure a positive recommendation for analysis, there is no specific psychoanalytic 'method' of first interviews that guarantees the creation of a psychoanalytic dialogue. If the findings of our study are to be trusted, it seems that each patient–analyst couple must work together, using the psychoanalyst's technique but also their individual capacities, to find out whether a psychoanalytic dialogue is possible, or could become possible in the future. It is the quality of the developing dialogue that determines whether patient and analyst can reach a belief that psychoanalysis can take place and become beneficial. Because of this highly individualized indication process, together with its ability to promote deep change, we regard it as especially important to keep psychoanalysis alive as a potential treatment for a broad group of psychic disturbances.

The confrontation with so many real-life first interviews has broadened the WPIP members' understanding of the nature of competent psychoanalytic functioning, and has been a healthy process forcing us to overcome an idealized and to some extent crippling ambition as to what psychoanalytic work should look like – an experience we hope to communicate in the following chapters and thereby pass on to the reader.

2 ARE YOU AN ANALYST, MA'AM?

Overview of the clinical issues with an example of a case study

'Are you a doctor, sir?' was the question that 18-year-old Katharina asked of Freud while he was contemplating the landscape during a solitary excursion up the Rax mountain near Vienna in the summer of 1893 (Freud 1893, Lagerlöf and Skale 2012). Consciously she wanted Freud's 'objective' medical advice on her physical symptoms but, as Argelander (1978) has shown, unconsciously she hoped that he would help her to 'dis-cover' her 'subjective' knowledge about the causes of her anxiety. Moreover, they were both caught up in a situation whose 'scenic' characteristics had many points of contact with Katharina's original trauma, and which probably played an unconscious role in her decision to approach him. Freud had begun to develop some initial theories about the causes of Katharina's symptoms but, as he was also discovering at the time, if he wanted to treat her, he would have to relinquish his usual medical investigative procedures and help her instead to tell her own story, as it welled up in her consciousness over the course of their conversation. Furthermore, he had to maintain this analytic function while involved in a potent transference and countertransference scene in which, notably, he was of the same generation as Katharina's abusive father (Argelander 1978, Skale 2012).

Argelander's penetrating analysis of Freud's captivating account thus describes, in a nutshell, the requirements that are placed on the psychoanalyst in any analytic setting, but perhaps most strongly in first interviews:

1. to have a psychoanalytic theory about unconscious levels of intra- and inter-psychic reality underlying the surface of everyday experience;
2. to use this theory to help the patient achieve a sense that s/he can 'discover' her/his own personal knowledge about this unconscious reality;
3. to be able to do so despite the unconscious transference and countertransference dynamics enmeshing the patient and analyst;

and, we might add in the context of first interviews:

4. to achieve all this in a situation that is totally new.

These are the capacities that we may imagine Mr. A. was hoping to find in the analyst who presented the following case material. To paraphrase Katharina, 'Are you an analyst, Ma'am?' is the question that he seems to be asking her throughout their interview.

The Handsome Man on Crutches: the interview

The analyst consulted her voicemail during a holiday period and found a message from Mr. A. requesting an appointment: 'I need psychoanalytic treatment'. Because he sounded anxious, she returned his call. During their conversation, he again said: 'I need treatment of some sort'. As the analyst wrote in her report to the WPIP Clinical Workshop:

> Sensing the urgency and the neediness behind that statement, I could readily understand the feeling I had had when I first heard his message on my voicemail. For initial interviews with a new patient, I prefer to have time to spare so that I can think about the patient and his request. Since I was at that point still on holiday, seeing him while I had so much free time ahead of me would be the kind of opportunity I do not always have. I decided to suggest an appointment a couple of days later, even though I would not normally do that, so as not to hurry things too much.

Mr. A. turned out to be a man in his 50s, handsome and distinguished, but looking uncomfortable and disabled, on crutches and with a splint on one leg. He explained that this was due to a traffic accident, but in such a confused way that the analyst 'found it difficult to know who had run into whom'. 'It's got to stop', he said. 'It's ridiculous. I'm hurting myself. It's all wrong.'

As she listened to him, the analyst found that there was 'something youthful about him, a little naïve, with a boyish note to his otherwise masculine voice – as though he would agree to everything anybody asked of him but from time to time could get really angry.'

He explained that he had obtained a list of names and decided to go and see whoever called back first. The broken leg was the latest in a series of incidents convincing him that he needed to talk to someone to 'find out what wasn't going right for him'. He had divorced some years ago. 'It's a nice divorce', he said, but was disturbed to realize how irritable he could be with his children, which reminded him of his father. 'I can see myself just boiling over, shouting and so on.' He had even felt himself 'getting all worked up' when he had to wait for a bus on the way to the interview.

Because he did indeed sound annoyed and irritable, and because she had had a growing sense of underlying violence, the analyst asked him whether he had been violent with his children or was afraid that he might be. He replied that no, he was not like his father, that he was only violent in words. After a silence he said, as if he had just discovered something new, 'well, words can be violent too, I'll have to be careful about that.' He added that he had lovely children, his one success as a father.

In quick succession he described a previous not very successful psychotherapy, the loss of his father some years ago just as he was ending the therapy, and, as if in association to his father's death, he said:

> And I'm in the process of ending a delightful relationship I have had with a woman friend since the divorce; it was like a clandestine relationship because I never intended us to be a couple, really. But it was good, because she made me feel that I was able to make a woman happy.

The analyst was struck by Mr. A.'s use of the masculine form of 'happy', which in their language came across as a slip of the tongue. She restrained an impulse to point it out. Thinking that it might be an expression of a nascent transference linked to some significant object, she preferred to take a 'mental note' of it to keep in the back of her mind, which would make sense in due time.

In a change of tone that surprised the analyst, Mr. A. went on to say: 'It's hard to let go of a woman when you've got nothing else in the pipeline.' The analyst wondered about the oral and anal undertones of this remark and their possibly pointing towards repressed violence against women or unconscious homosexuality. Mr. A. continued: 'We're now in the final phase of the break-up. That separation rekindles the depression I went through at the time of the divorce, when I felt abandoned.'

The analyst asked: 'What's a "nice" divorce?' Mr. A. replied that it was difficult because of the children. After a silence he said some more about the divorce, which had been initiated by his wife, and then associated with various accidents and illnesses. Again he remained silent for a while. Reflecting on the childlike fragility that seemed to be welling up now, the analyst asked him about his memories of his childhood and what his family was like.

He described how, at the age of six, when a little sister was born, he began to realize that his mother could be 'quite nasty', both verbally and physically. Later, his elder sister, who had been an important source of support, left the family to go and live with a woman. The analyst realized that the slip of the tongue could have been related to the sister's homosexuality, and was glad to have let this come of its own accord.

Mr. A. fell silent again, then said: 'I must tell you that coming here to see you wasn't easy.' With embarrassment and emotion he told how, a few months ago, he had been to see another analyst working in the same part of town. As he approached the address, a childhood memory came back of genital fondling by a mathematics tutor in that same building. Later, public charges were laid against this man. In response to his mother's questioning, Mr. A. had been too ashamed to admit that he, too, had been abused. The analyst

(continued)

(continued)

he saw in that building confirmed the facts and was the first person to inform him that the teacher had been tried and sentenced. 'And from my childhood on', Mr. A. said:

> I had buried that deep in myself. I think that analyst liberated me from something – perhaps the shame of being a victim. I've never had much of a talent for investigating things. I didn't expect to see that come up in reality.

'Suddenly,' the analyst wrote:

> he asked me how much time we had left, as if in a hurry to put an end to our discussion. I replied that we still had some time left, adding that it was perhaps difficult for him to talk about memories such as those.

After a silence, Mr. A. said: 'My family history is one of violence.' He talked at length about his temperamental father who could be not only tyrannical and demanding, but also physically and verbally violent, terrifying him. But he insisted that he did not want to be thought of as a maltreated child; this was just the way they were brought up in their cultural environment. He added, as though in passing, that 'there was no sexual perversion' in the father's attitude. This negation, as well as the associations between sexuality and violence, reminded the analyst of Freud's paper, *A Child Is Being Beaten* (Freud 1919b) and she made a mental note of these themes.

She asked if he remembered any dreams. He was a bit embarrassed, saying that he remembered an erotic dream from a few nights before: *'I was kissing the woman with whom I'm breaking up.'* He wondered what it might mean. *'But it was enjoyable!'*

The analyst reported:

> Mr. A. then waited for me to comment on our discussion. I did not say anything about what I call the 'pre-transference' aspects of analysis. I was thinking of the violence that I had so strongly felt all through this interview; there was a great deal of hysterical dramatization to all this, not particularly well structured. There was also an authentic request for help, with something childlike inside Mr. A. that was not particularly perverse (like his father!). I was, however, slightly worried about Mr. A.'s tendency to somatic manifestations.

Mr. A. interrupted the analyst's musings, asking anxiously: 'What do you suggest I should do?'

The analyst felt in two minds at this point. On the one hand, she felt concerned about Mr. A.'s vulnerability, particularly his psychosomatic manifestations, his accident and recent break-up, so she wished to meet him again before taking a decision. Then again, she was sensitive to his pressing request for help and thought that he would, in all probability, be able to undertake the analysis that he seemed to be looking for. She struck a compromise, saying that analysis would no doubt help him to see things more clearly, but that perhaps it would be better to give themselves a little more time at first, for instance starting at two face-to-face sessions per week, before moving on to analysis at three sessions per week (the normal analytic frequency in that region).

Mr. A. responded:

> Usually I prevaricate and end up regretting it, so why not begin right away? I'd prefer to take a decision right now – you were the first person to return my phone calls, so this is where I want to be.

Directly following this quotation, the analyst concluded her report with the following sentence: 'When we talked about session times and fees, he suggested a fee slightly lower than the one I had mentioned, but I found his arguments quite acceptable'.

Returning now to the clinical requirements outlined at the beginning of this chapter on the basis of Freud's encounter with Katharina, and working backwards through the list, this kind of material amply illustrates the challenges of requirement 4. The first interview is a totally new situation for both partners, in more ways than one. It is neither a normal meeting, nor yet psychoanalysis. Patient and analyst don't know each other; beyond the minimal agreement to meet, they do not yet have any predictable working setting (in this case, there is even the interesting problem of meeting just before the end of the analyst's vacation, which some analysts would consider to be an enactment). Despite this uncertainty, they have to find a way to meet around highly intimate issues in the patient's life. Even a sophisticated man like Mr. A. does not really know what to expect of the analyst; on her side, the analyst does not yet know if and how she will be able to work with him. Thus, in contrast to what may happen later on in an established analytic setting, the patient and the analyst are both completely unprepared for what may ensue between them (Wegner 1992, Møller 2014).

The unconscious expands into this uncharted territory, revealing both the possibilities and limits of psychoanalytic understanding. A whole life and mind are suddenly unveiled, giving even the reader of such an account the feeling that it is impossible to take it all in at once. A potent and enigmatic transference and countertransference scene of wishes, expectations and fears is immediately set up and can be very disturbing. Mr. A.'s unconscious associations brim over with infantile sexual phantasies about what might happen in analysis (kissing, a clandestine relationship, being abused). As a result, defensive reactions are equally strong on both sides. At first, Mr. A. seems to downplay his hopes and concerns about the encounter by suggesting that he will just see the first analyst who is willing to enter the pipeline; towards the end, he makes a counter-phobic rush into analysis. From her perspective, the analyst wonders about his potential for violence, so that her question 'What's a "nice" divorce?' might be taken to betray nascent countertransference fears.

The unconscious dynamics in the first interviews that we have examined turned out to be so intense that we have adopted Bion's (1979) expression of a 'storm' taking place whenever two people meet for the first time, as an apt description. We will describe our understanding of this concept in more detail in Chapters 3 to 5, but instances of it will be found throughout this book.

On the basis of our case studies, we have come to think that this 'storm' is so powerful that it can influence the psychoanalyst's analytic functioning, and perhaps always influences it to some degree in more or less subtle ways. As a result, it appears that requirement 3 on our list, i.e. to maintain analytic functioning despite intense transference and countertransference dynamics, may best be seen as an aim that is never fully reached in practice. In the case of *The Handsome Man on Crutches* we see how difficult it can be even for an experienced analyst, working with a motivated and capable patient like Mr. A., to hold a steadfast analytic position. When she hesitates about beginning psychoanalysis towards the end of the interview (which did in fact lead to a long and working analysis) this seems to be not only owing to her conscious concerns over Mr. A.'s psychic structure and his ability to use the analytic setting but probably also, as we will soon see, because at that point she was partly overtaken by the unconscious 'storm'. It is almost as if she temporarily lost control of her usual working setting and let Mr. A.'s counter-phobic rush into analysis get the upper hand. Such phenomena are part of what we can call the 'vicissitudes of the analytic couple', expressing the various ways that patient–analyst couples find to deal with the transference–countertransference dynamics and their impact, or even their hold, on both partners. We will have a lot to say about these vicissitudes in the chapters to come.

Moreover, we will describe in Chapter 6 how the 'storm' can often be seen, with hindsight, to be brewing already before the first interview, for example in the first voicemail message left by a patient and in the analyst's internal and overt response to it. It can begin to affect the analyst's functioning in seemingly enigmatic ways already at this stage. This was evident in *The Handsome Man on Crutches* when something in Mr. A.'s first message already impelled the analyst to respond slightly differently to how she would normally.

All this goes to show how difficult the circumstances are in which the analyst must strive to meet requirement 2 on our list. The task of helping the patient to gain access to an unconscious reality that can give meaning to his/her experience was what we called 'switching the level' in our earlier hypotheses about what happens during initial interviews. We thought of it as a process in which the analyst helps the patient to move from an ordinary kind of exchange to a psychoanalytic one touching the patient's unconscious inner world (Quinodoz 2001, 2003). This premise seems retrospectively to have been somewhat optimistic, as will be discussed in Chapter 3. As demonstrated by cases like that of *The Handsome Man on Crutches*, the actual dynamics seem to be much more complicated. For example, although it seems reasonable to think that Mr. A. did indeed come a little more in touch with the traumatic impact of violence in his childhood, it doesn't seem correct to say that he was previously unaware of it. It can also be argued that he was unconsciously testing the analyst to see whether she was able to take on board what he needed to bring to her. As we will elaborate in Chapters 3 to 5 and again in Chapter 9, much of the psychoanalyst's work seems to involve coping with and working inside the 'storm' without being too much thrown off balance, striving to maintain an analytic stance and to 'open an analytic space' in which it can at least potentially take on meaning. This work, which we have sometimes compared to 'facing' or 'weathering the storm', seems to be an essential component of 'switching the level'.

The ability to meet these challenges depends as much on the impact of the particular 'storm' that arises in each new encounter as on the analyst's theory and technique. The latter help the analyst to understand the 'storm' and to orient his or her response, but they cannot operate unless they are integrated within the analyst's working personality as an 'internal frame', an ongoing, often unconscious or preconscious, analytic functioning which we will try to describe in Chapter 5, with more illustrations in Chapters 6, 7 and 9.

Requirement 1, the ability to keep in mind the existence of an unconscious reality that affects our conscious experience, is probably best seen as one component of the 'internal frame'. Psychoanalytic theory is part of the living experience of the analytic relationship and not something that can be applied independently of that relationship. We will have more to say about this in concluding Chapter 10.

Even so, although the 'internal frame' helps the analyst to cope with the storm and work with it professionally, it may not suffice. Often, as will be described in Chapter 8, the analyst can find useful support between interviews in peer consultation with colleagues; in some settings such peer-to-peer consultation may even prove to be indispensable.

In other words, there is *so* much going on beneath the surface in initial interviews like this one, that the analyst just cannot be expected to take it all on board in one go. Much is bound to slip through her internal frame and to manifest itself in other ways, as for example in enactments such as those we will study in Chapters 5 and 9, in particular.

We believe that another way in which partly undigested interview dynamics become manifest is through their unexpected impact on third parties who study the interviews. Indeed, very interesting group processes arise when case material like this is studied in psychoanalytic peer-group clinical workshops. This impact seems to explain what happened when the analyst brought her process notes (of which the above account is a condensed version) to one of the WPIP Clinical Workshops.

We used such workshops as part of our research method, as we will describe in Chapters 3 and 4. Their aim is not for analysts to supervise each other, but to find out more about psychoanalysis and in particular about how we actually do our work (rather than how we would ideally like to think we work). In the case of the WPIP workshops, the objective is to deepen our understanding of how psychoanalysts really carry out first interviews. This is done by discussing process notes from the interviews in such a way as to bring out the participants' and the presenting analyst's preconscious understanding of the case, as well as their implicit theories about it (Sandler 1983). The aim is also to see if these insights can be formulated in ways that can be shared by analysts working across different models. When things go well, the workshop participants and the presenting analyst are able to perceive more of the dynamics in the interview:

The Clinical Workshop

The Clinical Workshop's reaction to this case was very interesting. The group was engaged, friendly and constructive, but for much of the first, free-associative workshop session, it adopted a subtly critical and sometimes nearly attacking stance, especially towards the patient, but also occasionally towards the analyst's technique. Some of this was perceptible during the workshop but much remained between the lines, only to become more apparent upon going back to the recording.

For a long time the group's thoughts were centred on what many participants considered to be a seductive, violent, intrusive 'rushing in' quality to this patient, for example in the discussion about the number of sessions and the fee, as well as in the combination of seductiveness and violence in his unconscious attitudes to women. There was a lot of talk about the hidden ambiguity of his request, about the 'excitement' in the session and even about 'raping' the analyst. It was as if the group wanted to protect the analyst from Mr. A., but also wanted to reproach her for being too eager by answering his phone call and seeing him during the 'private' time of her holidays; as well as for having let herself be seduced, as evinced by deciding on analysis in the first interview, in spite of her reservations.

This was intertwined with another more discreet thread in the group process, stressing instead the neediness and despair of this patient, the small boy in him, his fraught relationships with his primary objects, his psychosomatic suffering and his worrisome potential for self-destructiveness. This tendency came out more strongly in the later parts of the first workshop session, after the moderator had drawn attention to the group's interest in the theme of intrusiveness. But even so, in this aspect of the discussion the group still tended to be critical both of the patient, who was described as disorganized, undeveloped and unable to tolerate anxiety, as well as of the analyst, for giving Mr. A. 'special' treatment. It was as if the group recognized the presence of a needy child in the analytic scene, but felt that to take him seriously would be to spoil him.

It was only during the second workshop session, in which the group was asked to do more structured work based on a set of four discussion questions, that the climate really changed such that that it became possible to appreciate the richness of this analytic encounter.

The patient's contributions with his associations, insightful links and dream could now be acknowledged. It became possible to think of his seduction, excitation and debasement of women as a defence against his insecurity about his sexual identity and his authentic fears regarding his fragility, anger, depression and repetitive self-destructiveness. It also became possible to see his way of entering the analytic space as a way of conveying his own experience of being intruded upon and overwhelmed by his family's violence and sexuality, as well as by his mathematics tutor. The group could see that the depth of the interview increased over time; Mr. A. being able to bring in more material as he gained confidence in the analyst's ability to contain without intruding, in particular revealing more about the traumatic aspects of his experience.

Progressively the group came to appreciate the analyst's work of containing and processing the interview dynamics. The workshop pointed out her receptivity and ability to respond to Mr. A.'s deep anxiety and feeling of urgency by giving him a sense of space, which she created by listening carefully without reacting excessively and in particular without attempting to interpret, yet handling the interview in such a way that he felt understood. The analyst responded to this by stressing her opinion that unconscious materials like dreams and slips of the tongue are something 'very precious' which she wants to cherish by wondering what it means, and which she must not 'burn' by premature interpretations: 'I think it would be a mistake to answer.'

She did, however, experience the workshop's exploration of the themes of intrusion and being intruded upon as meaningful. She told the group that while writing up the case for the workshop, she had felt embarrassed about her hesitation over beginning psychotherapy at two sessions per week or analysis at three sessions per week. She had put this down to her hesitation over the patient's ability to bear analysis, which subsequent sessions showed to be unfounded. Over the course of the second workshop session, she suddenly remembered another factor that she had forgotten: at the time of the interview she had a doubt about when she would have the three open hours to begin the analysis, which was also what led her to offer only two sessions per week to begin with. When the patient insisted on three, she realized that she could in fact arrange her schedule so as to accommodate him. She thought that this moment of confusion perhaps expressed her discomfort about taking on the patient.

We have come to accept as additional evidence for the unconscious 'storm' the fact that it can continue to have a powerful and unexpected impact at later stages of the exploratory process; in the Clinical Workshops or in the WPIP Investigative Team meetings. It is our contention that one major way in which the unconscious storm can be seen to reappear later on is through the defensive group reactions of the kind that were manifest in this Clinical Workshop during its first working session, when it first tried to get a handle on the interview dynamics. We see this workshop initially taking on a fight–flight basic assumption mode (Bion 1961) in which Mr. A. was seen as an aggressor, until a remark by the moderator about the group's interest in the theme of intrusion, and later the requirement to answer four standard 'discussion' questions, helped to get it back into a working group mode. As we will describe in Chapter 4, our impression is that such group dynamics can be understood as 'parallel process' phenomena, repeating aspects of the unconscious dynamics of the original interview. This allows us to see them not only as defensive but also as expressive, and thus as a useful source of information revealing more about the hidden unconscious dynamics of the case material and its effect upon the group members, as for example in this instance the impact on the group of Mr. A.'s childhood experiences with traumatic intrusion. As we have seen, the analyst confirmed near the end of the workshop that the theme of intrusion raised by the workshop was meaningful to her and that it had helped her to recover a repressed memory about what had taken place in her mind near the end of the interview.

After each of the workshops the clinical material, together with the workshop proceedings, is re-examined by the WPIP Team using the same discussion procedure as in the workshops. As will be discussed in Chapters 3 and 4, this allows the WPIP Investigative Team to build on the work done by the Clinical Workshops – including the information carried by the parallel process phenomena – to pursue its study of the interview dynamics. Here is a synthesis of the research report written after the WPIP's own group work on the case material and workshop proceedings:

The WPIP's impression

The WPIP Team's account highlighted three interrelated themes: 1) the communication by projective identification of poorly symbolized experiences and phantasies; 2) in particular, a mix of oedipal and incestuous unconscious phantasies and traumatic experiences; and 3) envious superego defences.

The WPIP Team thought that Mr. A. was intrusive because he was anxious, telling the analyst both on a symbolic level and through projective identification that he was in trouble with omnipotent and intrusive internal objects and phantasies. On her side, the analyst worked with him essentially on a symbolic level, in triangular space, although at some points she could also be thought to have enacted. Returning Mr. A.'s call and seeing him before the end of the holidays could be seen not only as a reasonable response to his request but also as an enactment, expressing her maternal reaction to his anxiety and her own interest in him as a patient. Similarly, her confusion about the number of sessions she had available, and moving directly to analysis despite some misgivings, suggested that she had momentarily relinquished her mastery of the situation. Thus her internal frame could be seen to be working well, but also to have been a bit rattled at times, when less well-symbolized contents seem to have slipped through.

However, it seemed to be the workshop group who had initially lost the symbolic level, more so than the analyst, starting out as it did by feeling intruded upon and thinking that this really was an omnipotent and intrusive patient. In fact, while projecting this onto the patient, the group was acting rather intrusively itself. There was important information embedded in the group's reaction. The traumatic themes in the patient's history and associations were present but not explicitly highlighted in the analyst's written account, which she tended to formulate more in terms of unconscious wishes and conflicts. Thus the group may have been trying to get a grip on these aspects of the material, which were less well-digested in the analyst's presentation.

In particular, Mr. A.'s associations involved recurring oedipal and incestuous transference phantasies, expressed on all psychosexual levels: oral (the dream about kissing), anal (the pipeline) and genital (the associative links between the previous therapy, the father's death and the 'clandestine' love affair). Together with the theme of abuse (by his parents, by the mathematics tutor and perhaps by the very direct response from the other analyst), these phantasies form an interweaving, highly charged pattern throughout the interview. Mr. A.'s associations suggested envious debasement of women and sexuality, but they also showed how difficult it was for him to differentiate his own libidinal and aggressive drives and oedipal conflicts from the traumatic impact of his childhood experiences, which he seemed to deal with in part through a defensive reversal from passive to active. From her participation in the workshop, it was clear that the analyst had perceived these dynamics and elaborated on them internally to some extent, if less so in her text, but had not consciously found them particularly disturbing. Her enactment about the number of hours she had available, indicative of her unconscious wish to keep Mr. A. at a safe distance, suggested that there were certain aspects on which she had not been able to elaborate; as is, of course, inevitably the case.

The workshop group, impacted by these undigested residues, seems to have experienced some of the disturbance in her stead. It seems to have initially adopted an archaic superego defence (Bion 1957, 1959), unconsciously holding that such disturbances ought to be denounced and resisted, rather than analysed and understood. Although the WPIP Team realized that the next idea was speculative, it thought that this superego reaction might have been reinforced by envy.

Indeed, it was interesting to note that Mr. A.'s eagerness to enter analysis didn't seem only counter-phobic or exacerbated by the analyst's decision to

(continued)

(continued)

see him before the end of the vacation; he needed, and was able, to use the analyst to move right on to very potent unconscious material. This analytic couple seemed to have hit it off well; from the outset it was clear that they were working productively, so that the analyst seemed to have good grounds for accepting his idea that analysis was the right treatment for him. Mr. A. was motivated for analysis and could afford it, at a time when such patients are more rarely encountered. Moreover, during the workshop, the analyst gave the impression that she liked this patient as a person and as a man. The workshop may have envied this 'glamorous' couple and, aroused by Mr. A.'s unconscious material, experienced a guilt-laden wish to intrude on the primal scene. As a result they may have projected their own intrusiveness into the patient and adopted a superego stance towards both patient and analyst, as if it needed to find someone else to blame. The fantasy that this analytic encounter was all too easy is belied by the perceptible tensions in the interview, but in addition to the traumatic experiences, envy might have been another determinant behind the workshop's sense that there was too much 'rushing in'.

In short, the hypothesis is that Mr. A. anxiously brought undigested – and indeed difficult-to-digest – themes to the interview, asking for help from the analyst, whose adequate response nonetheless left much that spilled over which ineluctably ended up on the workshop's plate. At first the workshop balked at this demand, placed on its group mind, but with time it got down to rather successful elaborative work from which the WPIP Team could benefit in turn.

If our observations and our reading of them are correct, the confrontation with such undigested unconscious dynamics can be one of the sources of anxiety and defensive reactions in analysts, both individually and collectively. This unthought known (Bollas 1987) in the patient is doubly the unknown for the analyst, in that it is both new and has not yet found a thinker (Bion 1997) in the analyst who can give meaning to it. Independent of the traumatic historical factors at work in the case, confrontation with something which the analyst's mind is not yet prepared to deal with is by definition 'traumatic' in the wider sense of the term, and can lead to defensive reactions or to enactments. It should not be surprising if the demands placed upon the analyst are particularly great in first interviews, but this leads us again to the question of how the analyst deals with the unknown in such situations, which we will explore further in Chapters 5 to 9. It also raises the more general questions of how we can best understand psychoanalytic knowing in the psychoanalytic relationship, and how these findings pertain to the processes that initiate an analysis, which we will try to address in our concluding Chapter 10.

On the basis of our case studies, the most realistic assessment seems to be that, as in the case of *The Handsome Man on Crutches*, some combination of elaboration, defence and enactment is always present, on the part of both participants in the encounter. What counts is that the analytic pair manage to utilize this combination to somehow engage with the unconscious dynamics, so long as they perceive and work through the defences and enactments later on. As will be described in Chapters 5 to 9, we see cases in which this combination works more smoothly and others in which it appears to be more chaotic and disturbing for one or both partners. In Chapter 7 we will show how the immediate outcome of each new patient–analyst encounter is the creation of an original analytic couple, whose overall mode of functioning can range from a more triangulated, creative encounter to a more dyadic, narcissistic one.

Working through this cumulative material, one develops a sense that the work Mr. A. and his analyst were able to accomplish together was extremely valuable – something 'very precious' – as she said about dreams and slips of the tongue and, by implication, about analytic work in general. Putting ourselves in their place, we can imagine that, despite Mr. A.'s suffering and the tensions of analytic work for both of them, they may have experienced a form of relief about being able to delve so deep as a way of opening up possibilities for change in the patient. Their intense and thoughtful personal involvement could be seen as one of the specific and necessary components of psychoanalytic technique. In our 'evidence-based' epoch it may be worthwhile to defend such profoundly personal treatment processes. This is also why organizations giving access to subsidized psychoanalytic treatment, which we will describe in Chapter 8, offer an important public service.

To sum up, it seems that the unconscious dynamics of preliminary interviews can be so powerful and 'blinding' that they are impossible to apprehend all at once, but also that it is feasible and gratifying to work with them if we are prepared to take this reality in our stride by facing the internal challenges with which they confront the analyst. This makes first interviews all the more interesting and important as a distinct field of study. Our findings emphasize how complex and successful the work that Freud (1893) did on the Rax mountain actually was, and how the four requirements placed upon the analyst, as outlined on the basis of Argelander's (1978) study of that case, are underpinned by pervasive unconscious dynamics which we can never expect to fully circumscribe, let alone eliminate, and which, on the contrary, are central to our work. Thus Katharina's question resonates through the generations, to clinicians and researchers alike: 'Are we analysts?' The answer may be that we never *are* analysts, but that we are always involved in the never-ending process of *becoming* analysts.

3 THE LENS WE LOOKED THROUGH

Exploring a method for qualitative clinical research in psychoanalysis

To allow our readers to form their own opinion about how we arrived at the contents and conclusions of this book, this chapter will give an overview of:

- the context and origins of our study;
- our first working hypotheses;
- the development of our study methods and our experiences with them;
- our general findings;
- how these findings led us to hypotheses about the dynamics of initial interviews that were in some ways very different from the ones we started out with.

To avoid overburdening the text, we have put some of the more technical details in appendices at the end of the book. Appendix 1 contains relevant facts and figures about the study. Appendix 2 presents a summary of our prescribed group procedures, together with our reasons for adopting them. One important component of the method, the 'discussion questions' and their development, is detailed in Appendix 3.

Following up on this panorama, we will make more detailed observations about the psychoanalytic group investigative processes in Chapter 4, alongside a second case illustration of how they work, adding to the one given in Chapter 2. The description of these processes, as they appear and develop in the successive 'Stages' of the investigation, can be thought of as an integral part of our findings. We have come to think of them as a powerful investigative tool, a bit like a microscope or a telescope arrayed with a series of lenses. In Chapter 10 we will review our hypotheses, methods and findings, discussing how we think they are relevant for psychoanalytic practice and theory.

Context: the EPF's ten-year European Scientific Initiative

As described in the Introduction (Chapter 1), the aim of the European Scientific Initiative was to transform the diversity of psychoanalytic cultures within the European Psychoanalytical Federation (EPF) into a resource for research.

The EPF created Working Parties whose official mandate was to investigate scientific issues of concern for the EPF and the analytic community at large, and whose members were chosen for their expertise in the designated areas and their representativeness of the various EPF societies and psychoanalytic cultures. The Working Party on Comparative Clinical Methods (CCM), for example, was set up to investigate how psychoanalysts really work in everyday sessions and what their internal working models are, as well as to arrive at greater clarity between psychoanalysts about these questions (Tuckett et al. 2008, Basile et al. 2010). Similarly, one of the aims of the Working Party on Education (WPE), and later its End of Training Evaluation Project (ETEP), was to arrive at better descriptions of the aims of psychoanalytic education and of the criteria for qualification (Junkers et al. 2008, Erlich-Ginor 2010, Hinze 2015). As we explained in the Introduction, our own Working Party on Initiating Psychoanalysis or WPIP (Reith et al. 2010, Reith et al. 2012, Reith 2015) was asked to contribute to the development of skills for determining the conditions for advising psychoanalytic treatment and improving referrals for psychoanalysis.

Each Working Party was responsible for setting up a research plan and for developing methods appropriate to their object of study. According to the general Working Party model, these methods usually involved Clinical Workshops bringing together psychoanalysts from different psychoanalytic societies and cultures to study case material following specified methods appropriate to their aims.

This required the Working Parties to experiment with modes of group work designed to encourage the participants in the Clinical Workshops to adopt a 'meta-perspective', transcending their usual clinical reflexes and explicit and implicit theoretical models, so as to:

- increase their receptivity to potentially unexpected aspects of the clinical material and to explore them as openly as possible;
- create conditions in which they could hopefully come to a better understanding of each other's approaches to the material, and see how and why these approaches might be relevant to the process notes;
- promote an open dialogue in which they could relinquish the supervising dynamics that are often seen in such situations, for a more mutually enriching impact on their explorations.

Although the involvement of analysts from different psychoanalytic societies and cultures was one way to promote this 'meta' perspective, a prescribed working frame was also expected to be important. The development of such frames was part of the research process. The results of the Clinical Workshops were studied by the Working Parties not only to compile and analyze the findings, but also to improve the working frame if necessary. Plenary panels were also held as part of this effort, bringing together the Working Parties

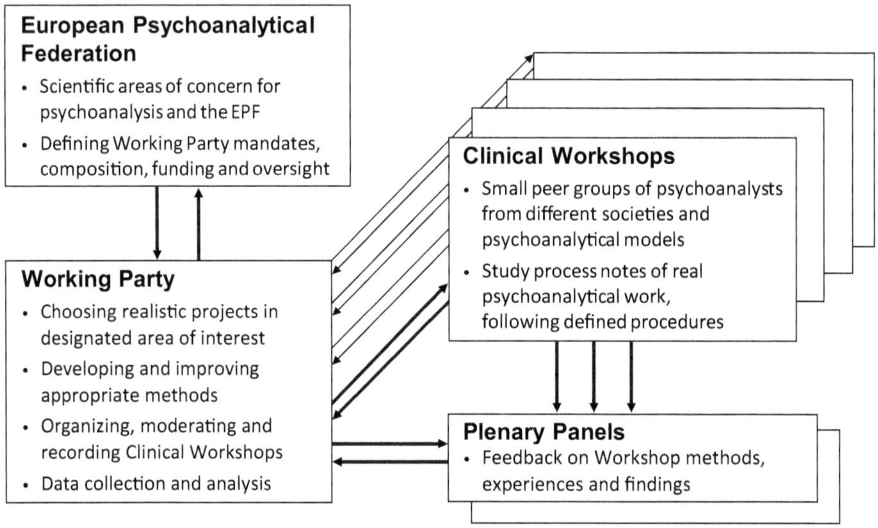

Figure 3.1 The Working Party model

and the Clinical Workshop participants to share workshop experiences and to discuss methods and findings, in a recursive process designed to improve the method and to clarify its relationships with the results (see Figure 3.1).

A palette of workshop methods was tried out, ranging from the very structured work of the CCM Working Party (Tuckett et al. 2008, Basile et al. 2010), to the purely free-associative group work of the Working Party on the Specificity of Psychoanalytic Treatment Today or SPPT (Frisch et al. 2010). The aim of the detailed questions of the CCM method was not to ask workshop participants to rate the clinical material according to pre-set criteria, as in standardized quantitative empirical research. It was instead to help them stick to their investigative task of precise and in-depth psychoanalytic exploration of the actual material, avoiding more impressionistic approaches in which preformed views would be more likely to take over and bias the findings or lead to obstructive group dynamics. With similar aims in mind, the SPTT Working Party chose a very different but equally disciplined discussion procedure, based on the 'weaving thoughts' method (Norman and Salomonsson 2005, Salomonsson 2012). Here, the idea was also to ensure that the actual psychoanalytic dynamics embedded in the material would be at the centre of the group associative process, and to keep the latter as free as possible of defensive individual or group dynamics by forbidding debate between group members and direct discussion with the presenting analyst.

Our own Working Party, the WPIP (Reith et al. 2010), chose an intermediate format, less structured than that of CCM and leaving considerable space for free-associative group work, but also asking the groups to respond to a few basic discussion questions as part of their task. This was partly dictated by logistics, as the conference time available for the WPIP workshops was too short to allow for the very detailed procedures of the much longer CCM workshops. Nevertheless, the implementation of some specific, prescribed workshop procedures was preferred to a purely free-associative method (see also below and in Appendix 2).

The aim of such procedures is to use something psychoanalysts already know how to do well, namely clinical case discussion groups, as a starting point for more disciplined and systematic forms of study, i.e. to turn clinical case discussions into a research tool. Although this is psychoanalytic research rather than conventional qualitative research, we do think that there are affinities with the latter.

Psychoanalytic research and qualitative research

Psychoanalytic work is a complex, contextualized and highly individualized process, largely dependent, moreover, on the patient's and analyst's subjective involvement. Much of it is implicit in nature and therefore difficult to capture (Pérez et al. 2015). Although many psychoanalytic developments seem unique to each patient–analyst encounter, we also think of them as instances of more general psychoanalytic processes, which it should therefore be possible to describe more explicitly and conceptualize in generally understandable terms. Such generative models of psychoanalysis should be based on actual observation and not only on theory. One of the challenges with which we are faced is therefore to identify, describe, explore and formulate dynamic patterns which enable us to find meaningful links between seemingly disparate phenomena in patient–analyst encounters, both within a given individual encounter and across different patient–analyst couples. Generating hypotheses about potentially meaningful patterns grounded in observation is one of the traditional aims of both psychoanalytic and qualitative research.

Unless they capture such dynamic patterns, controlled quantitative studies, which are based on the standardized assessment of pre-treatment and treatment characteristics and examine the statistical links between these characteristics, may neglect core aspects of the psychoanalytic process. This may be the case in standardized studies of first interviews, as we will discuss below. Similarly, in order to use single case studies to test our more general metapsychological theories (Hinshelwood 2013), we need to reach a min imal consensus about the clinical descriptions of what happens in psychoanalytic sessions. As this is notoriously difficult to achieve in practice, qualitative clinical and conceptual research may be useful in this area as well.

Qualitative research strategies (Harper and Thompson 2012, Ritchie et al. 2014, Silverman 2011, Varvin 2003, Wallerstein 2009) are designed to discover and conceptualize such dynamic patterns and may thus provide inspiration for appropriate research methods adaptable to our field. Within the range of qualitative methods, the approaches of Working Parties such as CCM and the WPIP are perhaps best described as attempts to develop 'grounded' theory (Glaser and Strauss 1967, Brown 1973, Tuckett 1994, Bryant and Charmaz 2007), most specifically constructivist grounded theory (Charmaz 2006, Charmaz and Bryant 2011, Tweed and Charmaz 2012).

The method of grounded theory research is to generate hypotheses on the basis of an intensive and methodological study of detailed cases, and to test these hypotheses using the similarly disciplined study of new and varied cases, including atypical ones or counter-examples. Hypotheses emerge and are refined in an iterative process involving inductive analysis of the data leading to theory construction, and testing the emerging hypotheses through new data collection and critical analysis. The robustness of the observations and hypotheses is repeatedly tested using comparative analysis across multiple instances within cases, between cases, and between levels of analysis. The process continues until the hypotheses are no longer substantially modified by new observations.

Because of the psychoanalyst's necessary participation in the perception and construction of analytic data, and the psychoanalytic researcher's similarly inevitable participation in the research process, a reflexive perspective, taking the influence of the research process on the findings into account, is an integral component of the method – not only as a safeguard but also as a further source of understanding. For instance, when the analysis of repeated patient–analyst interaction sequences leads psychoanalytic researchers to describe a pattern and to formulate a hypothesis about the transference and countertransference dynamics underlying this pattern, the potential influence on this formulation of the researchers' own countertransference responses to the sequences must be considered. This reflexive process, which is familiar to practising psychoanalysts, is described in similar terms in anthropology (Devereux 1967) and in constructivist grounded theory (Charmaz 2006, Charmaz and Bryant 2011).

The aim of the Clinical Workshops is to begin the study of process notes from psychoanalytic interviews in this reflexive spirit, while that of the core Working Party is to pursue it and, if possible, take it further.

This psychoanalytic group work is different from the 'focus groups' used in sociological qualitative research (Finch et al. 2014, Wilkinson 2011). It produces complex and informative psychoanalytic group dynamics, which we will describe in Chapter 4.

We thought of such methods as one potentially useful approach in a palette of complementary research strategies in the field of psychoanalysis (Leuzinger-Bohleber and Bürgin 2003, Wallerstein 2009). We hoped that it might point the way to a more experience-near clinical 'common ground' (Wallerstein 1990) underlying the accepted theories and practices of the different psychoanalytic schools – 'common ground' being understood here not as a unified model of psychoanalysis but as a shared argumentative field (Bernardi 2003) and a process of public discourse (Habermas 1984) in which to compare psychoanalytic approaches and reach a more empirically grounded understanding of our differences and similarities (Tuckett 1994, 2004).

Aims: what really happens in first interviews leading to psychoanalysis?

It is part of the psychoanalyst's responsibility to ensure that the patients s/he takes into analysis, or refers for analysis to a colleague, will be able to benefit from that treatment and will not be harmed by it. However, decisions to recommend and begin analysis do not seem to be based on a diagnostic assessment of the patient in the usual sense. Empirical studies having failed to demonstrate any clear correlation between standardized measures of patient factors and the clinical decision to offer psychoanalysis (Caligor et al. 2009, Wallerstein 1994, Bachrach et al. 1991, Bachrach and Leaff 1978), something else must be going on during consultations that accounts for the interviewing analyst's decision to recommend analysis, which has so far remained implicit. It would be worthwhile to attempt to discover and describe potentially influential processes, so that they can be studied more systematically (Pérez et al. 2015).

As discussed in Chapter 1, this conundrum is also expressed in recent psychoanalytic literature, which has tended to abandon the concept of 'assessment' of patient characteristics in favour of more process-oriented views of first interviews (see for example Dantlgraber 1982; Ogden 1992; Wegner 1992; Rothstein 1994, 2002; Lagerlöf and Sigrell 1999; Quinodoz 2001; Levine 2010; Schachter 2012; Reith et al. 2012; Crick 2013, 2014; Møller 2014). We were therefore interested to find out if we could arrive at better descriptions of the actual *processes* leading the patient–analyst couple to judge that analysis would be possible and worthwhile.

The main aim of the WPIP's study was thus to try to understand what happens in first interviews that lead to psychoanalysis. We wanted to take a fresh look at what really takes place, using experienced analysts to study the actual work of other experienced analysts, and to describe this with as few preconceptions as possible.

More specifically, we were interested to see:

- if we could detect and describe any characteristic forms of conscious and/or unconscious dynamics taking place between analyst and patient in such interviews; and
- whether we could find relationships between such dynamics and the decision to begin an analysis, as well as the process of the ensuing analysis.

Our ultimate concern was to see whether some patterns would come to the fore whose understanding would help practising analysts in their daily work, or at least contribute to our thinking about the processes involved.

First hypotheses: 'initiating psychoanalysis' and 'switching the level'

Knowing that no research strategy is ever theory-free and necessarily begins with some first hypotheses about what one expects to find and which influence the study design, we began with some ideas about what we thought we might see. We developed these in 2004 in a preliminary study of cases brought by the WPIP's Team members.

On the basis of the literature and these preliminary case studies, we expected to see forms of psychoanalytic relationship in which the analyst works to 'touch' the patient meaningfully on an emotional level (Quinodoz 2001, 2003) and so open his/her receptivity to what analytic work can be. The experience of this quality of relationship during a first contact might be what gives the future analysand a sense of what psychoanalysis is about (Klauber 1972) and what it has to offer that is valuable and different from what can be found elsewhere.

We tentatively subsumed these processes under the umbrella concept of '*initiating psychoanalysis*', both in the sense of 'initiating the process' itself, and of 'initiating the patient *to* the process'. '*Assessment*', whether in the specific sense of evaluating a potential analysand's ability to benefit from analysis, or in the more general sense of judging the quality of interaction between analyst and analysand, would then be only one facet of what the analyst does, and would largely be based on how the patient responds to it.

As one main component of 'initiating psychoanalysis', we expected to see something we called '*switching the level*', in which the analyst would help the patient to look at his/her problem or life story in a novel and opening way, provoking a kind of 'Aha!' experience. This would presumably be the result of becoming aware of some central issue that was previously preconscious or unconscious, and would thus be accompanied by a sense of surprise. This new perspective would allow the analytic couple to move from an ordinary kind of interview to another, more productive and emotionally more meaningful, level of exchange.

We hoped to find out more about the exact nature of this change in the interaction; how it comes about and what kind of work is done to accomplish it. We thought that as the analyst and patient began working together there might be an up-welling of affective and representational derivatives of unconscious conflicts, increasing the overall intensity of the interview, until a point was reached where the analyst might be able to pick up on something central which touched or surprised the patient. Patient and analyst would thus have a sense of discovering something emotionally significant, which they might be able to capture in a 'meaningful common formulation'. The aim of the research process was to explore these hypotheses as rigorously as possible. Meanwhile, the idea of 'switching the level' was adopted as an intuitively adequate metaphor.

We also postulated that, alongside the differences between the initiation process in *'consultation for referral' settings* (usually institutional settings where the interviewing analyst will not continue with the patient) and *'private' settings* (usually in private practice where the analyst can take on the patient him/herself), there would also be process aspects that the different settings have in common, and 'switching the level' would be one of them.

These opening hypotheses influenced the first set of discussion questions that we submitted to the Clinical Workshops and guided our initial analysis of the findings. As it turned out, some of the hypotheses were not really borne out by our findings and had to be relinquished or at least substantially modified as we pursued our study, to give way to rather different descriptions of the transference and countertransference dynamics of first interviews. We will outline these towards the end of this chapter; they will form the core themes discussed throughout this book.

Methods: psychoanalytic exploration in peer groups

Clinical Workshop procedures

The WPIP Clinical Workshops are described in Figure 3.2. They brought together groups of 12 to 20 psychoanalysts. We took care to achieve as varied a distribution as possible in each workshop in terms of the analysts' gender, country of origin, linguistic background, psychoanalytic society, level of experience, and membership status, in the hope of bringing together analysts influenced by different psychoanalytic backgrounds and models. Apart from creating a richer workshop composition, we hoped that this would help to overcome the blind spots that might occur in groups of analysts coming from the same background. A few candidates were admitted to each workshop because we thought that their position and motivation would contribute a fresh perspective.

Each workshop discussion lasted 4 hours and was held in two, 2-hour sessions, separated by a coffee break. The first session was devoted to a case presentation of first interviews followed by a general free-associative discussion. In the second session, in addition to their free-associative work, the workshops were asked to respond to a few pre-determined 'discussion questions' as described below and in Appendix 3.

The total of 38 workshops that contributed to the study involved several hundred practising psychoanalysts engaged in over two thousand analyst-hours of group work (see also Appendix 1 on 'Facts and figures').

Two WPIP members were involved in each workshop, one as moderator and one as observer and reporter. The moderator's task was to hold the workshop frame, helping the group to maintain a secure, respectful and open working atmosphere, and ensuring that the discussion procedures were duly respected and that each 'discussion question' was attended to. The presence

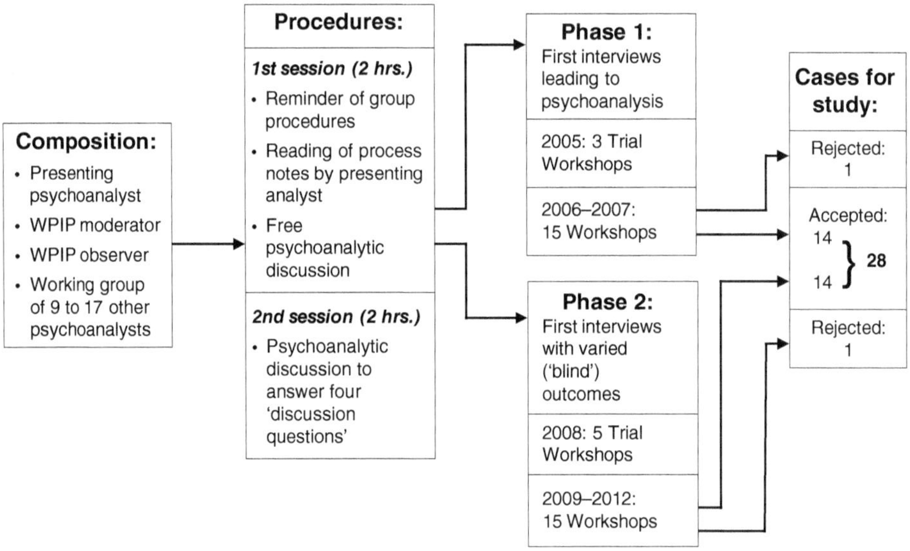

Figure 3.2 The WPIP Clinical Workshops

of an observer turned out to be an invaluable tool for capturing the group dynamics and for using this information in the subsequent analysis of the material by the WPIP Team.

The task of each workshop was to explore a different case of preliminary interviews, each submitted by an experienced analyst. We recruited presenting analysts working in both 'consultation for referral' and 'private' settings as defined above. The presenting analysts were asked to bring as detailed process notes as possible, but we refrained from giving them more detailed specifications because we were interested to see as much as possible of their own ways of working and of presenting their work, so as to respect the variety of existing practices in EPF societies and their respective institutes. It was also accepted that the patient–analyst pair might need more than one interview to arrive at a recommendation. We therefore investigated all of the interviews that the patient–analyst pair required in order to arrive at a decision. Their number usually ranged from one to two, but up to as many as five.

We asked the presenting analysts to prepare their case material so as to protect the identity of the patient, eliminating or disguising any personal information that would allow the latter to be recognized. Because their work would be subjected to scientific scrutiny, the presenting analysts were also informed beforehand that their own identity would be kept anonymous in all publications. The workshop participants were required to follow the usual strict confidentiality rules for supervision and clinical discussion groups, forbidding disclosure outside the workshops. The presenting analyst and participants were informed that the workshop proceedings were audio-recorded to allow later analysis. The presenting analysts of those cases meeting our inclusion criteria (see Appendix 1) allowed the WPIP Team to keep a copy of their clinical material for later study together with the workshop recording. All documents and recordings were destroyed at the end of the research process. Before publication, all case material extracts were reviewed once again with the presenting analyst to ensure that good psychoanalytic confidentiality practice was respected (Gabbard 2000).

As already described above in connection with the European Scientific Initiative, although we expected group free-associative processes to be an indispensable component of the psychoanalytic exploratory work that we wanted to promote, we did not think it would be sufficient for our research purposes. Together with the 'discussion questions', we introduced some other explicit prescribed rules of group procedure, which we summarize in Appendix 2. The reasons behind our choice of procedures were outlined above in connection with the European Scientific Initiative and are explained in more detail in Appendix 2. Their aims included bringing out the implicit theories of the presenting analyst and workshop participants, and providing a minimal basis for later comparisons across many different cases.

The purpose of these semi-structured discussion procedures and discussion questions was to function as a constructive frame for psychoanalytic group exploration in the workshops as well as later on in the WPIP Team, to which both primary process free-associative work and secondary process reflective and synthetic work could usefully contribute. They were not designed to impose pre-set categories in which the participants were expected to encode their findings, as on a scale or grid, but rather to stimulate their creativity and reflexivity.

We were not disappointed in this respect. Although at first sight there might seem to be a contradiction between the two modes of thinking, in which the more structured demands made on the participants might be expected to dampen their associative freedom, in practice this was not the case. What we observed was more like a necessary and fruitful tension, usually leading to open-minded, respectful and thoughtful group work. The international setting and composition of the workshops generated a free atmosphere in which the groups seemed less blinded by common theoretical backgrounds and less hampered by local group dynamics than they might have been in their home societies. Colleagues looked at the interview material through the lens of free association together with their experience, intuition, different theoretical backgrounds and creativity. Supervising dynamics could in most instances be avoided and replaced by genuine interest and curiosity. When other group dynamics in response to the material did occur, as we will describe below and in the next chapter, it was against the background of this working atmosphere.

Although participants sometimes complained when it was time to turn to the discussion questions, these did not diminish the psychoanalytic exploratory work and often had the opposite effect of relaunching and intensifying it, for example by setting off new insights and associations. However, as we describe in Appendix 3, finding good sets of discussion questions to serve this purpose was a trial-and-error learning process for the WPIP Team. We began our first round of workshops with a set of discussion questions that the participants experienced as too grid-like and restrictive, feeling they could not use them psychoanalytically, and leading us to devise new sets of questions facilitating more open forms of exploration.

As hoped, this group method often revealed aspects of the interview dynamics to which the presenting analyst had been blind, in the sense of not having consciously perceived them. There were also frequent instances in which the presenting analyst had had a sense of struggling with significant aspects of the dynamics but had not managed to understand or find words for them. When this happened it usually led to interesting clinical discussions, whose relevance was often confirmed by the presenting analyst.

Two phases of the study

At the beginning of the study, as a way of circumscribing our field of investigation, we asked the presenters to bring what they considered to be typical examples of preliminary interviews that had led to full analysis, either with the interviewer him/herself (in 'private' settings) or with another analyst (in 'consultation for referral' settings). This Phase 1 plan was applied to the initial Trial Workshops and the three subsequent rounds of workshops, resulting in 14 of the 28 detailed case studies retained by the WPIP Team for later re-analysis.

Two main considerations then led us to introduce Phase 2 of the study, in which we asked the presenters to bring any first interview that had interested them, but without revealing the outcome (psychoanalysis, some other form of psychoanalytic treatment, or no psychoanalytic treatment) before the end of the workshop. These considerations were as follows:

- There was an obvious risk that prior knowledge of the interview outcomes could lead to circular reasoning and confirmation bias. This legitimate objection had often been voiced by the workshop participants.
- Simultaneously, as we began formulating our observations about the 'storm-like' dynamics in first interviews (see below and Chapter 5), we wondered whether they were specific to interviews that had led the interviewing analyst to propose analysis, or whether they might characterize *any* first interview with a psychoanalyst.

We thought that studying cases with different outcomes, without sure knowledge of the outcome before the end of the workshops, might allow us to test our observations about the interview dynamics in different circumstances, and perhaps to refine them. This procedure was followed in the next series of Trial Workshops and thereafter in all new rounds of workshops, resulting in an additional 14 detailed case studies (see also Appendix 1).

We did our best to follow a similar procedure in the WPIP's re-examination of the cases, whereby the WPIP members who had not been in the workshop under study were also kept 'blind' to the outcome of the case until they had finished their assessment of it.

Although this was of course not a truly 'blind' procedure, we did find that both in the Clinical Workshops and in the WPIP Team exploration tended to be much sharper, with livelier and richer discussions, when it was not influenced by certain knowledge of the outcome. The aim of including cases with different outcomes in this small qualitative study was also primarily to intensify the examination of the psychoanalytic process.

Data analysis: further psychoanalytic exploration in the WPIP Team

The core WPIP Team was composed of eleven psychoanalysts from different countries and psychoanalytical backgrounds. In addition to their role as workshop moderators and observer/reporters, they met four times a year, at the EPF conferences and for long weekend retreats, to prepare the Clinical Workshop procedures and to study the material that had been collected.

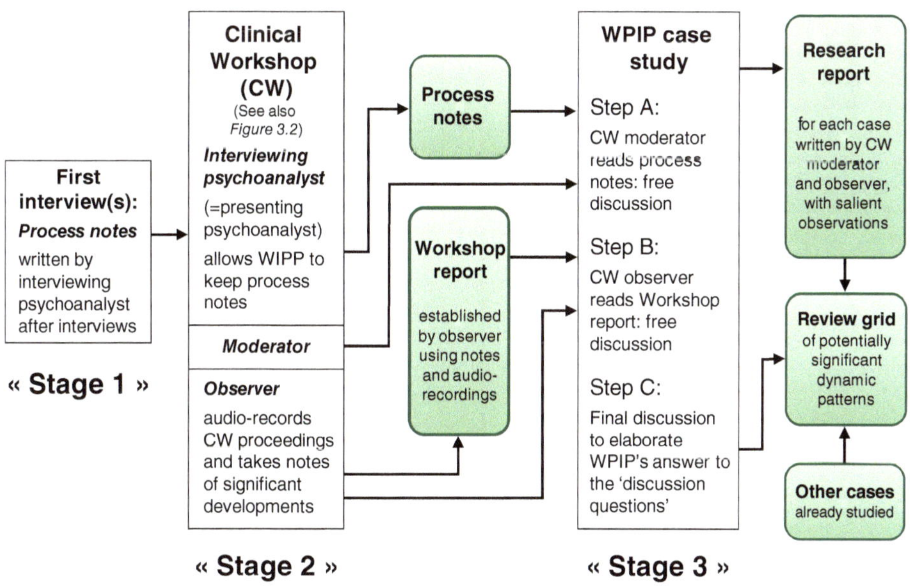

Figure 3.3 Individual case studies

After each workshop, the observer/reporter used his/her notes and the audio recordings to write up a transcript of the workshop proceedings, noting the flow of the discussion, the group process, and key passages such as salient moments or insights.

The clinical material, together with the workshop proceedings, was then re-examined by the WPIP Team using the same combination of free-associative and semi-structured discussion procedures as in the workshops: we found them to be just as useful to us as to the latter, providing a way of helping us to stick to our investigative task. The work was done in a prescribed sequence for each case, as shown in Figure 3.3. The resulting research reports were structured to summarize specific points that we thought were likely to be important, regarding the setting and unfolding of the interview, the workshop proceedings and findings, as well as the WPIP's answers to the discussion questions.

Step by step, as we moved on from case to case, and then during systematic case reviews, the findings were compared across cases with the hope of being able to detect, and ultimately to confirm or reject, emergent dynamic patterns. These could be general patterns that many cases seemed to have in common, or more specific patterns that seemed to distinguish some groups of cases from others. This confrontation of different cases, which is described in Figure 3.4, was also both free-associative and semi-structured.

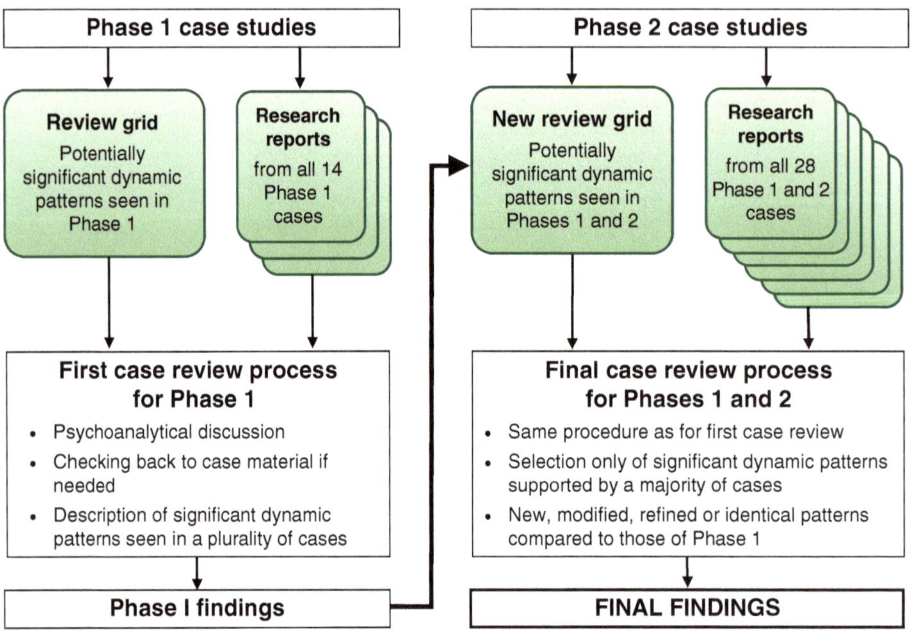

Figure 3.4 Case reviews

Often a pattern was first recognized during free-associative work, when some aspect of a case pointed to what seemed to be an issue of more general relevance and/or reminded WPIP Team members of other cases. When such a pattern seemed to make sense of many different clinical occurrences, it was noted as potentially significant and included in a case-review 'grid' listing the patterns we thought warranted re-examination in systematic case reviews. The first such review was carried out on the 14 cases of Phase 1; the second and final review was done on all 28 cases of Phases 1 and 2. Although systematic, such case-review work led to further free-associative insights and psychoanalytic elaboration. Only psychoanalytically significant patterns that were supported by a plurality of cases were retained for the findings that appear in this book.

For its first case studies, while it was still trying to find its way through the material, the WPIP Team needed up to twelve hours of discussion per case. Later on, this was often reduced to about four hours per case, not counting the meeting time devoted to the case reviews and the considerable working time devoted outside meetings to writing up the workshop and research reports.

Although systematic, time-consuming and challenging, these various parts of the WPIP's working procedure remained psychoanalytic, including through its impact upon us as psychoanalysts. Each observation struck us as novel and surprising, even when it seemed to confirm or disconfirm previous findings, moving us as though we were discovering it for the first time and giving us a sense that we were in contact with what psychoanalysis is really about.

Working with the case-review 'grids' was a learning experience on its own, similar to the work done to develop the discussion questions. It turned out to be a powerful frame, stimulating the Team to re-discuss and rethink its assumptions, often provoking a fresh psychoanalytic exploration of some of the case material.

Overview of our findings

We will now proceed to an overview of our core findings about the dynamics of first interviews, which will form the substance of the next chapters. Some other findings, concerning the group-investigative methods and their relevance, will be described in Chapter 4.

New hypotheses about the specific dynamics of initial interviews: 'facing the storm' and 'opening psychoanalytic space'

As we examined the clinical material and workshop proceedings to test our first ideas about 'initiating psychoanalysis' and 'switching the level', we were increasingly struck by a general observation, which imposed itself as a core issue for our study: namely, that in all cases we examined, the unconscious interview dynamics seemed to be even more intense than we had expected:

- On close examination there always seemed to be far more going on in terms of unconscious conflicts and transference and countertransference dynamics, than the analyst could possibly capture in the interview situation or even when writing up the process notes.
- Contrary to our first hypothesis that the analyst had to help the interviewee to allow an upwelling of unconscious affects and phantasies, it could be seen that these were powerfully present from the outset, including, as we will see in Chapter 6, in manifestations appearing before the interview itself.
- As we will describe in Chapter 5, these dynamics could strongly affect both members of the analytic couple, sometimes disturbing them and even momentarily overwhelming them. This made it difficult, indeed sometimes impossible, to 'switch the level' in the sense of becoming aware of something new, as we had postulated for this process. The 'meaningful common formulations' that we expected to see were only rarely achieved.
- Because of its intensity, we adopted the concept of an 'unconscious storm' to describe this phenomenon, borrowing the notion of 'storm' from Bion (1979). As we will also describe in more detail in Chapter 5, our new central hypothesis proposed that dealing with and working within the 'storm' was the analyst's crucial task in first interviews. It involved striving to maintain an analytic position despite the intense dynamics, in order to salvage the possibility of finding meaning for them. We came to think of this as striving to 'open psychanalytic space' or to keep it open, as an essential prerequisite to 'switching the level'. As our case material will show throughout the book, opening psychoanalytic space is a difficult task, involving both conscious and unconscious work at all levels ranging from the analyst's personal engagement to his/her reference to theory.
- We discovered that the patient–analyst couple seemed to find many ways to deal with this intense transference and countertransference field. These could be more or less defensive, for example through denial of what seemed to be a core issue and/or idealization of psychoanalysis, or on the contrary they could be open and non-defensive, with the possibility of taking on board more of the issues that were pressing to the fore. Having a strong internal and external frame could help, as well as having a concrete or symbolic third to rely on, as we will describe in many of our chapters, in particular Chapters 7 and 8. However, various degrees of enactment were also found in all cases (sometimes detected

by the analyst, sometimes not), as we will see in numerous examples and discuss in more depth in Chapter 9.
- Often some of the unconscious dynamics, present in the initial 'storm' but impossible to receive and transform at that time, could be seen to return later in the analysis seeking elaboration.

In retrospect, one can think of our hypothesis of 'switching the level', with its effect of discovery, surprise and 'meaningful common formulation', as reflecting a model suggestive of a pre-existing psychoanalytic space ready to be discovered and entered, such that the analyst's work involved finding a key to open it. What we saw instead was that an analytic space must be *created* and that this can be a challenging task.

Relationships between psychoanalytic process and outcome

The aim of including cases with different outcomes was to sharpen our examination of the psychoanalytic process, not to look for correlations between process and outcome. However, because we were struck by the differing, more or less defensive or open responses of the analytic couple to the 'storm', we were of course curious to see what impact these different responses might have on the decision to begin or recommend analysis or another form of treatment. The results were sobering:

- Many factors came to the fore from the cases we had studied which seemed to influence the choice of analysis, psychotherapy, or no analytic treatment, but these often seemed to be trivial, not fundamentally psychoanalytic factors, such as sociocultural background, whether or not the analyst had a vacancy, whether or not the patient could afford analysis or had access to subsidized treatment, and so on. These different situations evoked a lot of discussions both in the Clinical Workshops and the WPIP Team about the context of the first meeting in terms of financial, sociocultural and institutional issues. They were mainly individual situations, with anecdotal value, but which our study was neither designed nor equipped to investigate. We will not return to them in this book, except to explore the specific role of institutional consultation for referral settings in Chapter 8.
- As to the role of the specifically psychoanalytic dynamics that we saw in our case material, our tentative conclusion is the opposite of what much accepted wisdom might lead us to expect: namely, that there are no discernible relationships between the kind of process that develops in the initial interviews, and the treatment choice. Many different kinds of psychoanalytic process seem to lead to psychoanalysis, just as they can lead to other options. Treatment recommendation seems to be the

outcome of a highly individual encounter between patient, analyst and institutional setting. In particular, both parties seem to opt for the form of treatment which they think will provide them with the best possible conditions for dealing with the disturbing dynamics that they have encountered. We will discuss and illustrate our reasons for this view in Chapter 7.

These are not negative conclusions. While there may be a wish to provide indicators for 'analysability' from the nature of a first interview, and in that sense this conclusion is 'negative', our findings instead confirm the outcome of other studies and suggest that more fundamental dynamic forces are at work in these psychoanalytic encounters. As we will see throughout this book and will discuss again in Chapter 10, our findings can also be taken to support a view of psychoanalysis as a unique, highly individualized form of treatment in which an analyst is willing to engage fully and specifically with another person's difficulties, and to select the setting and mode of entry into the psychoanalytic process that seems most appropriate for this relationship. One of the things we have seen is that dynamics that were present in the first interviews but not picked up at the time were often dealt with later on in the analysis.

Discussion

The WPIP Team has been careful to test its hypotheses about any patterns by referring back to multiple levels of observation and comparison of the material. Nevertheless, the characteristics of the method, with its strengths and limitations, must be kept in mind when interpreting its results. This would have to be clarified through comparison with the findings when first interviews are studied with other Working Party procedures or other scientific methods.

For example, one possibility is that our impression of an unconscious 'storm' characterizing each of the first interviews examined was due to a bias in the presenting analysts' choice of cases. Although they were requested to bring typical examples of their analytic work, they may have hoped to find supervision in the workshops, or they may have been glad to have an opportunity to demonstrate a successful piece of difficult analytic work. This hypothesis is belied to some extent by the fact that in many cases the 'storm' was not experienced as such by the presenter during the interviews, even though it was later felt to be very much there by the workshops and/or the WPIP Team. Some presenters went home from the workshops feeling surprised or even shaken, with the sense of having discovered important yet unsuspected aspects of the transference and countertransference dynamics. The possibility of an unconscious need for supervision cannot be excluded by such observations, but on a conscious level, at any rate, some presenters certainly came away with the realization that the work was more difficult than they had thought.

The EPF Working Parties' approach has demonstrated that psychoanalysts working within different psychoanalytical models can exchange thinking about clinical material and reach a consensus about how to describe it. If their theoretical and clinical approaches are thought of as 'filters', then it is remarkable that something common can be picked up by each of them. The same can be said of the multiple emotional fields and perspectives produced by the dynamics of each 'Stage' in our investigation, as described in Chapter 4. When a pattern persists through all these filters, it probably does convey some valuable psychoanalytic information.

The working hypothesis which we have retained, therefore, is that the 'storm' in these interviews is active whether or not it is perceived, and that our research process worked as a good instrument to reveal it.

4 ANALYSTS BEING ANALYSTS
The group exploratory method in action

The frame provided by the discussion procedures, the research questions and the case reviews revealed extremely interesting group processes, both in the Clinical Workshops and in the WPIP Team, which could be seen to appear against the backdrop of the generally productive working climate and which could be understood as group responses to the clinical material.

An important point is that although some of these phenomena were noticed on the spot, most of them were first detected on careful examination of the workshop proceedings, or on re-examination by the WPIP of its own proceedings, for example during its systematic case reviews.

Having repeatedly encountered and examined these phenomena in numerous cases, we have come to think of them as a valuable source of information. There are, furthermore, interesting similarities between the group processes that we observed in the Clinical Workshops and the WPIP Team, and the internal processes that the presenting analysts described they went through during initial interviews. This may have something to do with the work required of the mind when dealing with unconscious dynamics that it is not prepared for – whether these arise in an actual first analytic encounter with another person, or in other situations requiring psychoanalytic work. It is therefore worthwhile to study these group processes in more detail before we turn to the internal work of the presenting analyst in Chapter 5.

We will outline two basic classes of exploratory group processes:

- those which seemed to flow more 'smoothly', where the elaborative work seems to be well contained by the working frame; and
- processes which became more 'turbulent', pressing towards enactment and threatening to burst out of the frame. In this second class we will include not only enactments, but also processes that appeared to become inhibited or blocked, when there seemed to be a sense that the working frame was in danger of being overwhelmed.

All groups tended to show both kinds of processes. We could see them in the Clinical Workshops from our vantage points as moderators and observers, but we could also experience them first-hand in our WPIP meetings. After describing these processes, we will illustrate them by following an example of case material through the three 'Stages' of investigation; from the first interviews, through the Clinical Workshop, to the WPIP research meeting. Finally, this will allow us to introduce a hypothetical 'Three-Stage' model of psychoanalytic research.

More 'smoothly flowing' exploratory group processes

In many case studies, one could observe an increasingly deeper insight into the case material as the work progressed, through the duration of the Clinical Workshop, and then in the WPIP's re-examination of the case building on the workshop proceedings.

Exploratory processes within the groups

Emotional resonance

Psychoanalysts in both kinds of group settings resonated emotionally with the material they studied, leading them to try to find symbolic representation for it, through reverie and other forms of elaborative work. Their emotional resonance could also be expressed in more turbulent dynamics, as we will describe further on.

'Associative' processes: reverie and free association

Primary process work involving reverie (Bion 1962, Ogden 1997) and free association could be seen to be important for the development of insight in the groups, as they collectively struggled to find representations for implicit or poorly represented aspects of the dynamics in the clinical material:

- One group member could be seen to respond to a specific sequence in the patient–analyst interaction, finding a telling image for it or voicing his/her fantasy about it, thereby setting off an associative chain in which other group members took part.
- Another workshop member would then respond differently to the same sequence, or indirectly by picking up a different sequence, setting off yet another associative chain. This produced a 'diffraction' effect (Kaës 2005) in which the personal sensibilities and diverse psychoanalytic models of the individual group members allowed them to capture different aspects of the material, much like a prism separating white light into its spectrum of colours.
- Several such chains could be seen to interweave (Norman and Salomonsson 2005), diverging or joining, reinforcing or contradicting each other, developing a progressively denser tissue of meanings with a few shared themes.

Fears are often voiced that introducing semi-structured procedures would interrupt this process. In practice, this is not what we observed. On the contrary, and in keeping with similar observations made by other groups (Tuckett et al. 2008), secondary process work could often be seen to enhance primary process work:

- Primary process, free-associative thinking could sometimes lead individual group members off on their own track, to such an extent that it could be difficult for the group to see the meaning of some of the divergent associative chains or indeed the links between them. The more structured approaches, such as asking participants to link their ideas to specific occurrences in the session material and to discuss them in terms of some predetermined research questions, could help the groups to retrace the origins and trajectory of individual associative chains, thus becoming more aware of possible common origins and meeting points.
- A strikingly meaningful discovery in the course of free-associative work could get the group into a hypnotic rut, preventing it from seeing other aspects. In contrast, a more structured approach could be seen to have the advantage of stimulating the group members to remain attentive to all potentially relevant aspects of the material, including aspects which they had wished to avoid or which seemed contradictory, producing a denser tissue of meaning.
- The discussion questions often helped individual workshop participants to become aware of previously preconscious impressions about, or associations to, the material and thereafter to find words for them.

'Reflective' processes: triangulation and the third-person perspective

Both in the Clinical Workshops and in the WPIP research meetings, the semi-structured working procedures also introduced a valuable 'triangulation' effect between the different group members and the material they were working on together, helping each participant to attain a more self-reflective, third-person perspective on his/her response to the material:

- Asking the participants to link their impressions to specific occurrences in the process notes and to answer the research questions made it easier to see how other participants could have quite different ideas or associations in response to the same aspects of the material.
- This provided a form of reality-testing in which individual group members could come to recognize that their own reading of the process notes wasn't necessarily exhaustive.
- The consequent linking of personal responses to those of others enriched the individual experiences of the material.

- Being invited to follow how other analysts using different models read the same material opened pathways for identification with their experience, promoting a better understanding of their thinking, from the inside as it were.
- This distinct viewpoint could then introduce a more third-person perspective on each analyst's own relationship to the clinical material, with more insight into how personal perceptions and understanding of the material might be influenced by explicit and implicit theories.
- When things went well, this triangulation could help to promote a shared third-person perspective on the diverse responses to the material and their common origins.

Exploratory processes between groups

The 'diffraction' and 'triangulation' processes could also be observed to take place between the successive research settings:

- Because the work was approached with a different group composition and from a new perspective, each new setting could pick up aspects of the interview dynamics that had not been seen before. Thus, the participants of a Clinical Workshop often became aware of a particular aspect of the interview dynamics that the presenter had not consciously perceived, or had not quite managed to pin down. Later on, the WPIP Team sometimes noticed further aspects that the workshop had missed or been unable to get to grips with.
- The process could also work the other way around. After the WPIP Team had worked on a first interview, it often discovered upon reading the Workshop proceedings that certain aspects had been captured, which the WPIP Team had not noticed. Thus, if the WPIP Team's associative chains had dried up, they could be refreshed or enriched by studying the Workshop transcripts.

Each group was thus able to build on the work that had been done at the previous Stage, and could function as a third with respect to the other Stages, facilitating insight and elaboration.

More 'turbulent' group processes

Alongside those that we have just described, interesting group phenomena also arose, both in the Clinical Workshops and in the WPIP Team, which could be understood as enactments in response to the clinical material expressing resistance, evacuation and/or proto-mental work, followed by increased awareness and elaboration.

These phenomena were usually temporary and appeared against the backdrop of a generally well-functioning working group. They rarely obstructed the working process but rather seemed to accompany it. Sometimes the moderator, the observer, or an attentive group member noticed them in real time, but many (more or less subtle or striking) instances were first noticed on examination of the workshop proceedings, or on re-examination of the WPIP's own proceedings during case reviews.

There was an example of this kind of group phenomenon in the case of *The Handsome Man on Crutches* reported in Chapter 2, wherein the predominantly engaged, friendly and constructive atmosphere of the Clinical Workshop temporarily became hostile towards the patient, and sometimes also critical of the analyst's technique. This cleared up when the Workshop group became more in touch with the patient's own experience of having been intruded upon and overwhelmed in the course of his development. The group had temporarily needed to defend itself against this theme of intrusion, and had done so in an enactment, by becoming intrusive itself.

At first, we thought that such group dynamics could be mainly nonspecific defensive reactions, belonging to the group's own equilibrium in the face of stressors not directly related to the clinical material itself. These various stressors certainly exist and include:

- the vulnerability of the workshop groups, who were asked to complete a clinical task before having yet been able to establish themselves as a group, composed as they were of participants newly brought together who mostly didn't know each other. The difficult task of establishing contact with the emotional life of a new group tends to create regressive reactions and psychotic anxieties (Bion 1961, Anzieu 1999). In one model of group dynamics, the phase of tension that arises as individuals adopt defensive positions to meet this challenge is described as 'storming' (Tuckman and Jenson 1977);
- the relatively large size of the workshop groups with 12-20 participants, which may have multiplied these anxieties;
- the short 4-hour time scale of the WPIP workshop setting, requiring the groups to accomplish much work in a limited space of time, perhaps reproducing the setting of first psychoanalytic interviews, in which the patient–analyst pair also have very little time to take in the impact of their encounter;
- the challenges of the 'meta' situation, where analysts were asked to explore material coming from ways of working that were unfamiliar to them, and moreover to relinquish their familiar explanatory models (Basile et al. 2010, Reith 2015);
- the research setting with its tension between primary and secondary process work, as described in Chapter 3.

However, similar phenomena were observed in the WPIP Team, even after it had long established itself as a trusting working group that had become familiar with its method and with the individual members' preferred psychoanalytic models and could afford to take more time over a case if it so required. This suggests that these more general explanations could not be the only relevant factors.

Enactment-like processes: description

Our cumulative case studies and group-work experiences pointed to a complementary explanation. Careful study of the workshop and WPIP proceedings suggested that such group reactions tended to appear at key moments, in response to precise aspects of the clinical material. This indicates that the group reactions performed specific unconscious functions in their efforts to deal with the impact of the material itself, and not only with the general investigative setting:

- One such typical function seemed to be *defensive*: for example to ward off the emotional impact of a traumatic aspect that was being discussed at that point, or to interrupt an associative chain that could lead to disturbing fantasies. Although such defensive reactions might reflect the group's own defensive reaction to the material, they could also sometimes be seen to reproduce defences used by the patient or the analyst.
- Another, equally typical function seemed to be *expressive*. Through a collective enactment, the group could be seen to give unconscious expression to important latent aspects of the interview dynamics which could not yet find verbal representation, such as an unconscious affect; a poorly symbolised unconscious phantasy; or internal object relationships, wherein some of the group participants behaved as if they were in concordant or complementary identification (Racker 1968) with one or another of the patient's internal objects represented in the analytic field. These forms of group response could be seen to perform an unconscious 'phoric' function (Kaës 2005), in which one or more members acted like 'messengers' for something important that the group was trying to capture and understand.

The 'defensive' and 'expressive' functions were found to be not mutually exclusive. The case material we report below, for example, illustrates how a Workshop group's defensive inhibition also expressed the patient's fears of being overtaken by an internal catastrophe. In the same case, through getting into an intellectual debate the WPIP Team temporarily interrupted its usual procedure to ward off the traumatic impact of the material, but thus also expressed the patient's phallic defences.

Inhibited versus enactment-like processes

These examples illustrate how the quieter, more inhibited group dynamics at one extreme and the 'noisy', more manifest forms at the other extreme may represent a spectrum of phenomena with similar basic characteristics. Whether through inhibition or more overt transgressions of the working frame, they seem to reveal a temporary threat to, or failure of, the containing capacity of the group. However, in doing so, they also revealed something about what it is that the group was struggling to contain. They could therefore all be seen as forms of enactment, in the widest sense of the term (on enactment, see Chapter 9 in particular).

Group enactments as parallel process phenomena

If we admit the existence of such defensive and/or expressive group reactions to the unconscious dynamics conveyed by the clinical material, then we may also view them as group processes working on important, but as yet poorly symbolized, aspects of the interview dynamics. Such processes can be thought of as paving the way for growing insight, although this is expressed at first in forms of enactment.

If we accept that this is what happens with enactments in ordinary analytic work, as the analytic couple struggle to become aware of and transform poorly symbolized aspects of the transference and countertransference field, it seems reasonable to think that the same can be true of research settings, where the Clinical Workshop and research groups struggle to become aware of the inter-psychic group field generated by the interview material. Thus we would be witnessing one of the ways in which the participating analysts conduct real analytic work.

We suggest that such group processes are similar to the 'parallel process' phenomena described in other settings (Searles 1955, Doehrman 1976, Gediman and Wolkenfeld 1980, Lagerlöf and Sigrell 1999), repeating and revealing something about the case material and its impact on those who discuss it, and thus pointing to important aspects of the unconscious dynamics carried by the material.

Parallel process phenomena as sources of information

These phenomena may be useful so long as they are noticed and subjected to elaboration. They must be taken into account not only because they are liable to complicate the research method, but also because they can enhance it once they are understood. In other words, what may seem to be unwelcome noise can actually carry valuable information.

In our experience, this information could occasionally be captured by the group itself when a participant pointed out the enactment, enabling the group to shift back from a defensive basic assumption mode to re-establish itself as a working group (Bion 1961), enriched by the intervening experience. This has particularly been the case in the WPIP Team and is well illustrated by the clinical example we will give below. The Workshop moderators could also help, for example with a remark about a theme that the group seemed to be particularly interested in.

More frequently, such events were captured on re-examination of the group's proceedings. This could be the case when the WPIP Investigative Team studied the transcript from a Clinical Workshop, enabling it to perceive parallel process phenomena that were not noticed on the spot. The Team could then build on the work undertaken by the Clinical Workshop, pursuing the workshop's elaboration of the case but also benefiting from the enactments, which promoted deeper understanding.

The same could happen when the WPIP re-examined its own meeting notes during its case reviews, once the passage of time allowed it to function as a third with respect to itself. Each time we detected such phenomena in our own group, on the spur of the moment or during case reviews, it contributed to a sense of insight and understanding, corroborating our findings with the direct evidence of personal experience. Some of the most convincing instances of parallel process were those in which we were involved ourselves, as illustrated in the case described below.

To sum up, having studied and compared many such observations and experiences we have come to see group dynamics in a research context such as ours, not only as an original creation by the group itself, expressing the group's own dynamics and equilibrium, but also as a useful source of information about the unconscious dynamics carried by the clinical material. Clearly defined 'prescribed rules of procedure' (Norman and Salomonsson 2005) and attentive moderation (Salomonsson 2012) are necessary to prevent gross destructive and obstructive dynamics, but on the basis of our observations they cannot control the expressive and defensive parallel process dynamics, which will inevitably infiltrate the group processes. One cannot stop the unconscious.

Indeed, and taking these ideas one step further, one might see these phenomena as forms of proto-symbolization in which the groups unconsciously played out (in the form of group scenarios) aspects of the interview dynamics which could not yet find verbal representation. This might be compared to the 'scenic function' of the ego as described by Argelander (1970) and to the understanding of enactment as a scenic production or 'staging' ('mise en scène') (Donnet 2005). It could almost be seen as a third, 'enactment' mode of thinking, interacting with the 'free-associative' and 'reflective' modes. This theme of enactment-related processes will reappear throughout the following chapters.

The Self-Assured Academic

The following case study, from Phase 2 of our project, exemplifies the investigative process, illustrating how each Stage can contribute to a deepening exploration of, and insight into, the unconscious interview dynamics. It is also an example of how parallel process phenomena can occur at each Stage, pointing to the work required of all participants' minds (patient, analyst, Clinical Workshop, WPIP Investigative Team) to take them on board and elaborate them, including enactments that repeat aspects of the unconscious dynamics.

The case study is based on first interviews that led to an analysis at four sessions per week, which the analyst experienced as satisfactory and which permitted significant improvements in the patient's life. If our understanding of the research process and its findings is valid, material like this also illustrates how a productive psychoanalysis begins while patient and analyst are both struggling to make contact with some of the most disturbing unconscious transference and countertransference undercurrents. It is not surprising that analytic work in first interviews would leave important dimensions unelaborated or untouched, but it is interesting to observe what a powerful impact these can have on those who later opt to study the material.

The interviews

First interview

On the phone Ms. B., a university researcher, had told the female presenting analyst 'that she felt in a crisis, and that she was at risk of ruining her life because she didn't really know herself'. However, at the first interview, the analyst met 'a young, quite pretty woman, dressed business-like, looking directly at me. She had a rather self-assured appearance, but also seemed tense and anxious.'

In response to the analyst's suggestion that she tell about herself, Ms. B. began, in what struck the analyst as an angry tone:

> I'm one of those who love too much. I grew up in a very dysfunctional family. We had loads of secrets. This summer something happened that made it very clear to me that something was repeating itself and that I had to do something about it.

She described that she had broken up with her friend, P., with whom she had been living for several years. He was married when they met and had left his wife for her:

They have two children. I couldn't cope with them. I had big problems especially with his extremely provocative teenage daughter. When I finally had a big row with her, and he took her side, that was just too much. I left him and moved into my mother's house. I had the same kind of relationship with him as with my mother, the same mechanisms, but it's only now that I've become aware of it.

An: Yes?

Ms. B.: I try to adjust for too long and put up with too much. I can't say no. I can't find my own limits. My mother and P. couldn't stand each other, they had big conflicts and she was always criticizing him in front of me. She even threatened that I should choose between them.

An: It must have been difficult for you to move home; she might take it as a confirmation that you had realized that her criticism of P. was right and that you had chosen her?

Ms. B.: Yes. I went directly into the old pattern between my mother and me.

She described an egocentric and possessive mother not allowing her daughter a life of her own, thinking she could read her daughter's mind and always knowing better how she felt. Ms. B. had tried to engage her mother in a dialogue about this but her mother couldn't cope with criticism and had broken off all contact (this occurred some months before the first interview). She hadn't seen her since and didn't want to. She had seen 'a counsellor a couple of times, but he was only scraping the surface. I need something else, something that goes into the depths and makes it possible for me to find other ways of acting.'

An: Did you think about how come the counsellor didn't understand that?

Ms. B.: Hmm?

An: Could it be that it's not easy for you to express that you need to be helped?

Ms. B.: I think it's more than that – I don't recognize my own needs. I am much more attentive to other people's needs.

An: Recognizing your own needs might be risky?

Ms. B.: I had to make sure my mother was OK. She has a very difficult temperament, she always had.

Ms. B. described how her parents, who were shopkeepers, divorced when she was 7; her father's gambling problems; her mother's tendency to end difficult relationships. 'She says that she has no problem breaking with somebody. She calls it "cutting off".'

An: Either you accept being a part of her or you become a cut off part of her?

Ms. B.: I had a brother who was six years older. My mother and he always quarreled and had conflicts about everything. Once after a big row he

(continued)

(continued)

	went away in a rage and threw himself off a building. I was 12 then. I had to be big and sensible. I had to be the responsible and intelligent child who took care to reassure my mother that she was OK as a mother. She told me, that if I too was going to kick up a row, she would do like my brother.
An:	You said there were many secrets in your family. You must have felt very alone not having anybody helping you with sorting out all this.
Ms. B.:	On the surface nothing was wrong and nobody was supposed to know what was under the surface.

In a sense, Ms. B.'s last comment can be taken as a metaphor for the session, with a split between the well-organized surface of an in-control professional, and a life in severe crisis with a terrifying, life-threatening inner world. Although Ms. B. could reveal her traumatic family history, she did so projectively, attributing all violence to others and describing herself only in terms of adapting to them. She made a difficult-to-refuse offer of analytic collaboration to 'find out about herself', contacting the analyst in words that she thought would interest her: going into the depths in order to change unwanted 'mechanisms'. She did not seem to be fully aware of how dark and forbidding those depths could be, nor how upsetting it might be for her to dive there. She talked as if determination would suffice, evoking some kind of self-improvement plan based on popular cognitive-behavioural ideas.

Realizing that Ms. B. was on the defensive, vulnerable and fearful of intrusion, the analyst began at Ms. B.'s narrative surface, echoing her, with her first intervention about her mother: 'It must have been difficult for you to move home; she might take it as a confirmation . . . ', and then tried to switch the level by offering a step-by-step transformation of the behavioural narrative into one more in touch with Ms. B.'s intra-psychic conflicts, culminating in: 'Recognizing your own needs might be risky?' In this way, the analyst picked up on Ms. B.'s more fragile dimension and gave an implicit interpretation of her transference to the analytic setting. This allowed them to move on to the crude and cruel material about 'cutting off' and the horrendous event of the elder brother's suicide. The traumatic impact of that last part of the session, however, seemed to be so overwhelming that it led the analyst to back away from the negative transference, implicitly offering herself as a better object: 'You must have felt very alone not having anybody helping you with sorting out all this.'

Second interview, three weeks later

Ms. B. rushed ahead in her assertive style:

> I have been thinking that I have no doubts that I want to go into depth with all this and that the process has already started. I know it's going to take a long time, but I need to do it now if I'm to change the patterns that I'm stuck in.

The analyst responded with a receptive interpretation of her transference to the analytic relationship:

An: And it's important for you to make sure that I understand that.
Ms. B.: Yeah.
An: And what we spoke about, did anything particular turn up afterwards?
Ms. B.: It made a strong impression on me how angry I felt with my mother. I always thought I was angry with my father. That it was his fault entirely. My mother made us believe he was the cause of everything that went wrong in our family. I was taken aback by my anger towards my mother. I didn't know how angry I was. Anger has been a taboo in our family. I was also surprised that I mostly spoke about my mother.
An: Yes, you didn't tell me very much about your father?
Ms. B.: My father went downhill.

His gambling and money problems worsened after the divorce, and he underwent a frightening social decline. Ms. B.'s fortnightly weekend visits became increasingly stressful:

> His flat was a mess. He didn't really care about us. I felt I was a nuisance to him. I don't remember if my elder brother ever came along. He'd probably made up his mind that he didn't want to. After he died, everything was chaotic. I couldn't sleep at night and went into my mother's bed to sleep. It calmed me down. I must have been alone at my father's place once. I couldn't sleep and came into his bed. Suddenly I felt his erect penis against my hand. I was shocked and rushed into my own bed. Since then I never stayed overnight at his place again.

Gradually, Ms. B. lost contact with him.

'It was a relief for my mother. She was always sad when I went to see him. But it made my paternal grandmother very upset at me. She thought we should protect him.'

At this point the session became a bit confused, as if reproducing Ms. B.'s bewilderment about the role of the maternal figures in her life. Ms. B. seemed to want to say more about traumatic repetition with men, but the analyst responded in terms of fears of abandonment, reminiscent of the conflicts with the mother described in the first interview, which tended to dilute the traumatic impact of the father's frightening breakdown and the intrusive incestuous situation with him. This sequence culminated in:

An: *It's not easy for you not to be nice; you risk being abandoned.*

This return to the maternal relationship may be what led Ms. B. to bring up two dreams at this point:

Ms. B.: After I was here last time, I had two dreams:

> *I was in a hospital bed. The doctor thought I was dead. She was writing the death certificate. I couldn't move or make a sound to tell her I was alive.*

She cried while telling it. 'That's how I feel sometimes. In the other dream':

> *I was in my mother's shop. I was helping with the clients, doing exactly what my mother would expect me to do. The light coming through the shop window was very beautiful. My mother was very pleased with me and hugged me.*

Ms. B.: That's how she would like it to be.
An: Either you are dead or you are your mother's sweet daughter – could it be that you want to stop being her sweet daughter?
Ms. B.: Yes, that's how I feel. But I do want to continue to try and find out about my old patterns in order to get rid of them.
An: At the same time it makes you anxious?
Ms. B.: Yes. I'm afraid of losing control – of losing my mind. My brother lost control and died from it. He was too young to deal with all that he was grappling with.
An: And nobody was helping him?
Ms. B.: I have been thinking how anxious I can become when reacting differently. Nobody has been able to deal with my feelings – either they were wrong or my mother knew better how I felt. I think I have used my work to keep myself at a distance. In a way I'm relieved that I can feel anxiety.
An: Time is up for today. Let's make an appointment for next week and talk about what will be the most helpful kind of therapy.

In retrospect, the two dreams, with their ominous implications of idyllic primary narcissistic fusion leading to psychic death, point to Ms. B.'s unconscious transference phantasies about the dangers of the incipient analytic relationship. This may explain her subsequently voicing her fears of losing her mind and dying like her brother.

The analyst's interpretation of the dreams ('Could it be that you want to stop being her sweet daughter?') underscored Ms. B.'s ambivalence between her wish to differentiate from her mother and her fear that this will lead to abandonment. Implicitly, it probably also referred to the more fundamental ambiguity of her transference wishes of togetherness, protection and well-being in the consulting room/shop/hospital, together with her great fears that this might be what the analyst/mother wanted as well. These transference fears are perceptible with hindsight, but were impossible to grasp more precisely, let alone address more directly, in the session. Instead, through her comment, 'And nobody was helping him?', the analyst again implicitly offered herself as a better new object, to which Ms. B. responded by reaffirming her behavioural stance, stating that she wanted to face up to the work of changing her 'patterns'.

The Clinical Workshop

After reading the sessions to the Clinical Workshop, the analyst said that preparing them had put her back in touch with the feelings she had experienced at that time, several years before. There was from the outset a difficult balance; of connecting with Ms. B.'s distress while remaining aware of her need to be in control, and her fear that the analyst would 'read her mind', like her mother. She had had the sense that there was a lot of undigested material to contain with this patient, but also a risk of doing too much.

The Workshop was thoughtful, but in an inhibited way, and rather protective towards both the analyst and Ms. B. This was notable not only in the contents of the discussion, but also in the group's behaviour, with a tendency to engage directly with the presenting analyst and to avoid triangulations in which Workshop participants could interact with one another about the analyst and her work. The analyst was described in the Workshop report as 'quite interactive in a gentle and informative way with the group'. There was a slow start to the discussion, giving the moderator an uncomfortable feeling that the Workshop wouldn't be able to fill the available time. She had to restrain a wish to intervene, not only to let the group develop its own process, but also because she felt that she would be experienced as critical and intrusive if she did (as indeed the analyst had felt during the interview). When it was time to begin work on the discussion questions, a group member quipped: 'but we have already said everything!' The joke was repeated when it was time to turn to Question 3.

The Workshop's attention was concentrated on the maternal transference, with its themes of intrusion and rejection, and Ms. B.'s fear of her anger and violence, with phantasies of killing her mother or herself. The Workshop felt that the analyst was able to move into this maternal transference but also able to move back, trying to make a safe space. The primitive dilemma for the analytic couple – to fuse or to cut off – was underscored. Rather than these extremes, the analytic couple needed a more open space. But this space was also something which Ms. B. could fear, because of its attendant risks of letting in the image of 'a vulnerable and sexually intrusive father'.

Interestingly, however, the discussion seemed to shy away from this latter theme. In four hours of work, Ms. B.'s father was explicitly mentioned only six times, and always very briefly, as though in passing, within the context of more global comments about the maternal transference. His frightening personal decline and inability to care for his children were not discussed, with the exception of two significant occurrences. One was: 'In her case there was no holding father – what of the possibility of a father in the analyst?' But like other such comments, it did not really lead to a freer group associative process. In fact, in this instance, the analyst intervened to point out that 'no-one had yet emphasized the patient's very controlling presentation, both towards herself and towards the analyst!' – as if she felt compelled to turn the group's attention away from the deficient father. The other occurrence, and the only one in which the word erection was explicitly mentioned, was: 'The exposure to her father's sexuality – the erection – can be taken as a reflection of there having been no one there for her at the time, leaving her confused and with no safe object to turn to'.

The other third, the dead brother, seemed to be even more difficult to let into the elaborative space. His suicide was explicitly mentioned only four times in the whole discussion, and tended to be drowned in more general developments or lumped together with other points, as for the father. A significant link was made between Ms. B.'s conflict with P.'s adolescent daughter and her own age when her brother died, but it was left at this stage of sketchy impression while the group flowed on to other things. Ms. B.'s brother was mostly present in the associative space through indirect allusions to his anger, madness, loss of control and suicide, perhaps most powerfully in comments about her dreams: 'There is a confusion that her mother wants her dead and yet also wants her as a helper'; 'Might she see the couch as a death-bed, or a shop-prison?' The analyst responded to these associations with her own early impressions of the way in which Ms. B. had adjusted to others as a type of suicide.

Thus, although the Workshop evidently struggled to understand the father and brother images, their meaningful omissions and evasions also revealed how frightening it was to face them. One Workshop member had an image of 'a ballet dancer on a minefield', feeling unable to specify whether that referred to the patient, the analyst or the group. The sense of not finding a space in which to think was attributed to Ms. B., in terms which could have also been applied to the Workshop: 'she has lost a home, she is looking for one and hoping to find it with the analyst, but fearing that as well'. At the end of the Workshop, the group voiced its sense of 'darker aspects' and 'concern about potentially destructive possibilities in relation to taking this patient into analysis'. The Workshop reporter afterwards described the group as struggling with 'a dark underbelly'.

One way in which the Workshop did find some structure was through more theoretical reflections about psychopathology and psychoanalytic technique. There were discussions about Ms. B.'s narcissistic defences: 'I wonder if she might in fact be saying, in a pushing away narcissistic defence: "I don't need your compassion, rather I need your admiration"'. This led to an important point:

> This patient wants analysis and is determined to do it, but there is the danger of a 'fake analysis' if the analyst is not able to truly reach her emotionally. It will be very difficult to transform a narcissistic relationship into a true object relationship. A 'pseudo-analysis' is therefore a real possibility.

The WPIP research discussion

While listening to the Workshop moderator's reading of the first session, the WPIP Team was shaken by the brother's suicide: 'It is so hard to take in the suicide of her brother. To begin with you have a view of a normal patient with normal problems and then suddenly, BOOM, her brother dies!' Shortly after, it was noted how little was said of the father in the first interview, and how the relationship with the married boyfriend was an Oedipal choice. However, as in the Clinical Workshop, the brother's suicide was discussed in terms of a failed separation from his mother, and in relation to her frightening image of 'cutting off'. No overt link was made between this 'cutting off' and the father's departure from the home or his castrated image as a social and economic failure.

The tendency to revert to the dual relationship with the mother continued upon reading the second session, culminating with the statement:

> Separation from mother is the most central inner conflict. Ms. B. realizes that she has a split representation of her mother, she loves her mother 'too much' and is surprised to find she also has all this hatred and anger. The patient wants analysis – while the analyst is holding back ('we will decide next time') because she fears moving too quickly into analysis and feels there is more to talk about.

Something very interesting happened at this point. One of the male WPIP members spoke up forcefully: 'But this patient can do analysis!' An animated discussion ensued, in which other male Team members chimed in, for a competitive and pedantic discussion exposing their psychopathological and technical reasons as to why Ms. B. would be able to benefit from analysis – until a female Team member pointed out that this was an enactment. The WPIP Team's standard research procedure was to study the Clinical Workshop report with the Workshop's evaluation of the case *before* formulating its own conclusions about analysability and predictions about outcome, on the basis of all available material. As she put it: 'This sudden erection – where has this come from?' Did it have something to do with the men liking this pretty, self-assured young woman, and therefore wanting to take her in analysis, or was it rather their identification with her, rushing ahead into analysis as she did?

Becoming aware of this phallic enactment was quite a shock for the men in the room. In fact, the group didn't yet have much of a basis for the affirmation that Ms. B. could undertake analysis; she presented as self-reflective but without much evidence that this was really so, apart from her movement between the first and second sessions and her ability to symbolize a fundamental conflict in her two dreams. She also seemed fragile and very much on the defensive.

Reading the Workshop report put the WPIP Team back in touch with the shock of the brother's suicide, Ms. B.'s distress, her father's severe decline, and what she had experienced as his incestuous response. Rushing ahead into competence and foregone conclusions had been the Team's phallic defence against trauma, repeating Ms. B.'s self-confident decision to begin an analysis.

These diverse threads in the WPIP's discussion came together when the Workshop proceedings mentioned, 'there was no holding father – what of the possibility of a father in the analyst?' We realized that what the Workshop actually seemed to experience as missing was not a holding father, but a *structuring* one: '[Ms. B.'s] history tells of a malfunctioning mother, . . . but she also needs a structuring paternal function. This is the central theme.'

The concentration on the maternal transference, at all Stages, could now be seen as expressing a denial of the deficient father figure through the wish to offer a better maternal object:

> The central unconscious dynamic of the interviews is a pull to jump in and be the good mother, which is of course an impossible trap to be in. The need for the ideal mother is in fact the need for a father to rescue her from the real mother.

If we trust the findings of the research process, then we may surmise that the rejection of a structuring father-figure in her mother's mind, compounded with the traumatic impact of her father's departure and inadequacy, left Ms. B. with the unconscious phantasy of a castrated 'dark underbelly', lacking the creative penis-as-link (Birksted-Breen 1996) needed to give structure to triangular object relations and to open mental space (see Chapter 5). She experienced her internal mother as 'cutting off' the genital father, producing an internal world that was not only unstructured, but also the locus of active destruction, threatening to ruin her life. She could not decide who the owner of this destructiveness was, but on account of it she feared that entering an analytic space could mean psychic death, as represented in her dreams and the fear of losing her mind. Ms. B.'s response was to adopt a phallic position where the missing penis-as-link would not be a problem. This same fear of the castrated underbelly was what the men in the WPIP Team reacted to, with their own phallic intrusion. An alternative and more generous understanding of their reaction would place greater emphasis upon the triangular rather than the phallic aspect, as if they were saying: 'But hey, there are men in the room! They *can* be useful!'

Thus, the work done by the analytic couple and the Clinical Workshop allowed the WPIP Team to notice and elaborate its own phallic defence and transform it into a more genital position. Perhaps it was this experience which led the WPIP Team to formulate its positive 'prediction', concluding its research report:

> The analyst will offer analysis. There is a risk of either a 'fake' analysis, or of a breakdown, but not a catastrophic one. The analyst will find her feet in the course of the analysis, just as the patient's need in the analysis is for her internal mother to 'find her feet' and be able to be a real mother who can also acknowledge the lack of the paternal function and find a way to make up for this, such that internal structuring then becomes possible.

Summary of the investigative process

One might sum up the interweaving and emotionally powerful processes set off by this case as follows:

- Ms. B. came to request analysis in a phallic defensive position, hoping thus to overcome her traumatic experiences. The analyst was able to nudge her gently towards greater awareness of her difficulty with needing help and her fear of madness, but she also tended to offer herself as a better, idealized maternal object.
- The Clinical Workshop was particularly sensitive to the ambivalent maternal transference, with its fears of destructiveness and psychic death, but it had to overcome considerable inhibition to come to grips with Ms. B.'s traumatic history and its intrapsychic representation, and consequently it was protective of both patient and analyst. The Clinical Workshop had the intuition of the lack of a 'holding' father ('what of the possibility of a father in the analyst?') but could not take

this insight further. In terms of parallel process, the Workshop thus seemed to express the patient's anxieties and defences as well as the analyst's protective maternal approach to her. Preconscious awareness of this may have led the group to express its warning about the risk of a pseudo-analysis in which the most difficult issues might be avoided in a flight into sanity.

- The WPIP Team responded with a phallic enactment, similar to the patient's phallic defences. Work on this allowed the Team to understand that what the Workshop had intuited as missing was a *structuring* father. The dark underbelly was the frightening image of a castrated, totally inadequate internal father, which the analytic couple had been trying to compensate for by its idealization of a better mother object in the transference, and which the WPIP had tried to compensate for with its phallic reaction, thereby repeating the patient's defence.

Feedback

When we later submitted the above text to the presenting analyst, she wrote that it was 'extremely interesting to be at the same time part of the process and to share the third-person observation position', and that she was:

> very moved experiencing the effect of the unconscious dynamics in the two interviews on the workshop as well as the WPIP group – and the analytic work done. What unfolded in the groups was a condensate of the essentials of the analytic process. Everything was there from the very beginning – and was picked up by the group members.

A 'Three-Stage' model of psychoanalytic research

Developments like those seen in this case were the rule. Group phenomena like those demonstrated in this chapter, appearing both in the Clinical Workshops and in the WPIP Investigative Team, were not only extremely useful as a source of information; they were also a form of unconscious engagement with the interview dynamics, and seemed to be a necessary aspect of the work of containment, exploration and elaboration. Moreover, this work could be thought of as similar in some ways to that done by the presenting analyst, both during the interviews and later while writing them up. Each level seemed to build on the conscious and unconscious work accomplished at the previous one, pursuing some aspects and picking up complementary ones, generally resulting in progressively deeper insight and understanding.

This led us to formulate a 'Three-Stage' metaphor to describe this kind of psychoanalytic investigation, in which the unconscious interview dynamics were not only studied in three serial investigative 'Stages' or 'steps', but also played out and actively explored on what could be understood as three complementary theatrical 'stages' or 'scenes':

'Stage 1': the original preliminary interview(s) between patient and analyst, as written up by the analyst

During the preliminary interview or series of interviews, the presenting analyst has done considerable psychic work to perceive and process the complex dynamics of the encounter. He or she has done further work between or after the interviews, while reflecting on them and writing them up, leading to deeper awareness and clarity. Further psychic work was done when preparing the interviews for their presentation to the workshop.

'Stage 2': the Workshop study of the interview(s) with the presenting analyst in the Workshop

Through the combination of 'free-associative', 'reflective' and 'enactment-based' thinking processes that we have described, the Clinical Workshops were able to deepen the presenting analyst's understanding of the case.

This requires us to postulate that the preconscious and unconscious dynamics of the initial encounter continue to resonate in the clinical presentation, through the presenter's text and presence, affecting the Workshop participants who must elaborate them anew. Aspects of the original interview dynamics that particularly require additional psychic work by the Workshops are probably those that the analytic couple had not been quite able to symbolize or put in words, corresponding to what Sara and César Botella (2001) call 'session residues' waiting for elaboration.

The unconscious 'scenic' quality of some of this work seems in some ways similar to what happens when a session is replayed using psychoanalytic psycho-dramatic techniques for supervision purposes, allowing additional aspects of the dynamics of the session to be unfolded and given emotional and verbal form. To use a theatrical 'stage' metaphor, it is as though the same play were being produced with other actors in another theatre, so that some as yet unnoticed aspects of the script can be expressed and elaborated.

'Stage 3': the WPIP study of the interview and the Workshop proceedings, without the presenting analyst, but with the Workshop moderator and reporter

Quite involuntarily and unexpectedly, the WPIP Team often discovered itself to be functioning as a third 'stage'. As described in Chapter 3, the purpose of the re-examination and comparison of the cases was to look for common dynamic 'patterns'. But analysts being analysts, the Team members found themselves strongly involved with each case. Despite their familiarity with each other and with the work, it has become a common experience for one member or another, or even the Team as a whole, to feel much disturbed. Although at a further remove from the original interview, this seemed to express the unconscious or preconscious aftershocks of the tectonic forces carried by the clinical material, requiring us to capture and understand previously unnoticed but powerful aspects of the original drama, in a way similar to what happened in 'Stage 2' with respect to 'Stage 1'. The result was often very moving. Over time, we have learnt to treasure this process, despite its trying nature.

Our hypotheses to explain 'Stage 3' are analogous to those for 'Stage 2', even if the processes become more complex at each stage. The WPIP Team ('Stage 3') is responding not only to the clinical material ('Stage 1'), but also to the presentation process and the resulting workshop dynamics ('Stage 2'). Although it might be surprising that the unconscious dynamics of the original interview continue to resonate on 'Stage 3' in the absence of the presenting analyst, aspects of the original dynamics may be transmitted not only by the process notes and workshop report, but also unconsciously or preconsciously by the workshop moderator and observer, who worked with the presenter in 'Stage 2'.

The fact that at some point it may be easier to elaborate *without* the presenting analyst must also be taken into account, just as in 'Stage 2' elaboration is facilitated by the absence of the patient. This does not necessarily contradict the idea that prior work *with* the presenter is also necessary.

Hence, although new processes are no doubt created at each 'Stage', they can also be an opportunity to elaborate the 'session residues' of the previous 'Stages', leading to a progressively deeper understanding.

If this assessment is correct, then the 'Three-Stage' method can be thought of as an instrument to 'see' unconscious dynamics that are too 'blinding' or overpowering for the mind to take in on first contact. The work done in 'Stage 2' with the presenting analyst allowed for an initial elaboration of strong emotions carried by the material, thus enabling the work undertaken in 'Stage 3', further away from the interview and not so close to the fire, so to speak, to take on board even more of the dynamics with their power, pain and anxiety.

We wish to emphasize that it was precisely our methodical research procedure that allowed us to capture and analyse the expressive and defensive group phenomena that we have described, and which are of course ubiquitous, but might otherwise have escaped notice.

The differential impact of diverse investigative methods on group dynamics would be a worthwhile object of future study, but on the basis of what we have gathered we find it reasonable to postulate that inter-analytic exchanges of the kind that took place in the Clinical Workshop and WPIP research settings really can function as an effective research tool.

We have therefore come to accept as additional evidence for the unconscious 'storm' the fact that in some cases where it did not seem to be consciously experienced as very powerful by either analyst or patient, or even did not seem to be consciously experienced at all, it could nevertheless come out forcefully later on, in the course of the exploratory process, in the Clinical Workshops or the WPIP Investigative Team. It was as if the 'storm' had to be re-experienced, while the requirement to 'weather' it and 'open psychoanalytic space' could be seen to characterize the work not only of the analytic couple, but also of the investigative groups.

5 FACING THE STORM AND CREATING PSYCHOANALYTIC SPACE

The vicissitudes of the analytic couple in first interviews

Our aim in this chapter is to introduce and discuss our main findings about the unconscious dynamics that are at work in first interviews. We use the term 'unconscious dynamics' in a global sense to refer to all aspects of the transference and countertransference dynamics of the first encounter, and not only in the specific sense of the 'dynamic' point of view in Freud's (1915b) metapsychology. Dynamic aspects in the latter sense of the term are part of the picture, appearing as unconscious conflicts aroused in the patient, as well as in the analyst, by the request for help. These conflicts, however, take place on multiple topographic levels, involving various degrees of symbolization. Economic aspects are also very important, in terms of how much the patient and the analyst can contain and symbolize the arousal created by the encounter, and how much they end up splitting off and/or discharging through enactment.

This introduction will form the background for the more detailed discussion and illustration in the next chapters of specific aspects related to the significant events that take place before the consultation begins (Chapter 6); the diverse ways that the analytic couple finds to deal with the unconscious dynamics (Chapter 7); the process of consultation and referral (Chapter 8); and enactment (Chapter 9). In Chapter 10, we will try to draw some more general conclusions about the nature of psychoanalytic work.

Our findings are based on our cumulative case studies. We will illustrate them in this chapter using a detailed example, *The Mother's Son*. We will also refer back to the two cases that have been discussed earlier in this book, *The Handsome Man on Crutches*, in Chapter 2, and *The Self-Assured Academic*, in Chapter 4.

These examples will demonstrate why our initial hypotheses turned out to be inadequate to account for the observed realities, and how a different picture of the unconscious interview dynamics emerged. Numerous other examples will appear in later chapters.

The powerful unconscious dynamics of initial interviews

We described in Chapter 3 how we expected to see a process of 'switching the level' taking place in first interviews that led to psychoanalysis. The analyst's work would encourage the upwelling of unconscious phantasy, and so help the patient to become aware of something new, which was previously preconscious or unconscious. This discovery would allow the analytic couple to move from an ordinary kind of interview to another, more meaningful, psychoanalytic level of exchange. We expected this shift to appear in the material as 'meaningful common formulations' shared by patient and analyst.

Although we did see such 'switching the level' in some interviews leading to analysis, it was not present in all cases; or when it was, it did not necessarily take on the form we had imagined. Furthermore, when a 'switch' did take place, it was not always evident that it played as central a role in the outcome of the interview as we thought it would. Last but not least, in what was retrospectively an overly simplistic model of the process, we had expected to see such a 'switch' predominantly affecting the patient, whereas it rapidly became clear that it also fundamentally involved the analyst.

In our examination of *The Handsome Man on Crutches* in Chapter 2, we discussed how it didn't seem correct to say that increased awareness was the main factor in Mr. A.'s decision to begin analysis with that analyst; her ability to take in his story, without feeling too intruded upon and without becoming intrusive herself, may have played just as important a role. It did not seem one of the analyst's main tasks to point out meaning, but rather to remain open to its emergence.

Such requirements placed on the analyst were apparent in many interviews. How the analyst dealt with them appeared to influence the interview process. Indeed, a frequent observation was that it was the *analyst*, not the patient, who needed to 'switch the level' for the interview to progress. During successful work in such cases, it was the *analyst* who opened an internal door to become aware of his/her participation in something that was being played out in the interview dynamics. Sometimes the analyst's awareness seemed to arise spontaneously, as a sudden insight; but at other times it seemed to be acquired as the result of a struggle in which s/he had to do considerable internal work to reach some understanding of what could be at stake. The analyst could then use this understanding to regain an analytic stance. Whether or not s/he communicated something derived from this understanding to the patient, and if so what of it and how, were also important aspects of the dynamics.

These challenges are well illustrated in the account that an analyst gave of her encounter with Mr. C.:

The Mother's Son

By way of introduction, the analyst who presented the case of Mr. C. remarked how, compared to other analyses, she had kept especially vivid memories of their preliminary contacts. Her notes confirmed the precision of her memories, when she returned to them four years later. She wondered whether this was due to Mr. C.'s and her own strong cathexis of the psychoanalytical process, or to a traumatic quality of the encounter, with some kind of failure in symbolizing and working through, and therefore with little possibility of integration not only on Mr. C.'s part but also on her own.

A powerful pre-analytic scene (see Chapter 6) was set up during their first telephone conversation. The analyst described how Mr. C. had made a 'clear-cut and unequivocal request for analysis', which was 'not often what I have to deal with', and how he had given her the impression of being 'a polite and pleasant sort of person, who knew what he needed and was able to say so in a calm and dispassionate manner. In a word, he made a very good impression on me'. But then:

> When I suggested that we fix an appointment, I sensed for the first time a note of unease in his voice; he explained that he was not really in any great hurry, that he had a lot of work to do as the year ended and that he would prefer to 'leave it' until January,

i.e. two months later.

The analyst was affected by the sharp contrast between Mr. C.'s initially self-assured presentation and the anxiety that 'emerged as soon as we began discussing doing something about it':

> On the one hand, that contradiction awakened my curiosity; on the other, it left me with a certain feeling of frustration. I wondered whether we would indeed have our scheduled meeting, and I was to some extent eager to find out what lay behind all this. What seemed clear to me was that some kind of rapport between us had immediately been set up – at least on my part – during that brief initial telephone conversation. It was as though, when Mr. C. postponed the first appointment until later, the situation had to some extent been reversed, such that the request had almost shifted from him to me – *I* became the person waiting for what *he* could offer, *I* was taking the risk of being disappointed, not Mr. C. (or not *only* Mr. C.). In addition, there was a kind of subtle seductiveness floating over all of this: I imagined him to be a polite and pleasant person, and I was eager to meet him.

On the appointed day, Mr. C. arrived exactly on time. 'I found him standing right up against the waiting-room window, staring outside', in what the analyst took to be an anxious attitude.

She recalled two other 'highly vivid countertransference memories of that first encounter', based on Mr. C.'s appearance and demeanour. The first was that she was surprised to find herself comparing the 'image of an energetic and resolute motor-cyclist, a likeable man in his late thirties, in good physical shape, dressed in jeans and leather jacket', with quite another one:

> . . . that of a Woody Allen-type person, a bit gawky, hung-up and introspective. I thought to myself: 'Psychoanalysis is not suitable for that kind of patient'. I realized very quickly that, through this fantasy, I was keeping something at a safe distance – like an implicit rejection.

The other vivid memory had to do with 'the way in which Mr. C. dealt with the physical distance between us', both in how 'he leaned over towards me' while they were standing up talking together, and how he would 'inch towards me as much as he could' once they were seated opposite each other:

> I had the feeling that he was getting too close to me, that he did not respect the conventional 'distance', if you like. I felt 'invaded', as though I had to move further and further back – I had to fight against this so as not to be impolite and hurt his feelings. In short, I felt both persecuted and guilty.

Mr. C. told the analyst that it was his wife's therapist who had suggested that he contact her. He explained that ever since adolescence he had suffered from a whole series of 'dependencies' (this was his expression): cannabis to start with, then alcohol, cocaine and gambling. He was determined to put an end to this because it was having a harmful effect on his work, on his family life and on his health. He had seen a therapist some time ago who had said during their first meeting that he was 'committing suicide little by little'. 'He may have been right', said Mr. C. 'Yes', he went on, 'he probably was right, but it was too brutal a thing to say in our very first meeting'. He never saw that therapist again.

'I noted that he was telling me that he needed me to go carefully – otherwise it would mean separating.' It is worthwhile remarking upon Mr. C.'s implicit warning and the analyst's mental note that she must heed it, because shortly afterwards she found herself involved in an interpretative enactment (Steiner 2006) which deeply upset her as well as Mr. C.:

> Then, in a calm and convincing tone of voice – as though he were suggesting an explanation so obvious that I could only concur – he added: 'I've always been dependent – firstly on my mother, then on my wife, then on cannabis and all the rest.' He made that statement as though emphasizing a kind of equivalence or interchangeability involving the three types of 'dependencies'. Then, without any interruption, he went on to say: 'And I guess that now you are expecting me to transfer my dependent attitude on to you' ('to transfer' was again Mr. C.'s expression, although he was not working in our field). I felt that he was putting into *me* something that was

(continued)

(continued)

> actually worrying *him* – his fear of becoming dependent on me; that fear might, at least in part, feed into what I had thought of, when we spoke on the telephone, as his ambivalence towards analysis. I thought also that, by postponing his first appointment – and thereby putting me in a situation in which *I* was waiting for *him* – Mr. C. had succeeded in passing on his dependence to me, in 'transferring' it on to me (or we could say that I had taken it on board inside myself).

Because she thought that this was worrying him, and not yet fully aware of her own confusion, the analyst felt under pressure to respond. She explained to the workshop that at this point in the interview she 'felt the necessity to do something for this patient'. After giving it as much thought as possible in the here-and-now of the session, she 'chose a form of words that seemed to me to be a fairly acceptable and not too threatening way of putting things' and said:

> The idea of having to transfer your dependent feelings towards your wife on to me could indeed be a bit worrying for you.

Because of the patient's strong reaction and her own sense of discomfort, the analyst immediately realized that something significant and powerful had happened. She had to struggle to think about what it was. Wholly concerned with the need to tread carefully and to find a non-threatening way of putting things, she had found herself doing the exact opposite: she used a wording that confirmed Mr. C.'s idea that she was indeed expecting him to become dependent on her:

> The sheer intensity of his reaction surprised me. He seemed both frightened and ill at ease: it was as though *he* had not evoked that possibility but that it had come from *me*. In addition, I could see the implication behind what he had said: that I was expecting him to develop with me the same kind of relationship as he had with his wife, i.e. an erotic one. In other words, there was a two-fold reversal of the situation. Firstly, it was not Mr. C. who had suggested that I was expecting him to transfer his dependent feelings towards his wife on to me – quite on the contrary, indeed, it seemed as though the idea had come from me. Secondly, the very nature of that dependence had changed – it was no longer the attitude he had had towards his mother and later transferred on to his wife – but something clearly erotic in nature. A subtle change had been introduced into the meaning of the word 'dependence': it was no longer an emotional dependence but a sexual one. I felt that there was some perversion of meaning here, a kind of de-symbolization. The outcome of that two-fold transformation was that I found myself in the role of an active seducer.
>
> For a split second, I could not quite grasp what was going on. I had to make an effort to remember who had said what, who had thought what, how each of us had been able to think that the other was actually thinking what

the one had attributed to the other, and so on. I felt that the confusion in my mind was perhaps a reflection of Mr. C.'s own confused state. By putting so many parts of himself into other people, he no longer knew what belonged to him and what belonged to others. The same process was operating inside me: the very act of taking inside myself what he was offering meant that I no longer knew who was thinking what. It was destabilizing and frightening.

I said to Mr. C.: 'The way I understand it, is that *you* seem to be thinking that *I* am expecting you to transfer your dependence on your wife, onto me. I imagine that maybe the kind of dependence you are talking about is similar to the one you had first experienced towards your mother'. I think I made that statement above all to help Mr. C. out of the confusion he was in – and probably also to help myself get back on firmer ground. He did indeed seem reassured by what I said, and went on to talk about his mother. I myself felt quite relieved at this – the thought went through my mind that we had made a narrow escape. I did, however, remain very much on the alert after that unexpected *faux pas*, a small-scale state of confusion that stayed with me as an underlying threat.

The patient went on to say that 'his mother had been very close to him and had been a major figure all through his childhood'. He first described what sounded like 'a very happy childhood, with lots of freedom', but then:

went on to talk about his most painful memory of those days: waiting every evening, with his sister, for their mother to come back home from work. Every evening, in his grandparents' house, he would stand at the window for what seemed to him to be an interminable length of time; unable to move, or even to breathe, it seemed. He was convinced that if his mother did not arrive, he would die.

Later, when he was in his twenties and living with the woman whom he would later marry, he began having panic attacks:

He would need to return home, to the bedroom he had slept in as a child, and his mother was the only person who could calm him down. Then, suddenly, he 'veered' towards his wife; she then became the only person who could soothe him.

Mr. C. had always greatly admired his mother. In his eyes, she could do no wrong – but that was beginning to change:

His wife had pointed out how badly his mother had behaved at their wedding; she had been 'nasty' to his wife. With a completely innocent look on his face, Mr. C. said that he didn't know anything about the proper procedure

(continued)

(continued)

> so that, at the time, he had not noticed anything untoward, but 'apparently' the bride should be the one who enters the church first – at his wedding, his mother had gone in first, holding Mr. C.'s arm as she did so. That had shocked his wife terribly. He added that his wife was very important to him in his life; he kept nothing back from her. 'In a way', he said with a note of self-criticism in his voice, 'it is all too easy for me to unload everything on to her like that'. Henceforth, he thought, he would probably be telling everything to me.
>
> He then associated to his father. A very good man; Mr. C. never doubted for one moment that his father loved him. He added that his father had a heart of gold, but was very shy – the fact that he could not discuss things more with his father was a real difficulty for Mr. C. He was very moved as he said this – it was the only truly emotional moment of that interview, except for his anxiety; he was almost on the verge of tears.

The patient went on to talk about how his family life and work suffered from his absences, and his impression that there 'might be something self-destructive behind all that'. This prompted the analyst to explore his anger, saying that 'he had not spoken very much about his angry feelings'. He replied that 'he never got really angry', as if this feeling had always been foreign to him.

If we try to summarize what happened, through his unconscious verbal, paraverbal and non-verbal communications, this apparently self-possessed patient induced strong feelings in the analyst from the moment of their first telephone exchange. After their talk on the telephone, she found herself not only in contact with his anxiety about asking for help, but also having to deal with her own feelings of being both seduced and rejected by him. This was intensified during their first contacts in the waiting room and as they settled down for the interview, when she had to deal with additional, powerful feelings of being invaded by him, wanting to push him away, feeling guilty about that, but protective towards him as well. The analyst's initial interest in taking on this new analysand became somewhat destabilized. In spite of her free-floating introspectiveness (Wegner 1992), through which she remained attentive to her reactions and did her best to elaborate them, this complex state of affairs seemed to overwhelm her bit by bit. As she put it in the WPIP Workshop: 'I wasn't able to think; he was coming in like a truck and I didn't want to be destroyed.'

As a result of these stresses placed on her internal capacities, the analyst didn't realize quite how much she had been taken over by multiple projective identifications until, to her surprise and dismay, she found herself involved in an interpretative enactment in which she took on 'the role of an active seducer'. Moreover, although she had promised herself not to imitate the first therapist whom Mr. C. had seen, in a way she found herself intervening intrusively, much like he had done. She, the patient, and the patient's intrusive, seductive and rejecting internal objects had become confused with one another. For a while, the difference between subjective and objective experience had been lost; triangular space (Segal 1997; Britton 1989, 1998a) had temporarily collapsed.

Shaken, the analyst was nevertheless able to use 'listening to listening' (Faimberg 1996, 2005) to overcome her state of confusion between self and objects and to redress the situation as well as she could. Fundamentally, the 'switch' had taken place in the analyst. Her second interpretation, albeit a bit defensive and intellectualized, seemed to reassure the patient and allow him to explore his relationship with his mother. Subsequently Mr. C., now able to communicate more by verbalizing than by enacting, described how badly he had needed his mother, but how this had led him to submit to her as well. He could talk more freely; an analytic space had opened up between patient and analyst.

With hindsight, Mr. C.'s associations demonstrate how the early phases of the session had reproduced important dynamics from the patient's inner world and historical reality. The scene where he was staring out of the window in the waiting room was a re-enactment of his childhood terrors; it was also a way of communicating these to the analyst and thus of 'transferring' his dependence on his mother onto the analyst, as he had done before with his wife. This clinging to his mother seems to have been reciprocal, at least in his phantasy world, with intrusive and oedipal overtones. Through her interpretative enactment, the analyst had found herself trying to protect and to seduce the patient in ways that were similar to his relationship with his internal mother. Her first interpretation seemed to have been influenced by an unconscious pressure to become such a mother, and so came out as an attempt to show Mr. C. what a good analyst she could be for him. It amounted to taking him by the arm to lead him into analysis, as his mother had led him into church!

In her internal protective and rejecting reactions, the analyst had perhaps repeated yet another aspect of the mother–infant relationship, such as feeling threatened by the child's needs and drives, and thereby trying to regain control. The progressive opening of analytic space was confirmed towards the end of the interview when Mr. C. was able to talk, with emotion, about his father as a third with whom he would have needed more contact in order to help him out of the dual maternal relationship. None of this could be fully thought through during the session itself, but it could be seen and elaborated during the successive stages of the Three-Stage research work, in processes similar to those described for *The Self-Assured Academic* in Chapter 4.

Developments like the analyst's first interpretation can be seen from different, not necessarily mutually exclusive, perspectives. One perspective is that of a failure of technique (Steiner 2006) involving *doing* instead of *representing* – i.e. an acting out (sometimes called an 'acting-in' because it happens in the session). Another perspective is that of role-requirement and role-responsiveness (Sandler 1976, 1993) in which the analyst, unconsciously picking up a cue from the patient, responded as if she were identified with one of the patient's internal objects. A third, related perspective is that of countertransference enactment (Jacobs 1986) or mutual enactment (Tuckett 1997) as an inevitable aspect of the analytic process, involving the patient and the analyst in an unconscious proto-symbolic scene, which can then become a starting point and incentive for later symbolization. The analyst who saw Mr. C. held all these points of view: she was upset by what she considered to be bad technique on her part, creating a situation from which she and the patient had had 'a narrow escape'; she described how she 'felt under pressure to respond'; and she wanted to understand what had happened.

These complementary perspectives on enactments in first interviews will be discussed in more depth in Chapter 9. Meanwhile, in the present chapter, we will refer to such events using the general term 'enactment', and we will retain the working hypothesis that they always carry some form of proto-representation of important conflicts arising in the context of the interview and influencing the interview dynamics.

Cases like *The Mother's Son* illustrate how first interviews can be characterized by extremely powerful, and sometimes overpowering, unconscious dynamics, which can affect not only the patient's unconscious behaviour, but also the analyst's unconscious response, to the point of inducing the analyst to enact. In fact, we found such intense dynamics to be the norm rather than the exception. Contrary to our first working hypotheses as described in Chapter 3, our findings did not suggest that the analytic couple had to work to permit an up-welling of affective and representational derivatives of the patient's unconscious conflicts, but rather that these conflicts and their verbal and non-verbal expressions were immediately and intensely active. They were so strong and omnipresent that it could be difficult, or even impossible, for the (by definition) unprepared analyst to capture and understand them fully in the here-and-now of the interview; they could be described as 'blinding'. The question was therefore how the analytic couple managed to take these intense manifestations of the unconscious in their stride and how they dealt with them as they tried to work together.

Before we proceed, a more systematic description of the form and contents of the dynamics may give the reader a better impression of their nature and intensity.

Towards a description of the unconscious dynamics

Onset

As demonstrated by the cases described so far, the expression of the unconscious dynamics usually began before the interview: during the first telephone contact(s), in the first scene in the waiting room, or in a patient's significant enactment before the appointment. This 'opening scene' phenomenon will be studied in Chapter 6.

Origin and content

As was also illustrated by the cases examined so far, the unconscious interview dynamics seemed to be closely linked to the request for help and its fantasized consequences. The fear of what could happen in an encounter, characterized by need, vulnerability and the unknown (inside the consulting-room window), was represented by the patient in unconscious phantasies referring to past experience and/or expressing recurrent object relationship patterns (outside the window) (Tuckett 2011).

Thus, Mr. A. in *The Handsome Man on Crutches* unconsciously imagined analysis as a situation where he could be abused or become the abuser. Ms. B., in *The Self-Assured Academic*, feared that needing help would mean giving in to a narcissistic maternal relationship and, ultimately, psychic death. Mr. C. in *The Mother's Son* was afraid of being dependent and abandoned, as well as of being seduced and taken over.

Such a synthetic account of the origins and contents of the unconscious phantasies at work in these interviews is, however, mainly possible *après coup*. Such *après coup* understanding is part of the normal analytic work done over time; in our study, it was a result of the work done in the Three-Stage research process described in Chapters 3 and 4. During the interviews themselves, it was not possible to perceive the dynamics so clearly, or sometimes impossible to do so. The same was true when the Clinical Workshops and the WPIP Investigative Team first heard and read the process notes. Whole lives were being revealed in these interviews, with many themes pressing to the fore, in what could at first sight appear to be an inextricably complex picture.

Questions remain about the links between these dynamics, as related to the request for help, and the core conflicts of the patient's inner world. Although it seems likely that the anxieties related to the initial encounter will be expressed in terms of central conflicts in the patient's life, this would require further study. It is also possible that other important unconscious conflicts are less strongly aroused in first interviews, or remain hidden there. In particular, the confrontation with the unknown in a first encounter, including the unknown of how the other will respond, may bring to the forefront primitive anxieties about finding a container (Bion 1962, 1967) and/or memories of traumatic experiences. This seems to be so in our cases, although other conflicts, including oedipal ones, were expressed there as well.

Mode of expression

The dynamics were communicated by the patient and, usually to a lesser extent, by the analyst, in various ways ranging from verbal to para-verbal and non-verbal communication, including scenic communication (Argelander 1970, 1978; Wegner 1992) and enactment. Several forms could be active at the same time.

Thus, to continue our examination of *The Mother's Son*, Mr. C. not only told the analyst about aspects of his predicament in his conscious self-presentation and unconscious associations, but also demonstrated these by postponing the appointment and by staring through the window in the waiting room scene, as well as through his general physical behaviour. Massive projective identification also played a role. In these ways, he unconsciously created a scenario in which the analyst was impelled to take part. Her involuntary involvement through role-responsiveness and mutual enactment gave her a direct experience of the unconscious dynamics, including a sense of identification with Mr. C.'s subjective experience and with his internal objects – at the cost however of a transient identity confusion, followed by a more lasting sense of threat to her analytic functioning.

These multiple forms of communication also seem to express similarly varied and simultaneously active levels of conscious and unconscious mental functioning, ranging from well symbolized unconscious phantasies, through less well symbolized object relations phantasies with splitting and projective identification, to nearly raw experiences looking for a container. For instance, although predominantly well-symbolized phantasies were reported in *The Handsome Man on Crutches*, less well symbolized experiences also slipped through and affected the Workshop and WPIP Team as shown in Chapter 2. The same was true in *The Self-Assured Academic* in Chapter 4. Thus the analyst, listening at one level, could nevertheless be affected by other phantasies or aspects that were communicated at other levels.

Awareness and elaboration

Our initial hypotheses about 'switching the level' could not adequately account for the interview processes that we observed. The actual dynamics were much more complex:

- There were many cases in which the patient seemed to be conscious of a key issue, albeit vaguely. S/he did not need to be made aware of it, but seemed relieved or interested to discover that the analyst had become aware of it too and was willing to talk about it. Often, as in *The Mother's Son*, this required the *analyst* to 'switch the level' internally in order to discover what the patient was trying to convey.
- Furthermore, many important developments seemed to take place unconsciously, for example in the flow of the patient's associations or in dreams between interviews. Sometimes the analyst noticed these but did not consider it useful to point them out; at other times, as in *The Self-Assured Academic*, the analyst remained partly unaware of them, but tolerated this situation.
- Finally, there were cases in which there didn't seem to be any clear work on a central conflictual issue, but rather a more general process in which the analyst demonstrated his/her ability and willingness to share the work of symbolization, verbalization and elaboration, perhaps conveying a sense of hope that something chaotic and unbearable might find a container in an analytic relationship. Under various guises, this more global form of psychoanalytic work seemed to be important in all cases, forming the essential background for the other developments.

The most global description of the process, across highly varied situations, might be that it did not necessarily lead to a 'switching of the level' in our original restricted sense, in which the patient would become conscious of something that was previously unconscious, but in a more general, encompassing sense, in which the patient's conscious and unconscious self-knowledge *took on a new dimension* in the context of an analytic relationship. This new relationship held the promise that the patient's self-knowledge *could potentially* find more meaning, even if this was not the immediate outcome.

Mr. C. was already aware of his dependent position in his relationships to women, as well as of his submission to his mother's controlling and seductive attitudes, but he did not know what to do about it. He feared to repeat this with the analyst and needed to see whether she could deal with it and explore it with him. Thus, the analyst's second interpretation could not really be seen as a 'meaningful common formulation' in the original sense of finding words for something previously unknown that she had helped Mr. C. to discover. Instead, it was better understood as the outcome of their joint effort to come to grips with something that they had both been experiencing up to that point as a concrete, inescapable reality, and which they had been afraid they would be unable to deal with.

There were three important developments later on in the session, but these took place in the patient's associations and did not correspond to instances of a real 'switching the level', in the sense that it is not clear whether the patient was aware of their significance. The analyst took note of them, but did not point them out, merely helping Mr. C. to tell his story.

The first development was when Mr. C. recounted his childhood memory of waiting next to the window for his mother to come home; this explained the waiting-room scene, but it is not clear whether he was conscious of the link between the two scenes.

The second development was when he spoke about how his mother took him into church for his wedding; this was a good description of the mutual enactment that had taken place towards the beginning of the session, but neither patient nor analyst made that connection, which only became apparent later on in the research process.

The third, and perhaps most important, development was when Mr. C. spoke about his yearning for a better relationship with his father. The space that the analyst's work had created for him made this triangulation possible, pointing to a way out of the fraught dyadic relationship. This amounted to a real 'switching the level' in a psychodynamic sense, but whose significance was not verbalized by the analyst (in fact, doing so might have spoilt its impact). However, this movement allowed them to talk about Mr. C.'s suppressed anger, which may also have been something that frightened the analyst when she felt he was 'coming in like a truck' and she was afraid of being 'destroyed'.

Containment by the analyst

On the basis of such findings, the analyst's work seems best described, not in terms of key moments when s/he helped the patient to discover meaning (which also happened), but in more global terms, of creating and maintaining a psychoanalytic relationship in which the patient had the experience that meaning could possibly emerge, through the specific nature of the relationship itself. We could describe this work on the analyst's part as an inner effort (and sometimes a struggle) to maintain the analyst's receptiveness. This involved tolerating anxiety and not understanding, as well as paying careful attention to the analyst's own reactions; in the form of internal resistances that might prevent meaning from emerging, or countertransference reactions and mutual enactments that might hold clues to the unconscious interview dynamics. When an intellectual effort to understand was momentarily required, it had to give way again to a more receptive position.

The analyst in *The Handsome Man on Crutches* was aware of this effort, but not too disturbed by it, although she was perhaps more affected by the dynamics than she realized. The same could be said for the analyst in *The Self-Assured Academic.* In both cases, however, some of the disturbance came out more forcefully in later Stages of the research process. Near the other extreme of the spectrum, Mr. C.'s analyst in *The Mother's Son* was profoundly shocked and disturbed to discover that by failing at first to capture the meaning of what was going on, she had enacted and frightened her patient. She experienced the internal work that she had to do in order to regain her balance, emerge from her confusion, and re-establish psychoanalytic contact with Mr. C., as a difficult struggle.

These analysts thus demonstrated an ability to contain the interview dynamics and to survive them as psychoanalyst; cultivating, maintaining or striving to retrieve their ability to think about what was being played out. 'Containing' was not only a spontaneous activity involving reverie; it was also active, challenging work (Cartwright 2010).

This combination of characteristics seemed to explain the intensity of these interviews. Such findings resemble the special difficulties of first interviews as described by other clinicians. Antonino Ferro (2012) offers lively metaphors for unconscious contents overflowing and jumping out of bounds. Agostino Racalbuto (2012) describes how, when he first enters the novel scene of the first interview, the analyst is so confronted with the unknown in the other, as well as in himself in reaction to the other, that he can undergo a transient loss of identity. Thomas Ogden (1992) opens his paper by underscoring that the analyst is perpetually a 'beginner' (p. 225) and concludes with the dire observation that:

> all that the patient says (and does not say) in the initial meeting is understood as an unconscious warning to the analyst (and to the patient) concerning the reasons why the patient unconsciously feels that each of them would be well advised not to enter into this doomed and dangerous relationship.
>
> (Ogden 1992, p. 246)

The concept of an unconscious 'storm'

The general observation that such potent, disturbing and sometimes overwhelming transference and countertransference dynamics are active in preliminary interviews has come to stand out as one of our most robust findings. As we studied one interview after another, we were struck, each time, by the fact that the unconscious dynamics that we saw at work were even more powerful than that which we had expected. The closer we examined each case, the more we observed going on, the higher the stakes being played out seemed to be, and the better we understood how both patient and analyst could feel at the brink of both great possibilities and great dangers.

In his paper, 'Making the Best of a Bad Job' (1979), Bion describes how a 'storm' arises whenever two people meet:

> When two personalities meet, an emotional storm is created. If they make sufficient contact to be aware of each other, or even sufficient to be unaware of each other, an emotional state is produced by the conjunction of these two individuals, and the resulting disturbance is hardly likely to be regarded as necessarily an improvement on the state of affairs had they never met at all. But since they *have* met, and since this emotional storm has occurred, the two parties to the storm may decide to 'make the best of a bad job'.
>
> (Bion 1979, p. 247)

The more we progressed in our study, the more this interested us as a particularly apt account of the interview dynamics that we observed.

Although Bion's exact expression is 'emotional storm', by which he refers to psychic changes taking place at an unknown, undifferentiated level, the word 'emotional' is somewhat unsatisfactory because it can evoke the manifest 'affective' storm of clinical semiology and of some exceptional cases of first interviews. In adopting Bion's term, we specifically intend to refer to an *unconscious* 'storm', but not necessarily a conscious or manifest one. In our observations, whether or not the 'storm' found manifest expression, it was often experienced *internally* by one or both protagonists, and it *always* seemed to be active *unconsciously*, whether or not it was noticed in subjective experience. We therefore prefer '*unconscious storm*' as a better descriptor of our observations (unless otherwise specified, this will be the implicit understanding of the term whenever we use 'storm' in this book).

The 'unconscious storm' could be observed to take place even in interviews which at first sight appeared calm and straightforward, and where it could influence both participants without their realizing it. In such cases the research process revealed how the analyst and patient had dealt unconsciously with powerful dynamics aroused by their encounter, in a way that was possible for them at the time, often to discover only later on in the analysis what had been at stake. In this sense, some decisions to begin analysis might be seen as one kind of mutual enactment, or as a mutual denial of more difficult dynamics which patient and analyst could not deal with at the moment (hiding away from the 'storm', as it were), but which they had to work through in the ensuing treatment.

The metaphor of an 'unconscious storm', with its image of disorder and turbulence, seems a good way to describe the multiple and simultaneous forms of communication, levels of mental functioning, and intense intersubjective phenomena including projective identification and identity confusion, role responsiveness and mutual enactment. It also helps to put a telling image on the challenges facing the analytic couple as they attempt to 'make the best of a bad job'. Facing the 'storm' and working within it is not an easy task; the analytic couple may find different unconscious approaches to it, in what we might call the various 'vicissitudes' of the analytic couple. We will return to these in Chapter 7.

How the analyst works within the 'storm': opening psychoanalytic space

Our observations, together with the metaphor of the unconscious 'storm', have led us to postulate that psychoanalytic work in first interviews involves a process of '*opening psychoanalytic space*' so as to create a relationship in which the 'storm' can be dealt with and may have a chance of finding meaning.

'*Switching the level*' in the sense in which we understood it in our first approach to the problem would be only one aspect of this more general process and would not always be achieved.

The concept of psychoanalytic space

Before returning to our findings, it is worthwhile to discuss in some detail the concept of psychoanalytic space, which has a long history, beginning with Freud. In *Remembering, Repeating and Working-Through*, he described the transference as a 'playground' that 'creates an intermediate region between illness and real life from which the transition from one to the other is made', and which allows for 'a piece of real experience, but one which has been made possible by especially favourable conditions' (Freud 1914, p. 154). Furthermore, it can be argued that the one-person topographical model described in his metapsychological paper *The Unconscious* (Freud 1915b) also contains an implicit metaphor of a new space in which the unconscious minds of the patient and the analyst can meet, in a two-person transformational model of the analytic couple (Reith 2013).

While Freud's view of psychoanalysis could still be seen as an archaeological one (Levine 2010) in which unconscious meaning was there to be discovered through application of the analytic method, Viderman (1970, 1979) introduced a view of analytic space as a 'construction' by patient and analyst, influenced by the interaction between the setting and the transference and countertransference. The function of this space was to *create* meaning, as opposed to a veridical reconstruction of past reality.

The creation of meaning in the relationship with the psychoanalyst has become a central concept in many psychoanalytic models. Klein's psychoanalytic play technique (Klein 1926, 1930) could be seen as a way of helping her child patients to find symbolic representations for their unconscious experience. Bion (1962, 1965, 1967) compared the analyst's work of helping the patient to find meaning, and to build a mind of his/her own capable of finding meaning, to the mother's work of receiving and containing the infant's projected proto-mental states and transforming them through her reverie. Winnicott (1971a) integrated the notions of a play-space and of an intermediate region between phantasy and reality into his concept of a transitional space between mother and infant, which allows the growth of the personality and of symbolic meaning; he extended this concept to that of potential space between patient and analyst, with similar functions.

Ogden (1986, 1989, 1994a, 1994b, 1997) combined the theories of Bion and Winnicott to describe psychoanalytic space as a shared dream space in which the patient's experience could achieve representation in the subjective meeting of two minds. He compared this space to the 'matrix' (Ogden 1986) in which the mind develops, as well as to a new 'mind (more accurately, a psychosoma) that is in a sense the creation of two people' (Ogden 1997). He understood the subjective experience that arises there as a new co-creation, the 'intersubjective analytic third' (Ogden 1994a, 1994b, 1997), which patient and analyst have in common, and yet is experienced by each in their own way, and to which they have access through their reverie.

Segal (1997) and Britton (1989, 1998a, 1999, 2003) added the equally important and complementary concept of triangular space (not to be confused with Ogden's analytic third). This introspective space is needed to achieve a third-person perspective on one's subjective experience. Triangular space is based on the oedipal triangle, in which the relationships between others are observed, making it possible to think of the self as having similarly observable relationships. Over time, this enables a growing awareness and understanding of subjective experience in relation to self and others – not only the subjective experience of the self but also that of others. Integrating the subjective and objective perspectives promotes symbolic understanding and personal identity. Green (1975) had already described triangulation with a third object as a potential capacity of the infant psyche, but which depends on the parental couple for its development. Green (1975) and Britton (1989) both show how failed triangulation leads mental space to collapse into persecuting, all-or-nothing forms of experience. Birksted-Breen (1996, 2016) introduced the 'penis-as-link' as an unconscious metaphor for the structuring function of the internalized parental couple.

Ogden's concept of the 'analytic third' also involves an introspective third-person perspective, since it requires self-monitoring to recognize that something new has arisen in oneself in the context of the intersubjective relationship: '"I" as unselfconscious subject is transformed into "me" as object of analytic scrutiny' (Ogden 1997).

Psychoanalytic space is asymmetrical both because it is concentrated on understanding the patient's subjective experience, and because it is the analyst's task to carry the work of receptiveness to subjective experience and introspective third-person perspective on it, sometimes for a long time until the patient can take over this work. The analyst's self-analytic work is a necessary precondition for the growth of the patient's own self-analytic capacities (Campbell 2015). This work begins during first interviews, and even during the preceding events (see Chapter 6). Bolognini (2006) describes the interviewing analyst's function as a 'concave' receptor and container. Wegner (1992) describes the analyst's third-person perspective on him/herself in the form of 'free-floating introspectiveness'. Dantlgraber's (1982) concept of an 'empathic triadic relation' can also be seen as integrating receptivity to subjective experience with triangular space.

Ideally, psychoanalytic space can thus be seen as a virtual space created by the patient and analyst working together in the psychoanalytic setting. Compared to ordinary space, it has an extra dimension, introduced by the progressive analysis of the transference and countertransference (Reith 2016).

Just as it takes three-dimensional space to turn over a two-dimensional sheet of paper to see what may be written on the other side, so the fourth dimension of psychoanalytic space is needed to allow the analytic couple to discover the unconscious scripts that govern everyday experience. Although virtual, it is a 'felt place' (Ogden 1997) of unequalled vitality and force of reality in which a transformational encounter (Bion 1965; Bollas 1979, 1987; Levine 2010; Reith 2013) can take place. Hitherto unconscious aspects of the patient's life, which were experienced as unthinkable things-in-themselves outside the patient's control, can be taken up into the analytic relationship, find a novel perspective and symbolic representation there, and subsequently be re-appropriated by the patient in new forms, enriched by a sense of greater meaning and mastery.

This description, however, is valid for the psychoanalytic space that develops in the course of an ongoing analysis. The special characteristics of first interviews, with their 'storm-like' dynamics and their confrontation with the unknown and unexpected, introduce particular challenges to the creation of psychoanalytic space, which we can now attempt to describe.

Problems of psychoanalytic space in first interviews

One might think of our early hypotheses about the processes at work in initial interviews as implying a conception of psychoanalytic space as something pre-existing, ready-made and available to be entered provided a key was found. Instead, as our observations demonstrate (and as could be expected from the theory), it should be thought of as a space that must be developed or co-created by each patient–analyst pair. This is of course what is implied in Viderman's (1970, 1979) notion of the construction of analytic space and Ogden's (1994a, 1994b, 1997) concept of the analytic third.

In retrospect, this conclusion makes perfect sense, since we are concerned with the unprecedented inter-psychic tensions arising within the unique unconscious bi-personal field (Baranger and Baranger 2008) generated by each new patient–analyst encounter (and probably in each new session). Each new field implies unprecedented challenges to the work of symbolization and elaboration, through reverie (Ogden 1997) and transformation into dreaming and narrative (Ferro 2012). Before this transformational work takes place, the field remains condensed, rolled up on itself, as it were, and so difficult to perceive; it is only in the extra dimension of psychoanalytic space co-constructed between patient and analyst that it can progressively unfold, be experienced, and find representation.

Until this has been achieved, the tensions in the field cannot be truly experienced as 'subjective' or 'intersubjective', in the sense that it has not yet been possible for the patient and/or the analyst to recognize them as something in which they are participating and, therefore, belonging to their own experience. They have not been able to 'appropriate' (Roussillon 2006) or 'subjectivate' them (Wainrib 2012). Cases like *The Mother's Son* demonstrate how powerful phenomena in the bi-personal field can strongly affect the patient's and the analyst's minds, and yet be transiently experienced as somehow strange, alien and upsetting – 'uncanny' to use Freud's (1919c) term – not fully recognizable as being part of their own subjectivity. These 'uncanny' experiences are characterized by a temporary breakdown of the distinction between phantasy and reality (Kahn 2004). They arise between the two members of the analytic couple but are 'interpsychic' (Bolognini 2011) rather than intersubjective. Until they are noticed and subjected to the analyst's introspective work, they cannot be recognized as 'analytic objects' (Bion 1962; Green 1975; Ogden 1994, 1997) for which meaning can be found. They may even be 'transpsychic' (Bolognini 2011), so overwhelming that for a while they are not captured at all.

In such situations, the unthought known (Bollas 1987) in the patient is doubly the unknown for the analyst, in that it is both new and has not yet found a thinker (Bion 1997) in the analyst who can give meaning to it. One possible consequence is that it can form a 'silent background' (Ogden 1997) to the interview. This may explain, for instance, why some of the deepest phantasies at work in *The Self-Assured Academic* could only be experienced and elaborated during later Stages in the research process.

Observations on how psychoanalysts open psychoanalytic space in practice

Our case studies amply demonstrated that '*opening an analytic space*' in which to unfold each new bi-personal field was a challenging task, even for experienced analysts. We might compare it to erecting a tent in very bad weather, or to rebuilding it after a real storm has torn the pegs loose from the ground.

In our report on Phase 1 of our study (Reith et al. 2010), we described preliminary findings about how the psychoanalyst accomplishes the work of setting up the psychoanalytic tent in these circumstances. When we pursued our study, using our findings from Phase 2, as well as reassessing our data from Phase 1 (see Chapter 3 for the description of Phases 1 and 2), we realized that the preliminary findings from Phase 1 were largely based on what the peer groups in the Clinical Workshops (as well as the WPIP Team at the time) seemed to have considered to be satisfying analytic work. In retrospect, they were a somewhat biased selection from a wider spectrum of working styles, taking place not only across different cases but also at different moments in each case. These other forms will be described in Chapters 6 to 10.

One reason why it was easier to pick up the types of work described in Phase 1 may be that they were reassuring for the investigating analysts – because they were similar to what we tend to think of as 'good' psychoanalytic technique, and familiar, through their appearance in the literature. Less familiar forms of work may have generated more anxiety, making it more difficult to notice, tolerate, describe and understand them. Colleagues studying Comparative Clinical Methods (Tuckett et al. 2008; Basile et al. 2010; see also Chapter 3 in this book) have described how 'the "otherness" involved in listening to clinical material' from ongoing analyses 'is fundamentally allergenic, even xenocidal' (Basile et al. 2010, p. 9). Our own study has suggested that confrontation with the unconscious dynamics of first interviews can be a major source of anxiety in its own right, which can cause defensive reactions in analysts, both individually (Møller 2014) and in groups (Reith 2011b, 2015; see also Chapter 4).

Our preliminary observations from Phase 1 are nevertheless worth recapitulating here, because they remain valid as descriptions of some aspects of real psychoanalytic work, and because they can stand as a backdrop against which to examine other aspects.

First-person participation

As discussed above, the intensity of the unconscious dynamics invading the initial encounter and the variety of their modes of communication put considerable pressure on the analyst. This was the case both in the analyst's internal experience, and through the pressure to react in various forms of verbal or non-verbal enactment. Far from being only a neutral observer, or a specialist performing a technical function, s/he was also a participant in a human drama.

Sometimes the analysts who reported these phenomena in their case presentations described how they perceived the pressure to react internally or concretely, but managed to contain it. At other times, however, they did not understand that something specific and significant was happening, until they found themselves having strong personal feelings or fantasies, or had been involved in a form of enactment, which compelled them to wonder about the origins of their response. Some analysts reported that although the resulting situation could be disturbing, it seemed important for the purpose of understanding the encounter that they were able to *let* themselves be affected, or even disturbed, as a source of an understanding that was not only intellectual but also personal. When the analyst did *not* feel disturbed, this sometimes gave the analyst, or later the Clinical Workshop participants or the WPIP Investigative Team, a sense that something was missing, as if it were being defended against.

In some cases, the sense of being affected seemed to be related to the analyst's being willingly 'in tune' with the patient and receptive to the latter's conscious or unconscious inner experience. In other cases, as in *The Mother's Son*, the analyst could feel temporarily 'altered' by unusually strong feelings, unusual fantasies or involuntary involvement in an enactment, in ways that could be experienced as more disturbing or alienating. Whatever the precise mechanisms that seemed to be at play in each individual case (neurotic projection or projective identification by the patient; primary identification or introjective identification by the analyst), it might be appropriate to describe the analyst as 'resonating' with the patient or with some aspect of the latter's internal world. Sometimes this left the analyst with a sense of something unexpected that could threaten his/her internal equilibrium. However, even when that was so, the analyst usually reported that it pointed to something significant that the patient was bringing to the encounter and which they wanted to understand. The resultant understanding might be thought of as based on a form of 'identity of experience' (Loewald 1960, Emde 1990) with the patient and with the patient's internal objects.

It could be difficult for the analyst to remain open to such experiences in order to elaborate them, as opposed to avoiding them or shutting them out. We have come to compare this process to 'facing', 'working within' or 'weathering' the 'storm', as opposed to 'hiding away' from it.

Spontaneous elaboration

Many analysts felt that it was important to trust their ability to digest the experiences and enactments in an evenly suspended manner. The triad of 'free-floating attention', 'free-floating responsiveness' and 'free-floating introspectiveness' (Wegner 1992) aptly describes some aspects of this process, as is evident in the cases discussed in this chapter. An important and fundamental aspect of this form of work seemed to be a spontaneous elaborative process of 'reverie' (Bion 1962, Ogden 1997) in which the analyst 'transformed' (Bollas 1979, 1987; Ferro 2012) raw un-symbolized experience, physical sensations, affective states and impulses into potentially meaningful dream-like, metaphoric, scenic and symbolic forms of representation and thinking, as for example in the analyst's imagery about the 'resolute motorcyclist' and the 'gawky' 'Woody Allen' figure in *The Mother's Son*.

The ability to tolerate anxiety and not understanding can be seen as an integral aspect of this function. As we have seen for example in *The Handsome Man on Crutches*, some presenting analysts cherished their ability to wait in order to let experiences build up until they made sense of their own accord.

Self-observation: finding a third-person perspective

Another important aspect seemed to be a frequently reported and perhaps more active self-monitoring and self-reflective function, in which the analysts periodically strove to 'take a step aside' from the immediacy of the interaction, in order to observe their overt and covert responses and to place them in the context of a more 'third-person' perception and understanding of the developing patient–analyst relationship. Such work, which was intuitively recognized by the presenters and was commonly referred to, was discussed above in connection with the theories of psychoanalytic space.

This third position is partial, transient and variable, more or less insightful and thought-through. It can be more difficult to attain in the here-and-now of the session and easier to achieve afterwards, especially when consultation with others is available, as for example with a peer-group in a psychoanalytic clinic. We have also seen how it could be promoted by group work in a research setting, as for example in *The Handsome Man on Crutches* in Chapter 2.

Important as it appeared to be, this self-observing position didn't seem to work well without the analyst's more direct first-person involvement. Being involved and feeling affected provided the impetus and the material for self-reflective work. In other words, analysts found that they must function fully both as participant and as observer (including self-observer), and that they needed to sustain the inevitable tension between these poles. This may correspond to what has been described in other work (Sullivan 1954, Tuckett 2005) as the ability to maintain a 'participant-observer' position.

Finding support in theory

In our material, the role of the analyst's reference to a theoretical template seemed to be quite variable. Some explicitly referred to theory in their case reports or seemed to keep it in mind actively as part of their reflections during the interview. Others didn't have it at the forefront of their minds, but did seem to have recourse to it from time to time in order to make sense of their observations and experiences. Yet other analysts seemed to use it mostly implicitly.

Usually, this explicit or implicit reference to theory seemed to have a helpful structuring function as a means of 'triangulation' – as a platform from which to attain a third-person perspective on the interview dynamics (Birksted-Breen 2008, Tuckett 2011). Sometimes, however, theory seemed to invade and obstruct the analytic space, as when a theoretically coherent account seemed to cover up potent unconscious undercurrents of which the analyst was unaware at the time but discovered later on in the analysis. Keeping theory actively in mind was not a guaranteed way of 'facing the storm'.

Intervening to further the associative process

In many of the cases studied, the analysts were careful about what they communicated back to the patient. Much of the analyst's thinking and understanding remained unsaid. What *was* said was usually formulated prudently so as to take into account the patient's ability to use it, and was thereafter followed by 'listening to listening' (Faimberg 1996, 2005) to assess its impact.

Even apparently spontaneous words or gestures like handing over a box of tissues were often accompanied by self-monitoring and subsequent attention to the impact on the process.

One might say that the analysts tried as much as possible to 'respond' rather than 'react' (Symington 1990). When, despite their attention to the interview dynamics, analysts caught themselves 'reacting', as for example in *The Mother's Son*, they strove to transform their reaction into a more thoughtful and integrated 'response'.

Some interventions were aimed at communicating a tentative understanding in order to help the patient or to see how s/he would respond, but many reported interventions were aimed mainly at helping patients to develop their own account of who they were. The analyst's internal work could be used for example to offer words for something the patient might be experiencing; to promote the associative process; to help the patient achieve a more self-reflective position; or to ask questions about areas that the patient seemed to need to talk about but was avoiding.

Interpreting the transference to the psychoanalytic process and setting

When analysts did say something of a more interpretative nature, this was often with the specific aim not of communicating understanding *per se*, but of exploring and/or promoting the patient's ability to use the psychoanalytic relationship and setting. This could involve addressing the patient's anxieties about the request for help and its meaning or consequences: conflicts about needing help, fantasies about the analytic relationship and setting, or ambivalence about the results that it might bring.

An example of this kind of interpretation of the transference to the process and setting was seen in the first session in *The Self-Assured Academic* in Chapter 4. The analyst had picked up the transference anxieties in Ms. B.'s account of her relationship with her mother. Her interventions were indirect, referring explicitly only to the counsellor and, through the context of the exchange, to Ms. B.'s mother, but they implicitly referred to the psychoanalytic setting and process as well ('Did you think about how come the counsellor didn't understand that?'; 'Could it be that it's not easy for you to express that you need to be helped?'; 'Recognizing your own needs might be risky?'). Ms. B. did not respond directly, seemingly still talking about her mother, so she may have remained unaware of the transference meaning of the analyst's interventions, but it seems likely that, unconsciously, she captured the analyst's message regarding her transference fears about the setting and process. If so, this may have helped her to engage more deeply with the analyst, moving on to speaking about her traumatic family history.

In contrast to such interpretations of the transference to the process and setting, more direct interpretations of the transference to the analyst tended to be avoided. When they did occur, they could worsen the 'storm' or at least make it appear more threatening. The developments seen in *The Mother's Son* are particularly interesting in this respect. The analyst had intended to interpret Mr. C.'s transference to the psychoanalytic process, but to her surprise and dismay, this first came out as an interpretation of his transference to the psychoanalyst, which Mr. C. heard as a concrete invitation by the analyst as a person, and not as a symbolic reference to the analyst as transference object. This worsened the 'storm' or, in what might perhaps be a more precise image, prompted it to break out, temporarily overwhelming both participants. The analyst's second interpretation, by triangulating Mr. C.'s fears about analysis with his childhood relationship to his mother, helped him to see that she was talking about a phantasy that could be understood in the analytic process. He responded positively and was able to associate productively in the analytic space that had thus been created. The end-result was favourable but, as the analyst wrote, they 'had had a narrow escape'.

Sequences such as this one illustrate the conceptual difference between 'seduction by the person' and 'seduction by the method' (Donnet 1995, 2005), which will be examined in more detail in Chapter 8. The concept of 'seduction by the person' refers to the phantasy that an exclusive personal, narcissistic or sexual relationship with the analyst as a real person will cure the patient, whereas 'seduction by the method' refers to the patient's experience of a developing psychoanalytic space and process, based on a setting and method, with an analyst who can be invested for his/her carrying out a psychoanalytical function.

In the 'stormy' situation of first interviews, unconscious wishes and phantasies are intensively actualized in the bi-personal field and tend to be experienced as really happening; it is more difficult to locate them as taking place in phantasy. This 'threat' is amplified by the fact that the patient is unprepared for what will take place in the interview, and that patient and analyst do not yet have an established, agreed-upon working setting. In such a situation, interpretations of the transference to the analyst can be experienced as a real 'seduction by the person', as opposed to the 'seduction by the method' that may be facilitated by interpretations of the transference to the setting and process.

The differential use and impact of interpretations of the transference to the analyst, as compared to interpretations of the transference to the setting and process, will be further discussed in Chapter 8. Whether or not this depends on the context of the first interviews in 'private' settings, where the interviewing analyst can continue with the patient, and 'consultation for referral' settings, where the interviewing analyst will not continue with the patient, will also be examined in that chapter.

Summary and discussion: the vicissitudes of the psychoanalytic couple

The working model that we have developed on the basis of our study is that while 'switching the level' indicates a successful psychoanalytic process in some first interviews, for this movement to be possible, the analyst–patient pair must somehow manage to 'weather' the 'unconscious storm' of the intense interview dynamics, and use these dynamics as an opportunity to 'open psychoanalytic space', rather than 'hiding away' from the 'storm'. Even when 'switching the level' does not take place, in the sense of becoming conscious of something unconscious, 'opening psychoanalytic space' may be sufficient to initiate the psychoanalytic process (Reith et al. 2010).

This could be because the interview introduces the patient to a way of working with a psychoanalyst through which something in the patient's experience, that was initially felt to be meaningless, could take on at least some promise of meaning. The patient's discovery that aspects of internal reality *might* find representation and elaboration in the relationship with an analyst could be a sufficiently powerful motivation to pursue this form of treatment. The analyst's ability to tolerate the 'storm' and to work within it might be what gives the patient some measure of trust and hope in psychoanalysis, even for patients who do not yet think quite symbolically.

One might compare 'switching the level' to the lifting of repression that becomes possible once mental conflict has achieved some degree of representation, and 'facing the storm' to the ego's ability to hold together and to function in the face of less well represented drive derivatives or traumatic experiences. If the ego risks being overwhelmed it must maintain repression or find other solutions such as splitting, disavowal and projection, or discharge in enactment or acting out. This working model seems similar to Levine's (2010) 'two-track' perspective on beginning or intensifying the psychoanalytic process: 'switching the level' would correspond to his 'archaeological' model of psychoanalysis in which psychic contents are uncovered; while 'facing the storm' would correspond to his 'transformational' model in which the mind of the analyst has an essential function in the analytic dyad, for the creation or strengthening of psychic elements. As Levine puts it:

> The creation of a given analytic patient will be a function of the degree to which the analyst will be able internally to create and maintain him or herself as an analyst with and for that particular patient.
>
> (Levine 2010, p. 1390)

This is not only a matter of psychoanalytic technique. Sensation and affect must be *experienced*, including by the analyst, before they can be symbolized and elaborated. The analyst's 'concave' receptor and container (Bolognini 2006) is not some abstract function: it involves his or her whole person, as we have seen in *The Mother's Son* in this chapter. This can be difficult for the analyst. But the patient needs this living receptivity by the analyst, so as to be able to *exist* with him or her; the contrary could lead to an experience of annihilation. This concave, asymmetric welcoming of a whole person by another whole person is part of the special pleasure and challenge of doing psychoanalytic work.

That being said, 'switching the level', 'opening analytic space' and 'initiating psychoanalysis', understood in terms of getting a psychoanalytic process going, should not be idealized, nor equated with actually beginning a psychoanalysis.

There were cases in which a high-frequency psychoanalysis on the couch was decided upon, while it wasn't clear whether a psychoanalytic process in the sense in which we have described above had really been initiated in the first interviews; as well as other cases in which a psychoanalytic process of this kind got started, but in which it was decided for good reasons to embark on treatment in some other setting.

Furthermore, however well the analytic couple seemed to deal with the 'storm' and to use it to arrive at meaningful treatment choices, close examination of the cases showed that in every patient–analyst encounter there were aspects of the 'storm' that they failed to notice and/or seemed to have warded off. Indeed, on the basis of our case studies, the most reasonable assessment seems to be that some combination of elaboration, defence and enactment is always present, on the part of both participants in the encounter. What counts is that the analytic pair manages to use this combination to engage somehow with the unconscious dynamics, as long as they perceive and work through the defences and enactments later on. We see cases in which this combination works more smoothly and others in which it appears to be more chaotic and disturbing for one or both partners.

In fact, it seems realistic to say that the analytic process observed in our cases is *never* smooth and continuous. It involves fluctuations and breaks between moments of bewilderment; moments of representation and elaboration, when analytic space is opened and 'switching the level' becomes possible; moments that are more chaotic, when something unexpected breaks through and the 'storm' manifests itself through projective identification, role responsiveness and enactment; and yet other defensive moments, when one or both protagonists withdraw from analytic space, for example when they are too afraid to get lost in the chaos of such poorly symbolized experiences. Such breaks and fluctuations should probably be considered to be an integral, inevitable and perhaps even necessary part of the process. These 'vicissitudes of the analytic couple' will be further explored in the coming chapters.

6 THE OPENING SCENE

From anticipation to initiation

This chapter considers the 'entrance' of conscious and unconscious elements before, or on the threshold of, the analyst and prospective patient's first consultation meeting. The unpredictable consequences of such meetings bring to mind one of William Shakespeare's most renowned monologues:

> All the world's a stage,
> And all the men and women merely players;
> They have their exits and their entrances [. . .]
>
> (Shakespeare, *As You Like It*, 2.7.146–147)

This is probably one of the most prominent and well-known metaphors in English literature. It is our contention that metaphor, the implication that one thing is the same as some other unrelated thing, can be a powerful device. In Chapter 2 we encountered the expression 'ballet dancing on a minefield', generated within the Workshop discussion, which conveyed dramatically the idea that what 'lay below' was both potentially violent and dangerous. As such, the WPIP has found metaphor particularly useful in conveying the nature of those forces generated when analyst and patient come together. None, perhaps, more evocative than Bion's 'emotional storm', which has been a central and guiding metaphor in our research and throughout these chapters.

Psychoanalysis as a chosen or desired instrument may rely on many prompts: contacts with others, prior reading or lecture attendance, movies etc. Perhaps even nowadays there persists an unconscious societal awareness, often caricatured, that psychoanalysis is about a world we cannot see, that invites understanding even if feared, and somehow gives permission not to know while simultaneously wishing to do so.

Keeping alive metaphors, such as those developed in our discussions, helps to focus and sharpen an awareness that the forces we work with as analysts can be unreachable, deceptively camouflaged, and yet powerfully affecting. We are reminded here of Freud's original metaphor of 'the potentially explosive chemical laboratory' (Freud 1915a), akin to Bion's 'storm', whereby two people sitting quietly in the consulting room, or taking a first telephone call, may be experiencing severe emotional pain and disturbance at times.

Freud wrote in 1913:

> The patient meets the analyst with a transference that is already established and which the Doctor must slowly uncover, instead of having the opportunity to observe the growth of the transference from the outset.
>
> (Freud 1913, p. 125)

Ogden (1992) similarly reminds us:

> the analyst is the object of the patient's transference even before the first meeting . . . just as the patient has a fantasied analyst before the first session the analyst also has a patient (more accurately many patients) in his own mind prior to the first meeting. In other words, prior to meeting the patient, the analyst has drawn upon such particulars as the sound of the patient's voice on the phone, the source of the referral, the analyst's relationships with his current patients, as sources of unconscious feelings about the patient that he or she will bring to the first meeting.
>
> (Ogden 1992, p. 227)

In this chapter we will try to demonstrate how the opening scene may be a first configuration created by the enactment of those central unconscious dynamics, brought by the patient to the anticipated meeting, and the impact of this on the analyst. The opening scene as a metaphorical stage reaches backwards into the patient's history and early object relations, and also forwards, influencing the specific way this patient and analyst might work together. This may provide the earliest indication of the future analytic process. The patient approaches the meeting with hope as well as fear. Internal object-relations are activated and projective pressures heightened. The opening scene is thus ripe for repetition.

This, of course, is not a one-way process. The opening scene is formed by patient and analyst; encompassing both of their anticipatory fantasies and their spontaneous reactions to each other. The seeds of a mutual enactment and working relationship may be sown at this point. The opening scene may now be a step into something new. As a metaphor it contains the drama of those crucial, initial interactions between patient and analyst and the possibilities and fate of the consultation/analytic process.

Seen from these perspectives, we thought it would be useful to try to extract from the clinical material what might, in all likelihood, already be happening in the minds of both analyst and prospective patient, as they approach their potential first meeting. What unconscious elements have been activated, whose preparatory configurations may have begun hours, weeks, sometimes even months or years before this meeting? In much the same way that we think of a dynamic process continuing to unfold, develop and transform in the spaces between sessions and during analytic breaks, even continuing to evolve after termination, we are focussing in this chapter on those dynamic processes already active before prospective analyst and prospective patient actually meet.

What happens before, up to, and upon the threshold of the first interview became a particular object of interest throughout the WPIP Team's research. During our case analyses it became increasingly clear that the opening scene was an important source of information, often only possible to grasp in retrospect, and containing the central dynamic patterns formed by the patient's pathology and way of relating, as well as the two analytic participants' anticipatory and spontaneous reactions to each other.

The 'three-stage' method of looking back at our clinical material, which demonstrated a repetition of these dynamic patterns through all Stages, revealed retrospectively that the opening scene was the first manifestation of the specific central themes in the analytic encounter. If registered and thought about, it illuminates, through the way the patient and analyst responded to each other, some of the important characteristics of the eventual analytic process. Thus, we thought interest in understanding the specific configuration of the opening scene might facilitate a deeper retrospective and reflective examination of the possibility of initiating an analysis.

As part of our research we wanted to illuminate how, before actual meetings, fantasy elaborations in the minds of both analyst and prospective patient begin to create the opening scene phenomena.

When referring to the opening scene in this context we are looking at:

> Any significant events or information available prior to the interview and the analyst's and patient's fantasies before the interview or immediately on meeting, that may have affected the patient and the analyst or interview process.
>
> (WPIP Research Protocol)

Drawing on Argelander's (1978) seminal study of the complex dynamics set in motion at the earliest intention and evident in the opening scene, Elzer and Gerlach (2014) offer this description:

> when the patient comes in contact with the therapist, he unconsciously presents his central problem as if he were on stage. He acts out his problem . . . This scenic information is a kind of acting out with high content, which comes about through the minimal situation structure of the interview.
>
> (Elzer and Gerlach 2014, p. 145)

They go on to describe, resonant with our own observations, that the therapist can quickly become an object of transference, or there could be a rapid revision of pre-transference manifestations, and significant aspects of the patient's central conflict or trauma can quickly trigger fantasies, ideas and feelings in the therapist's mind – that require countertransference attention (ibid. p. 145). We find it useful to think about what precedes the first interview in the same way – the patient and analyst, in anticipation of the meeting, begin to 'stage' and to fantasize about the meeting, influenced by largely unconscious stirrings that may or may not have been heralded by manifest external pre-meeting events.

To colour and concretize our 'storm' metaphor we may imagine an actual storm where, well before its arrival, premonitory registrations of a significant occurrence are evident. Frequently one may become aware of a stillness in the air, maybe of rising heat and humidity, the movement and sometimes silence of the birds, and the appearance of dark and ominous cloud formations on the horizon. A particular collection of atmospheric elements announces a powerful climatic event. Fanciful as it may seem, we might draw an analogy here to the building tension and sense both of dread and hopeful anticipation in the minds of prospective patients, commencing from that point where they become aware of powerful feelings of unresolvable psychic pain and conflict and so begin the search for a particular place or person where some hopeful resolution could potentially be found. One might consider the earliest anticipatory staging of important aspects of core dynamics begins at a point where the patient recognizes that another mind may be helpful, and the patient starts looking for an analyst. The patient seeks repair through an object; a search reaching back to, and arising from, early object-relationship history.

It is feasible that the embryonic initiation of an analytic process has a distant heritage. Its genesis may be set at points of significant loss or conflict. It is also feasible that the pre-scene contains both hope of recovery of that which has been lost or damaged, and brings the patient to the analyst, together with fear of a repetition of the loss or conflict, and that these ambivalent expectations are projected into the new object.

The WPIP study of clinical material about the opening scene – in the form of early approaches and communications, enactments and environmental influences, and particular referral pathways – provided much grist for our collective thinking about how various phantasies (and fantasies) might be setting the scene during the steps toward a first meeting.

Not surprisingly, anxiety in facing the largely unknown is a prominent feature (certainly in the majority of our cases) that could eventually be seen as the primary driving force activating the patient's enactment of his or her core dynamics and a counter-enactment by the analyst, that will run through all of the clinical material in different forms but with parallel content.

The Woman Who Planned

Ms. D. calls an analyst without leaving a message and later makes another call, this time leaving a message, creating early negative feelings in the mind of the analyst. The seemingly childish voice on the phone and the surname given by Ms. D., similar to that of a famous person, begin to colonize the analyst's mind. In a later call, Ms. D. explains how she obtained the analyst's name through another patient. The analyst's mind is again occupied, this time by thoughts about her earlier patient's eating disorder. Ms. D.'s name also reminds her of a famous restaurant. During the Clinical Workshop discussion, the analyst comments that such pre-fantasies are normal for her and their absence is often felt as 'a bad sign' for future analytic work. We learn in the workshop discussion that Ms. D. had in fact, somewhat extraordinarily, left her vehicle parked near the analyst's building the night before the first appointment, saying to the analyst, on meeting, that she felt she could be confused after the interview and so needed to have the security of her vehicle near at hand (the image of a getaway car comes to mind in the workshop discussion). It is later felt that this action reflects an ambivalent but also intense pre-transference investment of the analyst. It seemed that this analyst and her office building had already been positively invested as a potential container or transitional space, while more negatively the need to pre-park her vehicle may perhaps be understood as something of a self-rescue plan, indicating a possible range of fears connected with the first interview – losing her bearings, becoming confused and disorientated, and perhaps at a deeper, more claustrophobic level, some threat of attack that demands a getaway plan. This escape or rescue plan fails, however, as her carefully positioned vehicle is towed away the evening prior to their meeting, precipitating something of a rescue enactment with the analyst the following day, who lets Ms. D. know where to find her towed vehicle.

A dramatic illustration, perhaps, of the lengths patients may go to when scoping the prospect of meeting an analyst stranger and encountering their physical environment for the first time – indicative of complex pre-meeting transference assumptions.

In this case, an event that has occurred outside the consulting room is now active in the consulting room. While we hear Ms. D. described as a pleasant, sweet-faced, young woman, she has in fact burst into the analyst's room, quite distraught, immediately talking about her 'disappeared' vehicle in such a chaotic way that the analyst imagines her to be flooded by an experience of catastrophic, concrete and irreparable loss. It would be difficult not to include in our wonderings the fact that a clear 'no parking' sign was not seen by Ms. D. Her unconscious pressure to enact some irreparable loss seems to suggest that she hoped to find a transforming reception with this analyst. As a matter of fact, while the analyst recounts being drawn into an immediate rescue scenario, she describes how she let Ms. D. know that the parking area is private, that any cars left parked there are likely to get towed away, and that if she were to look carefully there is a sign that specifies where the car may be found.

When this opening was considered along with the Workshop material at the later WPIP Team meeting, it seemed that, though on the surface a simple event, this dramatic opening exchange was significantly more complex. Along with the analyst's own reflections, this opening seemed not only disorganized and persecutory but also strangely seductive, pressuring the analyst into a rescue posture wherein reassurance is given. One could imagine the analyst in this situation even feeling accused of involvement in the removal of the car, while worrying at the same time just what sort of patient she was encountering. But neither feeling seemed to have been prominent in the analyst's thinking. Instead, as she informed the Workshop group, she had felt it important to listen to this patient's anxiety so as to try and understand it. Certainly, she had many unspoken fantasies about Ms. D.'s distress, yet made a decision not to attempt any exploration, at that time, of the patient's anxiety, nor the meaning of her actions. She felt that Ms. D. would have experienced interpretation, or alternatively silence, as a refusal to recognize the impact of reality, while any prospective interpretation may well have been both wild and defensive.

Moments similar to these are never easy, yet such 'storm' conditions are so evocatively engaging that they thus became a major focus in the early workshop discussion of this case. It remained a strong focus throughout the research and became an important first configuration of a central aspect of the process.

Looking back on this situation the analyst's response can be understood in different ways. On the one hand the analyst's response could be seen as an enactment with avoidance of meaning and a flight into external reality. On the other hand, direct information to Ms. D. about the fate of her vehicle could be considered as having the value of an interpretation, possibly arrived at pre-consciously by the analyst, in which she restores hope to Ms. D. It is as if she were saying: 'you can find your lost objects and get them back', or even, 'you can find your past again', possibly implying that a traumatic history and experience of loss can be talked about and given meaning if one is helped to 'read the signs carefully'. Stretching our imagination still further, could this enactment also communicate to the patient that it is possible to differentiate external and internal reality, moving from one to the other, and thereby opening space for meaningful reflection?

A significant advantage in our three-stage research process was the opportunity to think further, wider and deeper than the analyst in the immediacy of such a storm, while endeavouring to imagine the rapidity with which dramatic beginnings activate a similar rapidity in conscious and unconscious processing. Considering the different ways of understanding the interaction, as delineated above, the Investigative Team wondered whether each hypothesis was probably inadequate in and of itself, and whether the analyst's decision could be thought of as lying somewhere in between – as a way of buying time, laying the groundwork for later interior work on its meaning, or possibly as a way of establishing or even salvaging a precarious relationship in which meaning might later be fostered. Hypothetically the analyst's implied message might then be thought of as something like, 'I recognize your distress and I take you seriously'. In the presentation we hear that after this initial exchange Ms. D. seems visibly relieved and the analyst thinks, 'all is not lost'.

Affected by such a 'storm' of distress as manifest in this case, analysts may find themselves in a similar quandary – to act or not act.

As it emerged in this case, the analyst's response appears to bring some relief for her patient and no doubt for the analyst herself, who has the thought, 'all is not lost!' Ms. D. said that she had been thinking of starting therapy for a long time, having felt so bad on occasions that she had contemplated suicide, but as she spoke the word 'su-ic-ide' it seemed to cause a knot in her throat. The analyst informs us that at this point a blank occurs in her notes, with a notation indicating she had either said something or had maybe thought of something to say. It is not too difficult to think that a tsunami of thoughts has quickly followed the opening 'storm'. The analyst tells the Workshop that she believes that if 'the words stayed in my pen, maybe they stuck in my throat as well (as the knot in Ms. D.'s throat) and I probably articulated at most a "mmmh"'. Retrospectively it is realized that something very powerful seems to have broken through at this point that momentarily could not be contained in thought or speech by either patient or analyst. If the implication in the analyst's original intervention was that it might be possible to find lost objects, then might we imagine Ms. D. telling the analyst she is extremely frightened about object relatedness; that her object relations are bound to end in catastrophe, or that she can't enter an object relationship for fear of losing her identity. It is fascinating to think that with her pen and memory the analyst has immediately replicated Ms. D.'s symptoms, as though at this very early stage of meeting she is so attuned to her patient that she has already begun resonating with her. A 'mmmh' may have been sufficient to convey such a resonance. As the presentation proceeds the workshop learns more of Ms. D.'s unhappy history. It is a moving and dramatic account of childhood experiences of loss at the time of her parents' separation, raising vivid fantasies in the analyst's mind of a mother and child 'huddled in a cave'. Ms. D. surprises herself; expressing a wish for some re-unification with her estranged, passionate and emotionally charged parents. Perhaps this indicates a capacity to step back a little and, at a symbolic level, express a deeper wish for internal integration. It is at this point that her analyst makes a very simple comment, 'and you . . . ', intuitively testing whether Ms. D. may also have the capacity to separate a little from her early objects and think more about herself. We go on to learn that she hated school, often playing truant, escaping through windows, displaying early reactive aspects of these struggles, while at the same time 'inside the consulting room window' (Tuckett 2011), in the transference, she also indicates a wish to run away from her analyst's invitation to explore individuation. Reinforcing these early impressions Ms. D. goes on to describe early moves to self-reliance and apparent independence, with a series of boyfriends punctuated by several tragic deaths. The analyst experiences this as a rather seductive and exciting tale of self-survival, prompting her own private and romantic James Dean fantasies.

This segment of the presentation, a dramatic story-telling and the analyst's corresponding private fantasies, builds a picture of a very chaotic inner life and relationships, much like a projection onto a movie screen, which the Workshop finds similarly stimulating.

The dramatic opening of the first session is repeated in the second, Ms. D. reporting intervening stomach pains and vomiting. The potential space between analyst and patient is immediately filled with tears and vomit. This sequence reproduces some of the characteristics of the pre-scene – the dramatic, concrete bodily manifestations replicating aspects of the concrete vehicle disappearance. The analyst is drawn again to consider how her equally concrete and immediate action had, on reflection, perhaps been an attempt to tune into an external reality while remaining open to deeper registrations of pain, rage, fear and precocious fragility. As the sessions unfold there also seems to be a lack, loss or shifting of boundaries, with movements in and out between patient and analyst. It feels as if Ms. D. has a tendency to merge in relationships, but when merged seems at points to fragment, losing her capacity to think, such that she has to break off a relationship again, or expel what she has taken in (this is consistent with her history, but a reflection only really formulated at our Investigative Stage). In the sessions there is a pressure to engage which is experienced by the analyst as an invasion. She feels the patient taking too much for granted, 'seeming to be in too much of a hurry'. Navigating sensitively between merging and meaning, something begins to form, described colourfully by the analyst as a 'coagulation'.

In her presentation the analyst seems powerfully activated, as if enacting the way her patient has flooded her emotionally from the first moment she entered the consulting room. Parallel to this, in addressing the research questions, the Workshop contends that a most fundamental meeting has occurred between both participants at a primitive level of physical sensation and emotional impact. At the same time, it is thought this analyst has demonstrated a capacity to weather a significant 'storm'. Ms. D. is considered fortunate to have found an analyst with a capacity for reverie in the midst of such tumult, remaining receptive to her emotional experience.

The pre-scene phenomena resonate through our work. In this case, it seemed to be tempered and facilitated by the analyst's capacity to stay in the room, in her mind, during the different manifestations of the original 'storm'. At times, however, reverie appears to give way to a type of sharing or mirroring of Ms. D.'s experience such as when something gets stuck in the analyst's pen and memory, like the word 'suicide' in the patient's throat, the image of coagulating, in experiencing 'the space between us filling up with tears and vomit', and a later exclamation to the patient, 'how much pain'. It felt as though processes of containment and transformation were enabled by this first step in the spontaneous sharing of experience between analyst and patient.

This analyst was able to attune herself to this patient and was able to resonate with her at a basic emotional level, as an antecedent to other psychic metabolism. One might think about the inner experiences resulting from this resonance as something akin to a meeting of souls, transformed into reverie and ultimately into useful intervention. It could be argued that such forms of empathy imply an observing position that is already one step removed from the more basic experience of vibrating with the patient – so close to our storm analogy. We think it possible to postulate that this analyst was doing something else, in the sense that with Ms. D. she was able to put herself in a state of active receptiveness, inviting projective identification as it were, or letting herself be affected by Ms. D.'s raw experiences, whatever fluctuating mode of communication the patient had available to her at any point in time.

We might deem this analyst's response to Ms. D.'s initial anxiety about her lost object as an enactment, an interpretation or something in between; but while still experiencing these possibilities, the analyst is nonetheless able to step outside sufficiently to look at what was happening. The response was spontaneous but also accompanied by intense reflective processes. If portrayed as an enactment, in the sense of a shared experience requiring symbolization, here we see an experience that is in the process of being symbolized. It was in fact this analyst's way of staying in the 'storm' so effectively that enabled the Workshop and the later Investigative Team to also look 'in between', imagining this patient becoming sufficiently comfortable because she felt the analyst was able to respond well to her emotional situation, both internally and externally, seeming not too afraid of the patient nor of her inner world. It was concluded that patient and analyst were able to meet directly and effectively on a profound level, where significant switching of the level or meta-communication about the relationship seemed neither possible nor necessary. Rather resonance, enactment and simple interpretation appeared to occur simultaneously or in rapid alternation, depicted as a recursive process, leading ultimately to better symbolization.

This type of resonance is not quite the same as collusion, but can rather be seen as a first step facilitating later reverie and containment. Stretching our metaphor, she was able to 'stay on the bridge', mind open to the 'storm', maintaining a course, based on experience, toward a possible analytic destination. This analyst was able to maintain, or regularly re-establish, her capacity to think throughout the interview process.

Here we witnessed an analyst creating an analytic setting and a transformation of a person in crisis to a patient in analysis. A similar transformation seemed evident in the Workshop process, enabling members to freely express contrasting viewpoints, while not evoking difficulties in managing group tensions, in contrast to other Workshops where the enactment of uncontained and untransformed material activated similarly uncontained and reactive responses.

So, besides the repetition of the dynamics brought into the consultation process, this case also demonstrates how the analyst's transformational function is shaped and adapted to the patient, and we get a sense of the vicissitudes of a new process towards finding a safer parking lot.

A more stable picture is developing of the patterns of Ms. D.'s enactment of her conflicts, her fears and hopes, and also of how this analyst is dealing with her 'counter-enactment'. The parking of the vehicle in the vicinity of the analyst's office, a place where parking was prohibited, can thus retrospectively be used as a flexible metaphor for aspects of Ms. D. and for the interview process itself. It broadly encompasses an intrusive rescue-plan, transgression of borders, ambivalence in the search for a secure container, and the spontaneous reciprocal adaptation in the analyst's reactions, thoughts and interventions.

The first incident can be understood *après coup* both as a representation of what the patient brings and of a transformational meeting where something new is able to develop.

The Maiden Challenged

The following case demonstrates in another way how aspects of the opening scene make an immediate impact on the analyst and form her fantasies about the patient's dynamics and ideas about what is expected of her – somewhat disturbing, somewhat precise – before she has seen the patient. Something is forcefully projected into the situation and the analyst's anticipation of the relationship. The image of a 'very important referral' flatters and pressures the analyst, who is at once occupied by a wish to live up to expectations and a fear that she might disappoint. The huge impact of the referral – of which the analyst seems somewhat apprehensive while also impressed at having been chosen – can in retrospect be seen as a first version of what reappears in different interactions during the consultation, the workshop and the research process.

The first event in the opening scene is a phone call from a prominent and distinguished university professor, from another field, who asks if the analyst has a vacancy for Ms. E., the daughter of her best friend, herself a distinguished academic. A traumatic childhood revolving around the separation of the girl's parents and an eating disorder is described. The analyst has a vacancy. The analyst feels both flattered and intimidated, wishing to prove herself worthy of the trust placed in her, but fearing that she may disappoint.

The impression is that the analyst was overwhelmed, not only by the important public figure choosing her, but also by something about what was communicated to her about the case. Her sense of being overwhelmed and needing to perform and impress an esteemed parent-like figure can be seen as the motivating force at the beginning of the presentation, in which the analyst prefaces the discussion to the Workshop group with her own more intellectual reflections concerning initiation.

Thereafter the analyst describes how, when Ms. E. arrives, she is struck by her smallness, both physically and in terms of maturity – looking like 'a little girl who had been playing with her mother's makeup'. As Ms. E. begins to speak, the analyst is jarred by the patient's throaty, grating, almost masculine voice and wonders whose voice it is, or whether it could be due to compulsive vomiting. Again, the analyst goes into theorizing about difficulties that arise on the threshold to adulthood. The analyst's eagerness to understand, and her use of the image of Persephone separated from her mother Demeter, perhaps also reveals her early identification with the young woman's situation and her already detailed anticipation of what central dynamics will be at stake in the analytic process.

As the Workshop discussion evolved, it became apparent that the analyst's description of the referral and her equally powerful, dramatic and theoretical introductory remarks had already activated an emotional reaction that coloured and formed subsequent reactions to the clinical material.

The analyst presents a picture of a young woman in difficulties. In addition to the strong identification with Ms. E., there is a maternal countertransference, which quickly infiltrates the presentation. The analyst presents in an engaged manner; she tends to respond immediately and directly to early thoughts and questions from an equally eager group, despite the moderator's request that she allow herself to sit back and let a dialogue develop within the group. The analyst reports that she felt anxious from the outset and, perhaps projectively, felt she must reassure the young Ms. E. She tells Ms. E. about her discussion with the referrer (the prominent friend of her mother), which while possibly intended to be explanatory, re-introduces her own earlier pre-scene anxieties. With some encouragement Ms. E. tells the analyst about her very successful academic career, but how, instead of the anticipated pleasure of university life, she had become preoccupied with eating and control, with episodes of bulimia and vomiting. The analyst is quick to reassure: 'you do not understand what is happening to you and that feels quite frightening'. Ms. E. agrees and goes on to describe feelings of isolation and difficulty in concentration, whereas she had expected a new freedom.

Again, the analyst is quick to respond, suggesting Ms. E. feels disappointed, bad and angry with herself; having sensed the thought 'if only I could pull my socks up' in Ms. E.'s refrain, she suggests that Ms. E. would like to 'shake herself up'. Ms. E. goes on to describe, in a slightly matter of fact way, her parents' separation when she was 10, and the conflicts that arose with the parents' new partners. She describes an ongoing, angry, unhappy relationship with the father who 'doesn't have a clue about me', and a famous mother who had encouraged her to seek analysis via an equally famous female friend.

Various other conflicts and dissatisfactions emerge. The analyst comments: 'How many mouthfuls you have had to swallow'. The young woman, sounding both surprised and disappointed, says that she thought she had digested her early experience, and then she promptly bursts into tears, sobbing, with mascara streaming down her face and now looking more like a 'sad little clown'. The hoarse, hard and slightly detached voice has collapsed. It seems the level of connection between analyst and patient has shifted and deepened.

In the second session Ms. E. is without makeup and comes across as pale, demure and frightened. The analyst is clearly affected and has to resist an impulse to 'pick her up' and say something to make her comfortable, feeling a tightness in her stomach. Ms. E. proceeds to talk about angry and frustrating exchanges with the father who seems to favour the 'sock pulling up' approach to life's difficulties, and seems out of touch with his daughter's distress. The analyst makes a statement about the impossibility of pleasing father; she feels she disappoints him but is not able to renounce the wish to seek his approval.

Violence then enters the session via a dream:

> I was watching my grandfather kicking hard and violently a child who had become like a ball, all rolled up on the floor. My grandmother was reproaching him for never having commanded respect from the child. What did he expect, she shouted, he got all he deserved for not behaving like a father figure, not teaching the child to respect him. I just stood there, observing, feeling helpless, feeling nothing.

Ms. E. offers no associations, as if helpless and feeling nothing. However, the analyst suddenly feels exhausted, as though having run miles and miles.

The analyst writes:

> I feel astonished and speechless. Paralysed, as if I have been forced to be the captive spectator of a brutal, violent, but also exciting game. I also glean some vague and obscure sexual titillation in the images reported. I feel emotionally bruised and somewhat horrified.

She tells herself that she must proceed carefully and with leaden feet. She concludes that she is dealing with a feeling of foreboding, as if sensing a threat while at the same time feeling intensely watched, a shadow perhaps picked up at the point of first contact and persisting. The analyst then makes what she describes as a non-committal comment, as if to take time, but in fact this has a very powerful effect on the patient. She says:

> It is strange and interesting, isn't it, how much one is prepared to do, how far one is prepared to go, to hold onto a (grand) father.

The Workshop group considers this a very powerful interpretation, with an almost 'sisterly joining and identification quality', again suggesting a persistent shadow, activated when she first heard about the patient and felt she would have to take 'very special care'. Ms. E. seems more relaxed but also feels ashamed about this recognition, which implies her continued dependence on her own parents in relation to where she might live and how future sessions may be funded. This pull towards dependency is mirrored in the analyst's inclination to take special care and, as it were, to pick her up. In a manner of speaking, Ms. E. had 'been in the analyst's arms' since the first referral call.

The group discussion had a similar quality of wanting to pick up and carry the process along, as if in collusion with the analyst's conviction that special care was needed. The lively dialogue developed between the analyst and the group might, looking back, to some extent have served defensive needs; as a reaction to the pre-scene pressure on the analyst to perform well and not disappoint.

During the presentation the group laughed repeatedly, particularly when Ms. E. took control at the end of the sessions, stating that she wished to start after Christmas and that she wouldn't be able to pay much. This occurred after the analyst had suggested taking some time to reach a decision and meeting after Christmas. Here for the first time the analyst exhibits a slight irritation, but also curiosity. A somewhat adolescent flavour seems to echo through the group, a bantering tone was often followed by a sense of relief when an insightful comment was humorously put. A couple of members adopt more of a teaching stance, possibly drawing back from these more excited elements, perhaps replaying the wish for an idealized, all-knowing authority figure vis à vis the patient´s adolescent or childish needs.

However, the group becomes increasingly ready to consider an underlying theme of violence, linking Ms. E.'s harsh voice and the violence expressed in her dream, and the question is asked, 'who is kicking whom?'. The analyst's irritation at Ms. E. dictating how a therapy might proceed is discussed as a powerful projective identification, in relation to Ms. E.'s experience of being moved around following her parents' separation.

The analyst's introductory excursion into mythology with the reference to Persephone is understood as her way of managing the pressure. Who is going into the Underworld? A group member remembers that Persephone had no choice, reflecting that in the sessions presented, 'everybody forced everybody'. The analyst felt she was left with no choice, neither when the important person called her, nor when at the end of the sessions it seemed Ms. E. had decided their future together.

A conflictual relationship between Ms. E. and her mother emerges as a major theme. The analyst's first interpretation to her patient, 'that there seemed to be too many mouthfuls to digest', reflected not only the impact of the opening pre-scene and first session, but also the initial impact on the listening group. Almost as a 'selected fact' (Bion 1962, Britton and Steiner 1994) it combined the contradictory aspects of the analyst's initial disturbance as she attempted to digest the special and violent nature of this case. The analyst's strong somatic arousal, in projective identification with Ms. E.'s eating disorder, may have been her somatized solution to the rage and fears around separation that Ms. E. subsequently 'vomited' into her mind. The violence sensed from the first contact, even a 'seductive violence' surrounding the referral, is represented in Ms. E.'s dream about a child being kicked.

A picture of a patient having both an inviting 'adopt me part' and also a 'violent part' could not be seen until the later part of the group discussion. The analyst felt a violent pressure in the pre-scene events, but was initially only able to attend to the 'adopt me part' of Ms. E., corresponding to the steps the group was able to digest. Following the thoughts about Ms. E. having both a nice 'adopt me' aspect and a violent part, the group could now begin to consider how, despite the slightly cut off entrance, there is an aspect of Ms. E. looking for someone who might help control this self-destructive quality. From the beginning this could be seen as inducing the analyst to be the 'saviour', repeating a pattern of maternal collusion against father. It was felt this also operated as defence in relation to incestuous anxieties about a father who, we learn, wanted her 'to share everything only with him'. This formulation helps us to understand Ms. E.'s resistance and need to control both setting and sessions.

Towards the end of the discussion another understanding emerges: somebody is going to intrude on somebody, and is going to overwhelm somebody, in a way that will challenge normal separation. This could be identified in several of Ms. E.'s significant relationships, particularly with the father, as well as in relation to the analyst. The intrusive impact of the referral was evident in the opening scene. Provocative and hidden violent intrusion has been, it seems, the eye of our now more clearly defined 'storm'.

The analyst's own 'storm' may have influenced the group processes strongly in a way that reproduced what had occurred in the interviews. People seemed to feel pushed around. Much of the discussion was focused on the analyst's (understandable) difficulty in digesting all that was put into her, and in the groups it became difficult to find sufficient space to digest and think. A tendency to rush around trying to 'put the ball into the goal' was strong, to make sense of the material rather than accepting that which we can't understand. There are 'too many mouthfuls to digest', which may lie behind the urge to go into a somewhat deadening intellectualization in the analyst and in the groups.

The perspectives of the Workshop and the Investigative Team were not quite identical; the former focused more on positive aspects of the analyst's work, the latter more on the difficulties. This can be understood as a reflection of opposite features – both in the conflict about growing up that Ms. E. has brought to the analysis, and in the analyst's own difficulties related to the pressures in the referral – finding space and a position from which these opposite needs could be seen and understood.

Concluding remarks

These two cases, with their especially prominent opening scenes, illustrate the immediate entrance of powerful projective forces, from the first steps towards contact between patient and analyst. They show how events in the opening scene can be understood both as the first enacted demonstration of central aspects of the patient's dynamics, and furthermore through the effect it has upon the analyst's functioning and adaptation to the patient and the situation (Wegner 1992). It is the first crude version of a mutual-enactment (Tuckett 1997, 2011) that will invariably constitute part of a prospective analytic process.

It is especially interesting in hindsight to focus on the details of the opening scene. On closer observation it becomes apparent that the earliest 'events' – the anticipation and initiation of contact in the consultation – can be seen as the first configuration of something that reaches back into the patient's past, the history and fate of the patient's object relations hidden in the repetition and staging of what the patient brings forward to the initial consultation, while simultaneously pointing forward towards the form and fate of the meeting of patient and analyst and the eventual analytic process.

The ubiquitous presence of mutual enactment in any first meeting suggests this is part of the analytic examination and process, a first representation of that which can be clarified and differentiated during an analysis. As Fairbairn (1958) puts it, the patient is 'press-ganging' the analyst towards a repetition:

> Thus, in a sense, psycho-analytical treatment resolves itself into a struggle on the part of the patient to press-gang his relationship with the analyst into the closed system of the inner world through the agency of transference, and a determination on the part of the analyst to effect a breach in this closed system and to provide conditions under which, in the setting of a therapeutic relationship, the patient may be induced to accept the open system of outer reality.
>
> (Fairbairn 1958, p. 385)

In the clinical examples above, the analyst's struggle in weathering the projections and pressure to repeat is obvious and dramatic. The enactment on the part of the analyst can be seen as an attunement, a reaction and a subsequent response that is possible in that moment. This understanding is in line with Stern (2004) who regards enactment as central to psychoanalytic work and implies that in enactment the analyst resonates with the patient's conflict.

Enactment can thus be seen as the first representation of what cannot be formulated or even thought, an idea similar to Bollas' 'unthought known' (1987).

What is staged in the opening scene, communicated in action and word, can only be fully understood *après coup* as the complex dynamics of the patient and the specific way each patient and each analyst find a way to work in the analytic relationship.

In hindsight, this configuration gains the quality of a metaphor, a representation with both concrete and symbolic elements of the past and the future. This understanding opens both an archaeological and teleological perspective on the process (Enkell 2010). The new meeting creates an opportunity for patient and analyst to see old patterns in new ways.

7 DIFFERENT BEGINNINGS

How is analysis initiated? What makes it possible for the analyst to reach a position where a positive recommendation can be made that will lead to analysis?

The following case vignettes of analytic beginnings were taken from the thorough analysis of 28 first interviews by the WPIP (see also Chapter 3). They are illustrative of the general finding that psychoanalysis is initiated on such different grounds that one cannot ascertain any single indicators or forms of interaction with which to predict the outcome of first interviews. There are neither identifiable characteristics of the patients, nor characteristics of the interaction between patient and analyst as seen from a more assessment-oriented perspective, that can predict the initiation of analysis. This makes it more difficult to discern the basic psychoanalytic principles underlying these diverse practices. How can the diversity of processes in analytic consultations be seen as springing from a common ground, from something specifically analytic? This diversity, at first confusing, has, through the working through of the cases, actually paved the way for defining more analytic ways of thinking about the consultation and what leads to psychoanalysis.

As described in Chapter 5, we found that in each consultation there appears, in one form or another, an interplay of two different aspects in the interaction, namely 'switching the level' of understanding and communication, and the immediate presence of a powerful unconscious 'emotional storm'. From the analyst´s perspective these metaphorical descriptions of the encounter are linked to the analytic function. The analyst brings the psychoanalytic theory of different layers of psychic functioning and of the existence of the unconscious into practice in the consultation process by facilitating a 'switching of the level' within the dialogue and by facing the 'unconscious emotional storm', taking a concave receptive position in an attempt to grasp the meaning of the interaction and to be able to make room for a whole person (Bolognini 2006; see also Chapter 2, Reith et al. 2010, Reith 2015). To be open and receptive in the first encounter necessitates the confidence in one's ability to stand the pressure of projections and uncertainty during the process, and the conviction that meaning can eventually be found. Seen from the patient's perspective, the crucial question must be whether the consultation creates an experience that opens the possibility of finding new perspectives, new understanding in the presence of someone who could potentially receive and contain the unmanageable. The result of each individual consultation must thus be shaped and conditioned by the respective ability of the two participants to create a meaningful dialogue and their capacity to bear all that remains uncertain and not conceptualized.

Our general findings in answer to the question 'how is analysis initiated?' can be summarized as follows:

- There is no specific way in which psychoanalysis gets started. There is no single indicator or form of interaction that can predict the outcome of first interviews, and no clear criteria to objectively explain why analysis is chosen. Psychoanalysis is initiated on different grounds, and the initiation depends on the highly individual characteristics brought to the encounter by the two participants and thereafter on the specific ability of the analyst to contain and metabolize these dynamics.
- The interaction between patient and analyst can take on a wide range of forms. The starting point of each individual couple can be placed in different positions along a spectrum, anywhere between the extremities from highly thought-through understanding in a more triangulated situation to a more enacted, collusive or narcissistic dynamic.
- The triadic situation in the initial encounter cannot be seen as a goal per se and should not be idealized. It was not a condition for beginning analysis, and an observing 'third position' can also be used defensively.
- Every encounter seems to have sequences with different qualities of interaction. There will be movements towards deepening of understanding and movements of distancing. A psychoanalytic consultation is not a smooth development towards deepening of rapport and understanding, and a reflective position is never fixed. Nor was this position constant in couples where a triangulation was possible. There are ruptures and breaks in co-work and understanding, to and fro between involvement and a more stepped back thinking position, shifts in the quality of interaction that can only be thought about afterwards.
- The initiation of analysis is often set in motion on the basis of a positive transference–countertransference position where disturbing material is not consciously considered, in a kind of benign, positive, mutual idealization.
- The analyst's recommendation of psychoanalysis with a given patient is influenced by the analyst's more personal characteristics in combination with his or her psychoanalytic culture.

The following case vignettes were chosen as demonstrations of the general points above and to show how varied and dissimilar beginnings tend to be.

The Wary Scientist

In this case the strength of the immediate creation of a repetition of the patient's central unconscious dynamic is very explicit, both in the interaction between analyst and patient and during the whole process of analysing the case material. The pattern created in the interaction can be seen as predictive of the analytic process in a potential analysis with this specific patient.

Mr. F. is 24 years old and single. He is in his final year of advanced studies in physics, following a study program for especially gifted students. The analyst is female, conducting the interviews for a clinic service that can offer reduced fee analysis, with an eventual referral. The consultation consisted of four interviews.

The analyst describes Mr. F. as a handsome young man casually dressed in a modern, slightly scruffy style. He comes over as intelligent, thoughtful, eager to talk, but at the same time the analyst feels she has to ask questions to keep the interview process going. She thinks this might be because he is anxious to know what she thinks. Early in the interviews Mr. F. expresses concerns over therapists who will be too eager to give explanations that could be wrong. During the whole consultation process there is a theme of being clever and of potential not being fulfilled.

Mr. F. describes his long-term anxiety that had worsened because he failed an exam. Recently he has broken up with a girlfriend and ended his counselling. He comes from a family with two younger brothers. His father is described as a scientist who, after a very promising start, did not really fulfil his potential. His mother works as a school teacher.

At 18 when Mr. F. was applying for university he started taking drugs and drinking, and the analyst had the impression that the parents did not take any notice of this. He has usually done well academically. After his first degree he was in doubt about what to do, he had difficulties in finding jobs, and finally decided on advanced physics, 'because his father was also a scientist'.

He talks about his anxiety of hierarchies, his critical attitude towards himself and others, his competiveness, but at the same time his fear of hurting others. He hates the weakness his anxiety gives him.

The analyst finds the interviews characterized by Mr. F.'s oscillation between engaging with the analyst, but then also retreating into an aloof state, which creates a feeling of discomfort and failure in the analyst. For example, after Mr. F. had mentioned the sense of weakness his anxiety creates in him the analyst asks whether he remembers any dreams. Usually he does not, but he recalls one from a few weeks ago that was disturbing. In the dream he is lying asleep on a chaise-longue and has wooden arrows in his feet; he tried to pull one out, and found a big splinter; then he could see his flesh.

He pauses, and the analyst comments on this vivid dream image as a wound opening up in him, and suggests his anxiety feels like a wound he has to cover up.

This leads him to talk about a childhood experience with a 'horrible' child-minder, who had spoken ill of his father; he had told his mother about this, but it was only the youngest brothers who were then removed from the care of the child-minder, while the patient was left with her for a few more years. The analyst suggests he must have felt angry and helpless, which makes him retreat into a more critical attitude, comparing the analyst with a bad counsellor – at this point the patient rejects further exploration.

The consultation process ran over three interviews and throughout these the same pattern is repeated: the movement towards a deepening of understanding, where the interpretations of the analyst lead to more information and more analytic dialogue, then followed by retreat. The fear of being dismissed was present all along, and defensive distancing kept taking over at times during the consultation.

In the Workshop group process there was an atmosphere of taking over, of competition about who would 'win' in the room, some sort of excitement from the start – even before the material about the patient and the setting were presented by the consultant. The group function continued to be tense; the question of control seemed central. This can be seen as a repetition of the presenter's feeling of discomfort and failure caused by this intelligent, thoughtful, eager, competitive patient, who repeatedly oscillated between engaging with her and retreating into an aloof state. There seemed to be a corresponding impatience and eagerness to know in the Workshop, to which the analyst reacted with a tense, rather controlling function, perhaps like a teacher. Something transmitted itself immediately to the group; there were a lot of 'experts' in the room and it seemed to resonate with the patient's competitiveness and ambivalence. The Workshop grasped the dynamics of narcissistic vulnerability; an oscillation between wanting to be taken on and anxiety about being dismissed. This was repeated in the WPIP discussion as the WPIP Team was at first unable to see how the Workshop process was a reflection of the material. During the whole process of this case there was an avoidance of relating, a movement of to-and-fro. Forceful dynamics, with difficulties acknowledging the contribution of others, went through all the three processing steps.

The outcome of the interviews was that Mr. F. was recommended for reduced-fee, five times weekly analysis. The WPIP later learned from the clinic that the patient had actually started in twice a week therapy which later developed into five times weekly psychoanalysis.

Although the analyst was drawn into the competitiveness and fear of closeness during some passages of the interviews in a way that could not be precisely conceptualized, she could also use the experience to understand what was central about Mr. F.'s problems, and what may become difficult in an eventual analysis. At the same time, she could preserve hope of development in this very open-ended situation. Seen from the two aspects of analytic functioning, described as 'switching the level' and 'facing the storm', one can see the 'storm' as filled with anxieties about intrusion from the father as well as the mother, and this affected the analyst's inclination to suggest analysis. She seemed to adapt to this and was capable of enduring the pressure to reach an understanding of Mr. F.'s anxiety behind the competitiveness, ambition and omnipotent defences, which for extended periods had concealed his wish to develop. Her experience and understanding made her able to give interpretations that switched the level of communication, thereby enriching and opening the dialogue. When the analyst could finally suggest analysis, it can be understood as based on her experience of the possibility of creating an analytic dialogue and a development in their interaction, in spite of Mr. F.'s recurring tendency to retreat. When one looks back upon the strong movement to and fro, on the fear of closeness both during the interview process and later in the group discussions, it can in hindsight be taken as a prediction of a specific quality in an eventual analytic process with this patient. This was not formulated explicitly by the analyst, neither in her recommendation of analysis to Mr. F., nor in her description of the consultations at the workshop. The consultation process gave her some experience of what analysis with Mr. F. would be like, it was also in this sense the beginning of analytic work, informing Mr. F. to some extent about what psychoanalysis could be for him.

What in this case is referred to as 'a movement to-and-fro' is evidently connected to Mr. F.'s central problems in relationships, and therefore stands out as a particularly evident characteristic, but it proved to take place in many first interviews. This can be understood as a result of the fragile quality of an initial analytic dialogue. In the first meeting there will probably be only short passages where the contact can produce interaction and understanding on deeper levels, where it can be analytic in a more narrow sense. Because of the special task of first interviews there will be more ruptures, fractures, shifts of themes, and levels of functioning that both participants contribute to, than there will typically be in an established analysis.

The Weaver Unravelled

The next vignette is in some ways akin to the case above; an example of analytic co-work that introduces analysis, it also features sudden breaks in the flow of the dialogue. The analyst was at times able to reach an observing third position, and there is one example where this actually was reached by a rather abrupt rupture in the dialogue. This case also has the hesitation, the to-and-fro movement of patient and analyst, with the latter often drawn into this process. The analyst's observing position seemed at first to serve him as a defensive escape, but he becomes aware of it, works on it, and is finally able to use it for his own independent thoughts and silent or outspoken interpretations; a sign that he has managed to recover and regain his analytic stance. This pattern seems to repeat itself several times in the first and second interviews.

The analyst's first impression of Ms. G. is her voice, pleasant but hesitant, over the phone. In the first interview she comes across as both self-conscious and inhibited, often looking at the ceiling. A relationship has recently been broken:

> She goes on to say that in every relationship, particularly romantic ones, she immediately notices the negative aspects. So, she saw that the young man involved had more defects than good qualities and that maybe he had even more hidden defects. In the end, it took her quite some time before she could see the positive aspects, her partner's good qualities – but, in both cases, it was by then too late, the relationship was over.

The analyst noticed this unconscious transference warning, but described it in a rather distant way referring to himself in the third person:

> While the psychoanalyst wondered internally about this strange way of entering a relationship, she became silent and surreptitiously changed the subject, describing how she came to contact me.

In the following text the analyst shifts back and forth between the first person and the third person when he refers to himself.

Later in the session Ms. G. talks about her choice of profession, she explains that she did not pursue the career for which she felt most gifted, that would have been too easy, she wanted to prove to herself she could do the other subject too.

> She describes the way in which she studies and does her research, going round in circles, as it were, and coming back to what she has already discovered – I begin to imagine a kind of Penelope figure, unravelling the weaving she has already done. When Ms. G. speaks, I can feel these to-and-fro movements – undoing what has been done.

In the second interview the analyst reported about the beginning:

> I notice that as she talks, she sits well back in her chair and looks up at the ceiling – she gives me the curious impression of a baby in a cradle, staring at the ceiling. I think that she really must have analysis, lying on the couch. But at the same time I wonder whether I should refer her to a colleague who is just starting out but whose work I appreciate and whose fees are very low since she is just beginning her career as an analyst.

These somewhat incompatible ideas ('she really must have analysis' and 'I should refer her to a colleague') were registered and reflected upon by the

(continued)

(continued)

analyst, which resulted in a deeper understanding of what Ms. G. was enacting in the relationship: an invitation followed by a rejection. His thoughts after the session were described as follows:

> This second session made me think more in terms of psychoanalysis, even though we did not talk about that. Ms. G. had a more structured narrative and it was actually addressed to someone this time. It was evident that she was trying to remember what she could. At that point, I thought about my initial idea of referring her to a colleague – realising then that perhaps Ms. G.'s problem has to do with the rejection she provoked in her family when she was a little girl.

The last remark shows why the analyst in the session did not take concrete steps to plan analysis and instead thought about referring her to somebody else; only retrospectively could he understand the way she provoked rejection.

In the details of the interview it is possible to see how Ms. G. helps the analyst to recover, especially at those moments when he seems to be stuck and resigned. Ms. G. responds very sensitively to the whole process and seems to be unconsciously aware of when the analyst is close to quitting; she then shows him a bit more of her wishes in order to bring him back on track. And she silently, but also accurately, uses these movements in the contact to make him aware of her inner dynamics of seduction and abandonment.

Only in the third interview does the situation seem to change:

> At the beginning of this session, there is a very long silence. Ms. G. wonders if she should say something! She has read the book on self-esteem that she had told me about before. What is written in it means something to her, and she wonders if the behaviourist approach outlined in the book might be more appropriate for her. I quite deliberately dodge the issue and ask her if she has any dreams she could tell me about. She thinks for a moment, then tells me of a dream she had three or four weeks ago: she is in a bar, waiting for the boyfriend she had then, the one she broke up with recently, which was a more or less secret affair that she didn't want to tell anybody about. In the dream, he doesn't turn up. She then orders a Spanish beer that goes by the name of 'Vilanos'. She doesn't drink it, but looks over the top of her newspaper. (Here the analyst makes the comment to the Workshop: 'no, I still don't take notes during sessions!') I encourage her to associate to her dream and, taking into account the elements I have already mentioned, say that she is desperately afraid of being abandoned

and left alone. She agrees, adding that her relationships always end up like that, in abject failure.

I tell her that what she is really waiting for is, in my vocabulary, called psychoanalysis. She looks straight at me – her eyes no longer looking up towards the ceiling – and says that she had already thought about that and had talked a bit to her sister about it.

At the moment when the analyst 'quite deliberately dodges the issue' he doesn't join in with her defences against the idea of psychoanalysis; he refuses to accept her abandoning him by her talk of behavioural therapy and asks her about a dream. She can pick up this question and use it to symbolize the whole situation of the session by remembering a dream. He did not join in being one of the 'Vilanos' and then she also could refrain from it: 'she didn't drink it' but 'looks over the top of her newspaper'. When the analyst says, addressing the Workshop group: 'No, I still don't take notes during sessions!' he acknowledges that within the session 'news' is produced between patient and analyst by their talking and thinking about the abandonment and the 'abject failure' which seem to make relationships so dangerous and often impossible for her.

Often such 'news' can only be produced after the unconscious dynamics of wishes and the defences against them have been enacted in the session, by the patient as well as by the analyst. In the above case it is only after an enactment that it becomes possible to address Ms. G.'s wish for psychoanalysis, though she had known of it for quite some time. Indeed, it was this wish that originally brought her to the first interview. She had to defend herself against this wish until she came to the point where she could readily admit it. Following this, Ms. G. again started building up defences that had to be dealt with in the following interviews, until she finally came to her decision to enter analysis.

This preliminary interview process is an example of a creative couple, formed by an analyst taking on an observational stance and a patient welcoming new experiences in order to find out more about herself. There is a clear development through the process, where the observational stance shifts from having a defensive quality vis-á-vis Ms. G.'s seductive–dismissive pressure, as the analyst's initial way to cope with the unconscious 'storm', to his realization of a mutual enactment of Ms. G.'s conflict of seducing and provoking rejection which places him in a real third position. At that point an analytic way of exploring is brought in, namely by asking Ms. G. whether she had any dreams. This makes a fruitful, albeit abrupt, rupture in Ms. G.'s defences, paving the way for the recollection of a dream and for receiving interpretations that move the dialogue to a different level.

In this, as well as in the case of Mr. F. above, the analyst came to realize the central aspects of the patient's specific dynamics through a process of mutual enactment that became increasingly clear to the analyst. Tuckett (1997, 2011) sees this mutual enactment of the analytic pair as something that is always going on, and suggests that a central analytic task is to realize and use this.

There are cases where the analyst did not succeed during the initial interview in creating a more constructive, one might say momentarily 'oedipal' co-operation, nor was the analyst aware of the mutual enactment, and was instead drawn into a more static narcissistic collusive interaction. One might suppose that this would make an impact on whether or not analysis could be initiated, but it turned out that identifying an oedipal or a narcissistic form of interaction could not be used as a predictor for the outcome of the interview.

The Elegant Woman

In the following case, psychoanalyst and patient formed what could be described as a narcissistic pair with a disturbing pull towards symbiosis; here joint defences, a strong mutual identification, and idealization were aspects of the contact which weren't addressed or 'solved'. It was a dialogue shaped by the overwhelming material of Mrs. H., its impact on the analyst, and the analyst's personal style facing a more disturbed contact. In spite of the raw, concrete quality of the first meetings, a psychoanalytic psychotherapy was started which later was transformed into four sessions per week psychoanalysis.

Mrs. H.'s urgency was already sensed by the analyst in the first phone call; she sounded stressed and was disappointed by the waiting time. The analyst wondered about Mrs. H.'s way of relating and commented in the workshop:

> She brings immediately something in about us . . . we are both familiar with Sara! (the referring analyst) . . . maybe there is a misunderstanding, I am not familiar with Sara . . . that was what I noticed . . . she thought we were friends in a way.

Mrs. H. likes the analyst's explanation that they first have to do some 'research together', which might anticipate mutual idealization and a push towards a symmetrical relationship.

The notes from the first interview begin as follows:

> Mrs. H. is tall, (taller than I am). She comes in examining me. I am immediately impressed by her elegant body attitude, her big grey eyes, and her being dressed in black (I feel small and girlish next to her). I discover her accent is from the south, where one consistently says 'our mum', 'our dad', 'our brother', 'our sister' instead of mum, dad etc.

The analyst felt both small and girlish, and becomes dismissive about the language the patient used. This description is marked by admiration and devaluation and gives a glimpse of the onset of a narcissistic atmosphere.

Mrs. H. is a woman in her early forties, who, together with her sisters, only recently started to say out loud that their mother has a psychiatric disorder. This realization, coinciding with their father's death, 'threw a bomb' into the family. Mrs. H. describes a chaotic life with this mother who could not listen, could not take anything in, and who attributed telepathic abilities to the patient. The analyst's first intervention is: 'Was there a psychiatrist . . . involved?', a question that conveys the disturbing, chaotic feeling Mrs. H. transmits and maybe a hope for some help.

The analyst's own remark in the Workshop to this intervention was that Mrs. H.'s material was overwhelming, but that she 'should also be welcome with all that'. The analyst seemed to have to go along with Mrs. H.'s material and defences, and she stayed with the patient's focus on the concrete details of her life. The analyst thus asks a lot of clarifying questions while Mrs. H. goes on to describe the very ill, psychotic mother who had turned her life into hell. The power of the material seems to leave no space for patient and analyst to get to the possibility of thinking about and observing what is going on within the session, both inside Mrs. H. and between them. The analyst describes in the Workshop that, 'I liked to go as close to her language as possible . . . and I felt her fear . . . how it is when somebody says, my mother is a schizophrenic'. A group member suggests, 'like telepathy?' This the analyst confirms.

During the sessions she has a vague sense of identification and pressure towards collusion, as in one session where Mrs. H. mentioned 'the others' in a way that made the analyst think:

> I notice strong images of the big Catholic families like we have in the south, and I notice a modus of an immediate understanding, like I should take that for granted, should know, understand that.

This is followed by a clarifying question: 'Can you tell me who 'the others' are?' – a question that seems to counteract the push towards a symbiotic, a priori understanding.

The feeling of an overload of concrete and confusing information and a 'storm' of anxiety difficult to contain was present during the whole process; a feeling of disturbance and chaos that was experienced both in the Workshop and in the WPIP Team meeting. In both groups there was some irritation, and the experience that the analyst was swept into a 'research together' and was doing too much.

After Mrs. H. left the first session, the analyst reports the impression that she likes Mrs. H., 'as if she knew her from a long time ago', but also that she 'felt dizzy and kind of puzzled'. She warns herself about Mrs. H.'s way of talking about her psychotic mother, with whom she seems to feel completely entangled and even mixed up with.

Throughout the whole process of the interviews there was no change in these dynamics; Mrs. H. sticks to her 'realistic' description of her demanding and overwhelming situation, and the analyst does not try to change the form or level of communication. She is thinking whether Mrs. H. is strong enough to go into this, and feels reassured by her impression that Mrs. H. is a survivor. The analyst sees Mrs. H. as 'a super-kid', an idealization she later becomes aware of in the Workshop. During the interviews the analyst had the hope for an analysis, not to begin at once, but something they could move towards. The analyst suggests this and Mrs. H. accepts, but insists on starting with one session a week, which seems to be comfortable for both of them and helps them to 'survive'. It was reported that after more than a year the patient entered into an analysis of four sessions a week. In the analyst's description of the later analytic process she underlines the continuing necessity to create a membrane between herself and Mrs. H., a reflection of the difficulties in creating space between them.

The encounter has a 'realistic' and 'matter of fact' quality, introduced by Mrs. H. but also taken on by the analyst. There seemed to be no 'transference offer' and no possibility for the analyst to try to create it. Then a pair is formed that can be described as a benign form of a narcissistic/symbiotic couple, where the analyst senses the lack of space between them. The optimism leading to an initiation of analysis is supported by a mutual admiration; the analyst's impression of an elegant lady and a super-kid, and by Mrs. H.'s experience of a close, friendly and to some extent equal relationship. They seem to share the idea that analysis was what could help Mrs. H., a fantasy of psychoanalysis as an idealized narcissistic object, as a huge strong container that can contain all breakdowns. In the WPIP discussion this was seen as a way to ward off a breakdown of Mrs. H. and a breakdown of the present situation. As if in this interview the thought of transference has to be avoided by both as a disturbing 'third' which must be excluded. The analyst had the idea of a step-by-step development towards analysis. The observational stance, an attempt to triangulate the dialogue, was felt as a threat that could cause chaos and therefore had to be postponed to a future psychoanalytic process. This can be compared to what Britton describes from one of his analyses:

> As a consequence it seemed impossible to disentangle myself sufficiently from the to-and-fro of the interaction to know what was going on. In the early years of her analysis I found that any move of mine towards what by

another person would have been called objectivity could not be tolerated. We were to move along a single line and meet at a single point. There was to be no lateral movement. A sense of space could be achieved only by increasing the distance between us, a process she found hard to bear unless she initiated it.

(Britton 1989, p. 87)

The dynamics of the interviews above were experienced directly in the group discussions; the material created bewilderment, a sense of frustration leading to criticism, questioning the analyst's technique and decisions. While the Workshop and WPIP Team sometimes tended to react enviously or with jealousy towards a creative couple where triangulation becomes possible, especially in the beginning of a case discussion, different forms of narcissistic pairs are always at risk of being attacked and devalued and seen as a result of poor technique.

Obviously there are the defences of both patient and analyst that pass into the inter-psychic dynamics of a first interview that leads to full analysis, but which at the same time contradict the classic technical ideals of observing and addressing the defensive dynamics in order to make the project of psychoanalysis possible. The analyst in the example above had a feeling of being too close, but this only emerges after her own idealization of the patient's capacity to survive and of the strength of psychoanalysis. She did not embark on any attempts to show a more specific analytic way of thinking and talking during the interviews – still she recommended analysis, and the co-work resulted in four times a week analysis. The analyst must have had a secure confidence in her own capacity to be in this process. She was overwhelmed by, but not too scared of, the disturbing material, and she possessed and communicated sufficient hope of development for the patient to accept the offer. One can easily imagine another analyst who would not, for different reasons, recommend analysis here. The analyst in this case believed in psychoanalysis as the most suitable treatment; for her psychoanalysis seemed to be a secure inner object (Caper 1997). Rothstein argues that this must be a precondition in order to be able to recommend psychoanalysis (Rothstein 1998a). And yet a psychoanalytic dialogue, in a more narrow sense, was not initiated during the consultations.

Regarding the instability in the interaction and its collusive quality for longer or shorter periods in analytic work, the situation within first interviews is especially complex because it not only relates to the patient's pathology and analyst's competence in functioning analytically, nor his trust in becoming able to do that vis-à-vis the specific patient, but also to a characteristic in the frame of the first interview, namely its place at the border between analysis and more concrete undertakings, between the internal and external (Racalbuto 2012, Møller 2014).

The Promising Patient

The next vignette has parallels to the case above because of what could be seen as an initial mutual idealization. Here it is not in a chaotic form, on the contrary, it is a seemingly calm and a very structured meeting. The agreement to start analysis is made on the basis of a kind of positive collusion where the more vital but maybe also more threatening issues are not, and probably cannot at the time of the interview, be addressed. This phenomenon, whereby more disturbing material was not addressed, was found to be much more common in first interviews than expected.

The analyst had a vacancy and was looking for an analytic patient; Ms. I. wanted analysis and had been recommended by a colleague to contact this analyst.

Ms. I. had sent a letter to the analyst before they met where she, in a short, focused and structured way, expressed her wish for analysis. The analyst was content with this and already from this point was interested in taking this patient into analysis.

The consultation could be characterized more in the direction of a fairly competent structural diagnostic interview than an analytic dialogue. The overall impression was that more dangerous parts and primitive anxieties were not being touched upon.

Ms. I. left her home town to find a job in the capital. In the letter she says: 'it is only now when I am away from my family . . . that I started to feel unwell, a lack of safety . . . a bad conscience and feelings of hopelessness'.

In the first interview she describes her difficult childhood with an unhappy mother, who functioned as a child, and a father who was drinking. She had been 'more like a mummy' to her mother. The analyst mentions analysis in this first interview and the possibility of being listened to; the patient reacts in an explicitly positive way, maybe a well-behaved sort of manner, to this prospect. She relates her need of someone who may listen to the lack of anybody who could listen to her throughout her childhood; the parents were preoccupied with their own conflicts, and she mentions a situation where she had to take a pair of scissors from her mother who was threatening the father.

In the second interview the analyst asks for any thoughts or dreams that may have occurred after their first meeting. Ms. I. says she is afraid of what is felt to have been revived, but reassures herself that 'it does come up all the same'. She has been anxious after the first meeting, has had 'good memories from her childhood', which gave her a terrible anxiety and made her rush to do the cleaning. She reports a dream where a friend's sister had died; in the dream he walked in front of her, searching and crying. The next thing that is reported is that Ms. I. says that she lets nobody come close to her, lets nobody touch her. She had also mentioned her utter loneliness in her room as a child, with the parents outside shouting at each other.

The analyst is ready to decide about psychoanalysis towards the end of the second interview, and suggests this. Recognizing Ms. I.'s rising anxiety as expressed in the description of scary thoughts welling up inside her, the analyst recommends a third meeting. Also in the third consultation a disturbing anxiety is present about what will surface in analysis. The analyst relates this partly to Ms. I.'s recent contact with her parents and partly to the prospect of analysis that stirs up unconscious anxieties.

During the interviews it became apparent at a manifest level that Ms. I. wanted a more coherent mother than her real one had been, and that the analyst, who wanted a patient at that time, felt moved to take care of her. The analyst structured the situation and Ms. I. complied with this structure.

On a deeper level, the core problem of Ms. I. – being a child that parented the parent – is discretely re-enacted, but not conceptualized. Although Ms. I. spoke about disturbing experiences and thoughts, the atmosphere that came across was calm; Ms. I. went along with the analyst's way of structuring the sessions. The match could seem *too* good, with untouched mutual idealization, while the conclusion about analysis could look like a rationalization, as the analyst does not mention or think about the risk of being overwhelmed by anxiety and aggression that cannot be contained. The analyst reported in the Workshop, that she had actually realized this later in the analysis. Ms. I. had by then been in analysis for eight months, and had not been such an easy-going analysand as the analyst had expected. But it had been possible gradually for both analyst and Ms. I. to work also with the more disturbed aspects of Ms. I.'s internal objects.

The fact that the analyst does not respond to Ms. I.'s fear of what the analysis will bring to the surface, a fear first expressed in the dream and then again in the beginning and end of the second meeting, seems to be part of her technique; she acknowledges that Ms. I. becomes anxious, she offers a third session because of the anxiety that wells up after the first offer of analysis, but within that situation she takes it primarily as a confirmation that the prospect of analysis makes ideas surface in Ms. I. Her attitude is confident; she does not seem warned or deterred, for example, by the patient's comment 'that nobody is allowed near her'.

In the Workshop discussions the analyst admits that she had decided to take Ms. I. on already, on the basis of the letter, and she became convinced in the interviews that Ms. I. was a 'parentified' child, who needed analysis. In a way, the analyst avoids going deeper into Ms. I.'s material because they will have more time later. The group commented on the structured way the analyst works and Ms. I.'s accommodation towards this: 'she accommodates to everybody'. The analyst needed the patient, Ms. I. needed analysis, but the collusive quality of the meeting of these matching needs was not considered.

In other words, it had been possible to get a working analytic process started without either protagonist being explicitly aware that core dynamics were repeated in the first interview. There was a mutual enactment here of the patient's primal difficulty; being a premature, well-behaved child that responded to the mother's needs.

Looking at all the cases that have been analyzed, an unacknowledged re-enactment of the central dynamics of the patient seems to be the case more often than expected. In the above case the analyst's positive motivation for taking on a patient, and the fact that her confidence in recommending analysis was not destroyed in the meeting with this specific patient, meant that her defences kept uncontainable anxiety and chaos at bay. Ultimately this meant that psychoanalysis was given a chance and, with the hindsight of the on-going analysis, this proved to be a good decision. It is debatable whether the analyst should have gone into the more disturbing material in the first interviews, or whether it was fine that she was there in the role of a structuring, understanding mother; there are also different attitudes to technique at stake here. However, this came across as a conscious choice from the side of the analyst; while the analyst seems to have been aware of some transferential phenomena she was not, at the moment of the interview, open to more primitive material.

The Man in the Middle

This is a case where the consultation ends with a recommendation not for analysis but for psychotherapy.

Mr. J. is a self-made man in his forties. His request is that the analyst take him on, which she in principle is able to do. The institutional and cultural context is immediately pushed to the forefront, both in Mr. J.'s request for analytic training in the first phone call and in the beginning of the analyst's presentation to the Workshop. He had been referred to her by a prominent member of another Psychoanalytic Society. The analyst struggles to promote IPA standards in a difficult 'anything goes' environment, at the cost of considerable conflicts inside and outside the group. Mr. J. no doubt knows who she is and what Society she adheres to. And yet he announces himself unabashedly as belonging to a 'wild' group, where he is already in training, without any real background qualifications. He comes because of difficulties with his wife, but he also wants analysis because he is planning to become an analyst himself.

Although during three initial interviews Mr. J. for the most part presents himself as though he has no real problems, it becomes evident for the analyst that he has a very fragile identity, living in chaotic sadomasochistic relationships, with powerful conscious and unconscious envious reactions. And he actually formulates rather disparaging remarks about analysis and analysts, causing the analyst to feel attacked. The impression is that perverse stories of sadomasochistic excitement, boundary violations and denial of psychic reality (the reality of psychic suffering, the need for proper training and growth, etc.) serve as a defence against terrifying issues, such as destructive rage, envy and greed, and/or abandonment by a narcissistic mother figure. The analyst, as well as the Workshop group and the WPIP, express doubt whether he will be able to give up his defences against this. He comes as if he has no need for analysis, and the analyst is recruited as a narcissistically invested object: to be offered help will be experienced as a humiliation.

The interviewing analyst's dilemma was, on the one hand, that she saw this man needed help and this was perhaps his only way to ask for it. On the other hand, she was aware that at moments she felt overwhelmed and blocked by her anger as well as by paranoid feelings about his cunning way of functioning, which made her seriously doubt her ability to help him. The institutional context of the request for analysis intensified this already very difficult situation. If she said yes to his request for analysis this would in a way be collusion with his omnipotent defence, and if she said no she would neglect his wish for treatment and his possibility for development. The consultation process could be described as Mr. J. and the analyst both looking for an appropriate frame within which to deal with Mr. J.'s desperate helplessness, despite the temptation to believe in omnipotence. This temptation is both internal in Mr. J., and external in the environment. Mr. J. is living in a corrupt world where a father is missing; he is looking for an omnipotent mother who can make him a 'man'.

The analyst is seen as maintaining an analytic position despite very difficult transference countertransference dynamics – created both by the patient's sadomasochistic omnipotent attacks and by the analyst's role in their mutual overlapping environment. The impression is that there is some movement towards revealing more of his vulnerability, his need and pain during the three interviews. However, the objects he turns to in his need between sessions are magical figures, such as God and fortune-tellers. The analyst offers once-weekly psychotherapy, at the same time leaving open the possibility for a slow development towards psychoanalysis.

This decision was based both on Mr. J.'s pathology and on the way his pathology interacted with the analyst's professional identity, closely related to her role in the institutional context in which she worked. Her analytic function was threatened in a way that made it difficult to separate his pathology from the professional conflicts that troubled her on a personal level, and this was instrumental in her doubt whether she could contain and work with his pathology in analysis. The severity of Mr. J.'s pathology gave rise to speculations about whether psychoanalysis could work for him, and in itself this could be used as a reason for starting with less intense therapy in order to see what Mr. J. could engage in and endure. The way this patient got the analyst engaged was of course a reflection of the severity of his narcissistic, sadomasochistic pathology. Her countertransference reactions could be used as a prediction of what would be difficult in an eventual analysis with him, but also as a sign that analysis should not be offered here. This was how the analyst thought about her reactions, and on one level also what led to her decision to offer psychotherapy. But what this case also shows is that, on the more subjective personal level, her decision was based on her feeling of not having a sufficiently secure psychoanalytic base, both in terms of experience and in terms of institutional foundation to start right away with psychoanalysis. Both the analyst and later the WPIP Team felt that her offer was the only feasible response in that situation. One could say that in a case like this there is not only a fragile patient but also fragility in the analyst's internal and institutional frames that contributes to the decision against an immediate engagement in analysis. There was an analyst present in the interviews, in the sense that she stood up against 'the storm' in the form of tough confrontations and Mr. J.'s direct attacks. She registered that she felt offended, helpless, angry, and yet she recovered. Though thinking about the interaction and finding ways of understanding and interpreting some of Mr. J.'s central difficulties proved to be a struggle, in shorter passages an analytic dialogue nonetheless seemed within range. This could be seen from a distance, when the case was discussed, but during the interviews the analyst did not feel secure enough to trust her analytic function with this patient. Had the analyst's internal analytic frame been more secure, or in another institutional context, analysis might have been recommended.

The Man with a Grievance

In many of the case discussions both in the Workshops and in the subsequent WPIP work there has been considerable disagreement between analysts about what would be the right recommendation in a given case. In the next case insecurity and doubt about what to recommend was outstanding during the whole process. It started during the interviews in a reduced fee clinic, where the consulting analyst's idea about whether Mr. K. could develop in an analytic process shifted from negative to more positive. The doubt continued throughout the steps in the discussion of the case, with disagreement in the Workshop and in the WPIP about how to understand the dynamics of the interview, and connected to this, whether psychoanalysis would work for Mr. K. There is however through all the steps of 'case analysis' a prevailing doubt whether Mr. K. will be able to develop in psychoanalysis, alongside a worry about his eventual passivity, his grievance and his wish to get something, to get compensation.

The information form sent in before the consultation stated that Mr. K. was in his mid-fifties, divorced with two grown-up children. His current relationship was breaking up. He described his problems as acute anxiety, bodily tension that disturbed his sleep, heavy drinking, suicidal thoughts when life felt too demanding; he characterized himself as one for whom it was a battle to continue with life. Positive satisfactions were listening to classical music, his children, carpentry work when he could muster the energy, and his work as a technology teacher.

The interview also started with a detailed description of a hopeless situation; Mr. K. had difficulties finding any point in life, but at the same time did not have thoughts about actually killing himself. It seemed difficult for him to formulate his problems, difficult to put words together. The analyst made a transference interpretation of the setting, suggesting he felt hopeless about the meeting and the prospect of getting things across. Mr. K. agreed, looking relieved, but added that he seemed to have a destructive effect on relationships. He went on to say that he had already felt depressed in the waiting room, which he had found shabby; he had wondered what kind of place he had come to. Again, the analyst made an interpretation relating to the interview situation, and suggested that Mr. K. had already met a familiar figure, old-fashioned, shabby, a figure from whom he did not expect much. This brought out more information about primary relationships, but the analyst was struck by the 'pat' tone ('pat' was the presenting analyst's expression, meaning 'glib', 'hollow'). The question of authenticity hovered over the whole interview, although the analyst subsequently found that this 'pat' quality diminished. The analyst seemed to make contact on a deeper level by catching Mr. K.'s negative expectation. An initial negative expectation in the analyst changed to a more positive one – evidenced in the fact that he actually referred Mr. K. to analysis – but the doubt about authenticity in the contact and whether hope was possible remained present all along. The referral might also have been partly motivated by a wish to find a male analysand; the consultant gave Mr. K. the benefit of doubt by referring to reduced fee analysis.

In the Workshop there was a general agreement that the analyst captured the immediate negative transference in an interpretation, which relieved Mr. K. and deepened the contact. The discussion started with a focus on signs that seemed to indicate that Mr. K. could profit from analysis: capacity for creative work, art, for projection and for repeating his main conflicts in the interview. He responds to interventions, he brings a dream, expresses a wish to be understood and is emotionally moved during the interview, and he has a good relationship with his children. As the discussion moved along, more comments on Mr. K.'s passivity, grievance, masochism and negativity were expressed. Attention was also drawn to the prediction that could be seen in the end of a dream, where Mr. K. was stuck in a boggy, marshy part of a field.

In the WPIP discussion Mr. K. was seen as a poor man fighting for free analysis, and it seemed uncertain whether he had a fantasy about a future or was just looking for compensation. Grievance is in the foreground; can a man looking for compensation be analyzed? The 'pat' quality that characterizes the atmosphere of the whole interview is seen to be the story of this man. This gave a feeling of sadness and hopelessness within the WPIP group. Was it sadness about how Mr. K. could manage his life in the future? Or sadness about the little he got from the future? Did Mr. K. perform a melancholic triumph with a 'no future'? The WPIP remained unsure about how much the unauthentic quality ought to be seen as the enactment of Mr. K.'s pathology in the transference and countertransference, and how much could be attributed to the analyst's assessment function. The fact that Mr. K. is assessed for low fee analysis with a candidate is very present, as is the need for male analysands. The analyst was relieved that Mr. K. seemed less disturbed in a psychiatric sense, but this relief might have made him overlook possible inaccessibility for other reasons. The WPIP Team, in an atmosphere of hopelessness (in hindsight a parallel to the patient's despair) skipped its normal procedure of answering the research questions and instead conducted a kind of vote among the WPIP members.

Each of the six present WPIP members described what would be their personal reaction and inclination were they to be confronted with Mr. K., and there were six different statements:

- *Not to offer analysis, because it would be too difficult to confront Mr. K. with his sad story, but instead offer short term psychotherapy to help him set his children free.*
- *Go more into the ambiguity of the motivation and get a better assessment of that.*
- *Not to offer psychoanalysis because of too disturbing negative countertransference feelings, though maybe refer to psychotherapy.*
- *On a rational level, there is a wish to take Mr. K. in analysis because of a belief that the patient could change. However, there is a feeling of ambivalence about actually going for analysis because of a reverie to the material that expresses hopelessness.*
- *The interview is too close to a psychiatric interview to be relied on for assessment for analysis. In analytic assessment one tries to see if there is something alive in the patient; to see whether there is something in him that blocks creativity that can be unblocked.*
- *Would want to take him on because the analyst is moved by Mr. K., but afraid of his own countertransference anger. Would give more time to the considerations.*

The differences mirror central issues in Mr. K.'s pathology. Furthermore, the way the group tried to manage the doubt and hopelessness, by skipping the normal work procedure, also reflects the strong negativity and destructive forces, relating back to the patient's pathology and his way of relating.

The patient actually started in analysis. The analyst who had taken on Mr. K. attended the Workshop, and at the time of the Workshop the analysis was in its fifth year. The analysis was described as very difficult, and the analyst could confirm the central issue of doubt, as it still seemed an open question whether Mr. K. could profit from analysis or not. In the evaluation process that followed the interviews there had also been some disagreement over what to recommend between the referrer and the clinic, whose task it was to eventually proceed with the referral.

At the time that this case was analyzed it was still 'early days' for the WPIP Team, and the Team had not quite left its initial assumption that the 'right' evaluation technique could be found to identify the 'analyzable' patient (Møller 2014). That meant that a critical and competitive atmosphere relating to the way we viewed interview processes could still sometimes intervene – this may explain why we became preoccupied with the extent to which the interviewing analyst's technique hindered some important dynamics from developing. We were still discovering to what degree every interview is formed by the enactment of the patient's core conflicts. Our own behaviour in working with this material shows that the WPIP Team also enacted these dynamics (Reith 2015).

But the six different reactions to the case material in the WPIP group also show the extent to which the decision to take or not to take a person into analysis is taken on an individual, personal and subjective level, closely connected to the analyst's experience of how it would feel to work with that patient (Dantlgraber 1982).

The specific difficulty in achieving a stable picture of Mr. K., and the kind of pathology that was at stake, demonstrates more clearly than with a less disturbed patient to what degree analytic recommendation is subjective. It is related both to the individual analyst, what he or she can work with, and to the psychoanalytic subculture the analyst belongs to. The last aspect seems especially to facilitate the competition about who gets it 'right'.

In the case of Mr. A. discussed in detail in Chapter 2, *The Handsome Man on Crutches*, the analyst felt shaken by the material in a way that created doubt over whether analysis was the treatment of choice. The form the doubt took was worry about whether the patient was too fragile for psychoanalysis. In that case it is evident that, on account of the special pressure the patient put on the analyst during the interviews, she hesitated to offer analysis and had thought about psychotherapy. If the sociocultural context had been a bit different, in the sense that it was more uncommon and rare to offer analysis, and if the analyst had been just a bit more insecure, with a less secure internal analytic frame (Parsons 2014), the result might well have been psychotherapy. It could even be argued that psychotherapy may have been a more prudent, but possibly less effective choice, in a different situation, where the analyst felt a higher degree of insecurity about her capacity to undertake a full analysis with this patient. There was in this case an analyst available in a concrete sense, and a working analyst present in a more symbolic sense, which contributed to the outcome that analysis was initiated.

All beginnings – but different

The above cases show how diverse beginnings are when it comes to central qualities in how patient and analyst work together.

One of our basic a priori hypotheses about what characterizes an analytic dialogue is that the analyst is able to switch the level of communication in order to deepen the contact, to reach the patient on deeper emotional levels and at the same time to show the patient something of what the undertaking of analysis will be like. One of the most outstanding findings in the case material is that the analyst must also be able to face an emotional 'storm', a recreation of the patient's central unconscious dynamics, as immediately created in the first meeting.

> These analytic capacities can be seen as three interlinked functions: a third position is needed to be able to deal with the emotional storm and this seems intrinsic as to whether the analyst may evoke a shifting of the level. To let this happen, it is of course vital not to close the intense dynamics of the first meeting. The so-called emotional storm will always evoke a resistance. This resistance in the patient is understandable and necessary. It is a kind of nodal point around which a process will develop. However, the emotional storm evokes a resistance in the analyst as well. The way the analyst deals with his own resistance is crucial and determines whether and how a psychoanalytic process will happen.
>
> (Vermote, paper read at WPIP panel, EPF Conference, Paris, 2012)

The capacity of the analyst's 'internal frame', to withstand the special type of 'storm' that arises with a given patient, seems to be one factor determining the ability of the analyst and patient to engage meaningfully with the unconscious dynamics. As demonstrated in the case vignettes above, only sometimes is a deeper level of thinking and communication reached during the consultation, and sometimes the 'storm', although always there, is not consciously experienced and considered by the analyst at the time of the consultation.

One way of describing the differences in the dialogue between analyst and potential analysand is along a line from an open, unstructured invitation to talk towards a more structured interview where the analyst also has the agenda of getting specific information. The cases with Ms. I. (*The Promising Patient*) and Mr. K. (*The Man with a Grievance*) are examples of this. These consultations may have more resemblance to a psychopathology assessment interview than, for example, the consultations with Ms. G. (*The Weaver Unraveled*). This seems primarily related to analytic subcultures and to the individual analyst's personal style, and only to some extent is this a reflection of a tuning in to the needs of the patient. Still, when analysts have commented on their consultation style, there is not always a correspondence between what they think they do and what they do. There is nothing that indicates that the structure of the interview can be directly connected to whether analysis is recommended or not, nor is there any indication that a situation where there will be a referral will decide the level of structure and/or the prospect of an analysis. The more open consultations have naturally more similarities with an analytic session, and must therefore *mutatis mutandis* be seen as a better demonstration to the patient of what analysis will be like.

Another a priori hypothesis was that, when the consultation should end in a referral (*'consultation for referral' settings*) instead of the analyst taking on the patient himself (*'private' settings*), the consultant would be more restrictive with transference interpretations. This idea was not confirmed; in both situations analysts gave transference interpretations, but primarily in relation to the setting.

As mentioned above, differences in the analyst/patient pair, along a line from more narcissistic, collusive encounters to a more Oedipal position of the analyst, could be identified. But these different levels of 'engagement' in first interviews, shaped by what the possible developmental level of interaction was for the two participants, cannot be used to predict whether analysis will be initiated or not; but it can most likely be seen as a prediction of characteristics of an eventual psychoanalytic process.

Whether a consultation results in initiating analysis or not depends, as Stolorow (1990) concludes, on the presence of some correlation between what the patient needs to be understood and what the analyst is capable of understanding:

> While there are doubtless patients who could only be analysed by the most gifted analysts, I believe that in principle, anyone with an intact nervous system can be analysed by someone.
>
> (Stolorow 1990, p. 129)

As mentioned above, the differences in the consultation processes are of course also linked to different psychoanalytic subcultures and related to this are the institutional/social contexts in which analysis can be offered, as well as to the individual patient's pathology (Crick 2014, Gibeault 2012). But we have come to the conclusion that it makes most sense to understand these differences from a specific analytic interactive perspective and to see each outcome of a consultation as a result of how analyst and patient adapt to the situation, including the broader cultural/institutional context, finding their way of coping with the dynamics of the unconscious storm that the patient brings to the encounter.

Each recommendation must be subjective, springing from what analyst and patient can bear. From the analyst's point of view a recommendation is based on the experience of being able, or at least a confidence in becoming able, to endure. In the case of referrals, what counts is a colleague's capacity to work psychoanalytically with the specific patient. This ability is linked to personal issues, experience and competence.

The analyst must be prepared to be drawn into a repetition and re-enactment of the patient's central problems from the very beginning. In 1971 Winnicott described the first meeting as a special moment, condensed with pure transference, owing to the fact that what the patient brought was still uncontaminated by the analyst. Our findings add to this realization that the analyst is sometimes not ready or able to take in and conceptualize the patient's projections from the start, because of the violence and rawness of the material. This is not what determines whether analysis will get started or not. That is dependent on whether there is an analyst present with confidence in his or her inner analytic frame to start such a process.

8 INITIATING PSYCHOANALYSIS IN INSTITUTIONAL SETTINGS

Introduction

There are three main routes into psychoanalysis: the first two may take place in private practice, where a person may identify an analyst from a professional register or by reputation and contact them directly, and then either go on to start an analysis or, after consultation, to be referred on to an appropriate practitioner. Bolognini (2006) describes this in terms of the consultant acting as a 'Ferryman'. The third route is through a psychoanalytic service or Clinic where the individual may self-refer or may have been referred by another professional, family doctor or psychiatrist.

A clinical service may be part of state provision, for example as a specialist part of mental health services, or may be attached to a psychoanalytic Society. Famously, after Freud in 1918 rallied IPA psychoanalytic societies to establish 'Free Clinics' (Freud 1919a, 1923b; Danto 2005), such institutions were set up in the early twentieth century by several Societies in cities across Europe. Nowadays, different countries have differing provisions through state insurance for funding or part funding of psychoanalysis, ranging from the relatively supportive to the non-existent. While not usually completely 'free', the clinics often attached to Psychoanalytic Societies now tend to offer psychoanalysis at a reduced rate and often the analyses are provided by candidates in training to enable them to fulfil their training requirements (see Box 8.1).

Box 8.1 Some psychoanalytic Clinics

Some of the Clinics attached to Psychoanalytical Societies include:

- Jean Favreau Centre for Psychoanalytic Consultations and Treatments, Paris, attached to the Paris Psychoanalytic Society www.spp.asso.fr (Bouhsira 2013);

(continued)

(continued)

- Jean and Evelyne Kestemberg Centre, Paris. Closely related to the Paris Psychoanalytic Society. www.asm13.org/Le-centre-de-psychanalyse-et-de-psychotherapie-Evelyne-et-Jean-Kestemberg;
- Vienna Ambulatorium, attached to the Vienna Psychoanalytical Society, www.wpv.at/ambulatorium (Diercks 2002);
- London Clinic of Psychoanalysis, attached to the British Psychoanalytical Society, www.psychoanalysis.org.uk. (Crick 2014, Pérez, Crick and Lawrence 2015);
- Winn Clinic, Sydney Australia, Sydney Institute for Psychoanalysis and Australian Psychoanalytical Society www.thewinnclinic.net.

There are many other organizations in numerous countries through which it is possible to have reduced fee or subsidized psychoanalysis; these are just a few examples.

The first meeting between an analyst and a potential analysand that develops into an analysis is inevitably going to be different in many respects to a first meeting arranged with a referral-on already in the mind of both. The latter sort of meeting is generally described as a 'psychoanalytic consultation', and is often carried out in an institutional context.

In 9 of the 28 cases studied by the WPIP, prospective patients were seen as part of an institutional service where both analyst and patient were aware beforehand that the meeting would result in an appropriate referral on for further treatment. In this chapter, we will use some case material from the WPIP to explore specific features of these institutional first interviews. Although the primacy given in *all* psychoanalytic consultations to the importance of unconscious communication and motivation makes different kinds of 'first meeting' not very distinct from a psychoanalytic point of view in terms of fundamental dynamics, studying both private and institutionally based consultations highlighted for us important themes about the process of 'initiating psychoanalysis' in *any* setting.

Why come to a Clinic rather than contact an analyst directly?

At a quite simple and conscious level, some may wish to see someone at a Clinic for a 'third party' consultation in order to have the opportunity to explore for themselves the possibility of psychoanalytic treatment without feeling under the sort of pressure to commit that may be experienced in seeing an individual in private practice. The 'institutional setting' may also be more attractive for less conscious reasons.

A defensive need for distance regulation? Or a communicative need for a reliable container?

In some of our cases it appears that the patient decides to go through the intermediary of a Clinic because of an anxiety about making a direct link with a psychoanalyst with whom they may then also go into treatment. There is sometimes the need in such cases for some tangible 'distancing' of the object; in others, there appears to be the need for a containing third object, perhaps one with the authority and security which an established organization with a good reputation is perceived to have over what may feel like the more 'uncertain' prospect of seeing an unknown individual. This may be to do with a particular fear of the unknown, that may prove to be of a paranoid type, or it may be a rational choice by a cautious or naïve individual in order to get some expert and impartial advice on how to get help. Or it may be more to do with the person's psychic need to first make contact with a mediating object to contain the anxiety about a more specific and direct contact.

The Hopeful Man

Mr. L. had a history of loss of a reliable and sane parental couple from when he was five years old, with many arguments, and his father's manic-depressive illness, finally leading to his parents separating in his adolescence. When in his mid-twenties, and overwhelmed by feelings he did not understand, could not control and from which he felt estranged, and not having a clear sense of his identity, he again sought help from the counsellor who had seen him for about two years over the period of his parents' separation. A recommendation from this trusted and reliable figure to the Clinic allowed him to anticipate that the Clinic would be similarly reliable and containing to him in his desperate state, rather than leaving him feeling he had to take his chances by approaching an unknown and unpredictable individual.

A Mysterious Arrival

Ms. M., having had previous experience of a therapist who she felt had tried to manoeuvre her into a treatment she did not want, together with a general sense in her history of not feeling secure in the reliability of anyone who could support her autonomy, seemed to need to find a way of taking control of her search for a helpful object. This was manifested at her initial contact, which was unusual in that she did not telephone or email first, but just came into the Clinic building in person and reported to the receptionist, in

(continued)

(continued)

a familiar way, even though she had never been there before, that she was 'depressed again', as if she had found for herself an institution she could trust and she had decided would already 'know' her and be 'on her side'. In the workshop discussions, a recurrent theme was to do with the question of whether Ms. M. *wants* or *avoids* close one-to-one contact: does she look for someone to help her, or perhaps the Clinic, not identified with any one specific person, is perceived as an 'impersonal' institution, her anxiety about immediate one-to-one contact thus being mitigated? As if the persecutory projection that would be intolerable in a direct one-to-one meeting can feel 'safer' to bring to the broader base of an institution.

Her subsequent arrival for her first interview created a powerful opening scene (see Chapter 6) conveying a sense of uncertainty, mystery and persecution that later resonated through the interview process. The analyst's own words convey this very well:

> When I came to the Clinic, about a quarter of an hour before time, I saw a young woman in front of the entrance, whom I thought might be the patient, but I wasn't sure. She appeared to be a bit insecure, looked at me, but didn't ask anything and didn't indicate she also wanted to get in, so I went in and left her outside. Then she rang on time and with a nod she made it clear she recognized me as the one she looked at in front of the main door. When she sat down she seemed to be rather anxious, insecure, desperate and somehow lost and dreamy.

The patient explained she had been waiting outside for her husband to bring the Clinic's questionnaire, that she had not only not filled out, but had forgotten to bring with her on the day.

In the first of two meetings, Ms. M. came across as anxious, insecure and speaking in a rather desperate way about a variety of situations in which she clearly felt the victim of persecution, struggling with the authorities, tortured and alarmed but also rather dreamy and vague and unaware of what part she may play in these situations. Ms. M. began by recounting stories about intrusion and abuse, first by the previous male psychiatrist she had seen and had felt wanted to push her into treatment, then by her present female boss. In reporting the case, the consultant analyst spoke of feeling she could not quite make sense of Ms. M. and her presentation, and yet that: 'I hesitated to ask more, but I felt it to be inappropriate, undermining, critical', and was bothered by a mixture of fascination and fear of being intrusive throughout the interview. Feeling as if she were drawn into asking more factual or 'psychiatric' sorts of questions, she was nonetheless able to find out more about Ms. M.'s childhood with a mentally ill mother and about a conflicted marriage. At the end of that session the consultant analyst found she had run over time: 'Then I realized the session was over and was surprised it was so late.' This, together with feeling more generally that she could not find a position from which she could address her sense of anxiety and destabilization or to reflect with Ms. M. on the process, led her to ask to consult with the Clinic staff group: 'During the interview, and also afterwards, I had the feeling I was drawn into something, not being able to grasp what was going on, so I decided to present her case to the group.'

The consultant's discussion with her colleagues prior to the second meeting enabled her, eventually, to gain a perspective from which she could see how powerfully Ms. M.'s seduction, as well as her persecutory projections, had affected her. The group had suggested that the patient had 'paranoid tendencies'. In the discussion, the consultant resisted this but then, during the second interview, the patient said:

> Just now, when I came here, I saw two men standing in front of the door and another one in a uniform who seemed to observe them. I thought immediately something strange was going on, something with drugs.

The consultant remembered the Clinic group discussion: 'The whole atmosphere changed into a vague and paranoid one, and only then did the Clinic meeting come into my mind again. I was surprised I had forgotten it completely.' She used her insight to formulate this interpretation: 'So you noticed something strange just in front of the building here, something that could make you suspicious about the whole situation here.' Ms. M. responded with considerable insight, and in accord with the consultant's sense of getting seduced. She said: 'I made also another observation a few days ago about how much I try to entangle other people into my current situation.' She described such situations at work and with her husband. Then she said:

> There is another thing I thought about, that I tend to change the meaning in nearly every situation. First, I can hear a positive comment in a positive way, but then I start thinking about and working on it, until it turns more and more into a critique, ending up with the feeling that it was a devastating comment, and that I missed that meaning in my first impression. Although sometimes I can see I was probably right in my first impression and that it *was* a positive remark, it doesn't help.

This allowed the consultant to say:

> So when you are thinking about starting psychoanalytic therapy or an analysis, and we are talking about it and I will tell you that I think it could be helpful for you to start an analysis and you might agree here, it could be that you will 'work' on it afterwards until you become rather suspicious about it.

Perhaps partly because the consultant analyst in this institutional context had no intention of even considering taking Ms. M. into treatment, with the help of colleagues she was able to find a position where she could stand back, register and metabolize the initial persecutory projections rather than then being at risk of rejecting Ms. M. as 'unsuitable' for analysis, and joining with Ms. M.'s persecutory suspicion. She could also respond to Ms. M.'s need for empathy and help with facing up to what she was able in the second meeting to come to understand about her own role in her difficulties. The triangulated space created by the institutional setting thus allowed the consultant analyst to 'weather the storm' and Ms. M. to subsequently be successfully referred into analysis.

Looking for the Right Place

Ms. N. comes apparently very uncertain of her sexual and personal identity, feeling frustrated by a lack of 'fitting in'. She is a young woman whose parents have recently separated, about which she feels very ambivalent, and she reports that the parents had little time for her and her siblings when they were young, leaving them in the care of a series of nannies. She has done a test on the internet which, she reports, concluded that she fulfils criteria for a diagnosis of a borderline personality disorder. She had made a start with another therapist in private practice but reports that she did not know what sort of therapy it was, and had dropped out deciding instead to come to the Clinic. In describing herself she keeps breaking off to say that she 'doesn't know', and conveys a sense of being unsure of herself, and having a difficulty in staying with anything or with anyone. The consultant notes her countertransference response of some impatience but also a curiosity and interest in trying to get in touch with Ms. N. The patient seems relieved when her consultant tells her that it appears to be very difficult for her to find a place that feels 'right' for her.

Ms. N. seems to be looking for a special place at a fundamentally regressive level, wanting to be welcomed and held, but at the same time terrified of being invaded. She appears to have no secure internal object, and it is as if she has a difficulty in finding 'a home' for herself in which to be and to discover herself. This was enacted by the consultant when, possibly in response to Ms. N.'s initial refusal of a couple of possible appointments that had been offered for the second of two meetings, she then made a mistake about the start time of the finally agreed second appointment, leaving Ms. N. 'homeless' for a short but meaningful period of time. Ms. N.'s decision to come to a Clinic could be understood as her need for a functioning parental couple who can work together to give her a reliable 'home', and she appears to use the triangulation offered by the institutional context as a defence against her fear of being engulfed in a narcissistic relationship. This case seems to be an example of one where institutional containment, both at the stage of consultation and then in the subsequent decision to offer her continuing analytic treatment at the Clinic, ameliorates the potential negative effects often seen in the intensive treatment of borderline patients; for example, in Ms. N.'s case the claustro-agoraphobic conflict in one-to-one private practice treatment may have been just too difficult for her to bear. This very concrete 'triangulation' allows a differentiation to emerge for the patient between what is felt to be a *literal* one-to-one relationship with the analyst, that is, an enacted satisfaction of the wish to be held, and more of a *symbolic* relationship where the patient can speak *about* her wishes (Milner 1952; see Chapter 5, on Psychoanalytic Space).

Interestingly, in the case of Ms. N., the Clinic consultant was, in fact, in a position to offer her psychoanalysis through the Clinic but the patient did not at first want to take this up and asked if she could see someone else, but then later changed her mind on meeting a possible alternative analyst. In her case, the consultation had been one where the patient was very moved by the encounter, and the contact with the consultant analyst had meant much to her – she said that she had not wanted to start working with the consultant as her analyst as she felt the contact had been so good that she feared coming to hate her analyst and so losing this important experience of 'goodness'. Ms. N.'s presenting problems – that very vividly included the fear of proximity and being taken over by the object and had motivated her to seek consultation at a Clinic rather than directly with a psychoanalyst – now played a part in her ambivalence in accepting the offer of long term analysis. It is as if Ms. N. worked through for herself a movement from the 'seduction by the person' where she felt afraid of spoiling something, towards a realization of 'seduction by the process' (see Box 8.2 for an explanation of this distinction) when she reflected on how the process itself may be of value to her, implicitly recognizing that she may well come to hate her analyst but that this would be part of the process rather than something that would destroy it.

Financial considerations: real resources and psychic resources

In some cases, in countries where there is little or no financial support available from the state or medical care authorities for psychoanalytic treatment, but there are psychoanalytic Clinics that can offer treatment at a low fee, it was apparent that the overt reason for the patient coming to a Clinic rather than a private individual analyst was financial; in such cases, this would be just about the only option for entering into analytic treatment. This was in reality true for Mr. L. (*The Hopeful Man*), a young student who, apart from his unconscious need for an institutional setting, had no other way of accessing psychoanalytic treatment unless it were at a low fee.

However, in some cases, the low-fee options may also be used in order to express more complex motivations.

The Man with a Grievance

Mr. K., a man in later middle age working only part-time and with limited financial resources, almost immediately conveyed to the consultant that he found the low-fee Clinic to be shabby and old-fashioned in its communications and appearance, unlikely to have anything decent to offer him, while at the same time almost making himself invisible in the waiting room, requiring the consultant to be active in identifying him. This representation of the institution as a transference object became more evident when the history unfolded in the course of the meeting, indicating Mr. K.'s difficulty in sustaining relationships, with parents who he felt did not connect with him, a school that expelled him, fall outs with friends, and relationships that did not last long. His turning to a superior narcissistic position from which he felt failed all round was all the more vividly confirmed in the account of a dream from a couple of nights before the first appointment: Mr. K. was carrying a rucksack which felt progressively heavier, the weight not changing but him becoming weaker, putting it down when he felt too weak to carry it further. His friend said, 'Come on, you must pick it up, it's not that heavy', and he then realized he had not put the rucksack on properly, there were straps that could be adjusted. He did this (that is, making use of the support of a friend), finding the rucksack was now lighter, and bearable, and he was able to continue on his way. But then he came to some marshy field where he became stuck. The consultant suggested that in the dream there may be some recognition of the patient's clinging to a grievance so that he deprived himself of relationships he knew could actually help him, and so remains stuck. Mr. K. was struck when the consultant linked this to the experience of finding the Clinic to be shabby, out of touch and his being in danger of writing it off as a place that could help him, and said he was aware of the rage and fury in him he knows is destructive to his relationships, and that his wish to get help now was his main reason for seeking analysis. His narcissism made it impossible for him to acknowledge that he has no money and has nowhere else to go.

This points to a general issue identified by colleagues working in low-fee Clinics, where it is evident that there are some who approach the Clinic who could pay a reasonable fee but who elect to go to a service where they do not need to pay or pay much. This seems often to be related to a narcissistic defence where a prospective patient feels an entitlement to being 'repaired' by an external agent rather than being able to bear experiencing the sense of a need in themselves for which they are prepared to make a financial and narcissistic investment. As many low-fee clinics are staffed by candidates in training, the issues highlighted in the related dynamics around the negotiation of such fees as are paid, are a very valuable opportunity for candidates to learn about the role of money and its meaning and management in psychoanalysis (e.g. Kestemberg 1985, Gibeault 1986, Krueger 1986, Klebanow et al. 1991, Herron et al. 1992, Berger and Newman 2012, Murdin 2012).

Consultation as assessment?

How do I know if psychoanalysis is right for me?

The aim of a psychoanalytic consultation is to 'consult' the individual seeking help or advice, in a psychoanalytic setting, in order to give the prospective analysand the opportunity to have a sufficient psychoanalytic experience to enable them to see if they can use this way of working (Klauber 1986; Donnet and de M'Uzan 1998; Ehrlich 2004, 2013; Bolognini 2006; Levine 2010; Crick 2014). A 'psychoanalytic setting' includes, of course, the consultant analyst's internal setting, their psychoanalytic stance and use of psychoanalytic technique. This may often include the general policy, as in many clinics, to see the prospective patient over two meetings, as a psychoanalyst will always want to 'hear' and further consider what an analytic intervention has provoked, in him or herself as well as in the analysand.

By this formulation, a psychoanalytic consultation is an 'assessment' but not necessarily as that term is usually used in the field of mental health. It is a chance for the prospective patient to 'assess' whether this way of working is something that makes sense to them and in which they may wish to invest. Equally it is an opportunity for the consultant analyst to use psychoanalytic technique to glean the 'data', make the psychoanalytic observations (of the patient but also of him or herself), on which to base their assessment of whether a person has the capacity to make fruitful use of a psychoanalytic setting. In this way, the two participants are then better equipped to be able to consider and discuss whether or not to proceed to psychoanalytic treatment. Of course, there will also be the need for an analyst to be making an 'assessment' of the patient and their symptoms, history, manner of presentation and mental functioning insofar as elements of these may suggest disturbance possibly requiring psychiatric intervention or support. But over and above this perspective, there is little in the literature to suggest that there are generally identifiable 'patient factors' that can be used to predict whether or not an individual is going to be likely to make good use of psychoanalysis, and so an 'assessment' of such factors is not the sole basis on which a treatment decision or recommendation can be reliably made (Caligor et al. 2009, Crick 2014, Erhlich 2004). What we found in this study, as described in Chapters 5, 6 and 7, is that the actual dynamics in a first interview and its outcome are to do with a very complex psychic interplay between the analytic couple.

Pressures on the consultant in the institutional setting

A Clinic will necessarily have its own purposes, needs, constraints and resources that at one level or another inevitably affect the consultant analyst in his or her work with a patient in this first encounter. In this section, some of the pressures to which consultants and first meetings are subject and how these emerged in some of our cases will be discussed. The primary task of some clinics may be to provide training cases for candidates in a related psychoanalytic training; some may have public sector contracts to fill in order to secure continued funding; others may be sought out as being a centre of excellence for psychoanalytic treatment. Some may have a mixture of all of these 'purposes'.

While it is of course important for any psychoanalyst to have in mind during a first meeting with a new prospective patient an assessment of psychopathology and the possible need for psychiatric intervention or support, this may be more likely in a Clinic or other institutional setting. In a Clinic, the consultant will be aware that they have a responsibility on behalf of the institution and towards colleagues who may be caring for the patient or making important decisions about his treatment in the future, and in this sense they may feel a particular kind of pressure to make an accurate assessment of psychopathology, risk and prognosis. If a case may be seen in the future by a candidate in training then there are more specific pressures to do with feeling the need to predict whether the patient will be a 'good training case', will remain in treatment for long enough to serve the candidate's training needs, will not break down and cause disturbance to an inexperienced and vulnerable colleague, or be unduly 'disturbed' by being seen under these circumstances. It is quite understandable for an analyst to feel anxiety and particular pressures when they have responsibilities to the needs, aims and resources of an institution that are broader than their responsibilities in private practice 'only' to the patient and to their own professional needs.

Correspondingly, while in any consultation there is the possibility that a more formal diagnostic, 'medical model' stance may be taken up by the consultant predominantly as a defence against the impact of the patient's disturbance, consultations in an institutional setting may be particularly prone to this. Bolognini (2006) draws a contrast between a 'concave' stance, which is respectfully receptive to the patient's communications, and a more 'convex' stance where, for whatever reason, the consultant is 'unable to tolerate the inner experiential contact with suffering or with the anxiety communicated' (ibid.) by the patient – fearing perhaps, in the institutional setting, that the resources of the institution cannot tolerate the patient. However, if the routine procedures in the Clinic include opportunities for case discussion with colleagues, this particular pressure on the consultant can be profitably examined. Crick (2013) writes:

> When overwhelmed by the impact of a patient's communication on him, the consultant may defend himself by reverting to 'irritable reaching after facts' in order to have something to hold onto; in the midst of the 'storm', trying to get his bearings perhaps by unhelpfully latching onto some 'judgement' to find certainty
>
> (Crick 2013)

and she goes on to point out the value in an institutional setting of working with a team of colleagues to mitigate this kind of 'judgementalism'.

In the case of Mr. K. (*The Man with a Grievance*), the material presented to the WPIP workshop was in the form of a report written by the consultant for formal purposes intended for the Clinic. It was detailed but more processed and worked through than other, more spontaneous presentations of notes on consultations, and the workshop questioned whether something 'raw' had been obliterated – was this to do with the consultant's defence against being more in touch with the patient's despair? The consultant in this case was very explicit in his account of the approach he takes for consultations with patients who are being assessed for psychoanalysis as a training case for a candidate. For him, consultations are 'rather like a projective test', 'a mixture of a session and information gathering. It is an interpretative encounter; alongside the analytic model of a session there is some information that has to be obtained from this one interview.' Notes or reports that give more of a sense of the 'raw' experience of working with a patient are of value.

Notwithstanding the consultant's clarification of his approach, the WPIP team was suspicious that in this particular case, with these 'processed' process notes, something of significance about the patient's hopelessness and despair was being split off and defended against by the consultant. In the course of the presentation the consultant had said he was relieved to find the patient did not show as severe a psychopathology in the interview as he had expected from the information he had about the case prior to the meeting. The WPIP wondered whether this consultant analyst's competence and interest in assessing the level of psychopathology had become a bit 'convex' – overriding a more subjective, 'concave' response to the patient – and thus overtaking the decision-making. This may have resulted in the hopelessness of the patient's severe problems in relationships not having been taken seriously enough (see also the discussion of this case in Chapter 7, Mr. K, *The Man with a Grievance*). Racabulto (2012) discusses how a 'technical' assessment can be a defence against the anxiety in the meeting and that adopting an 'objective' stance places a border between consultant and analyst, preventing an analytic interaction. Rothstein (1998b) holds similar views. Rather as 'theory' can invade and obstruct the analytic space, as described in Chapter 5, so perhaps does the adoption of a more 'objective' or psychiatric model line of thought in a psychoanalytic consultation.

However, this is by no means an artefact of all Clinic consultations: we found there were also such cases where consultants conveyed very clearly and much more directly in their reports their experience of the process in the consultation, of their encounter with and survival of the 'unconscious storm', sometimes going on to use this in developing their formulation, sometimes just reporting it for the workshop to then process (or not) and discuss. Like Pérez et al. (2015), we found there are great differences in how consultants write up their notes and reports of a first meeting. Sometimes, it is only in retrospect, when working through the notes in the process of writing up or perhaps discussing with a colleague (or in this case, the workshop presentations) that a raw, perhaps even visceral, subjective experience can be seen to have been indicative of a particular feature of a patient's pathology. This sort of triangulation can make it possible to think out of the 'eye of the storm' about something that had been difficult to make sense of, or even to attend to at the time.

We observed in some cases how the pressures to which a Clinic consultation may be subject may include the need to 'find' training cases for candidates, and that this has at least the potential to lead to overlooking elements of the consultation process, or the degree of psychopathology, that may otherwise have been usefully taken up. This may have played a part in the case of Mr. K. above, who did in fact go on to be a candidate's training case, and his pathology indeed proved over several years to be severe and apparently intractable.

The Wary Scientist

In the case of Mr. F. (described in more detail as *The Wary Scientist* in Chapter 7), a young man who was viewed in his chosen field of study as a 'high flyer' to be fast-tracked, we noted he had followed his father in choice of profession. He had a history of being identified as the 'successful child' in the family, and this had left him with a conflict between a sense of being pressured to fulfil the ambitions of others and his own success and ambition. The consultant seemed to be seduced into finding him to be a 'high flyer' in terms of being a potentially 'good training' case, perhaps influenced by the information she had received about him from the Clinic beforehand, and the workshop noted how, perhaps in response to the consultant's correspondingly positive and 'fast tracking' response to him, Mr. F. withdrew to be more defensive and aloof. In this way, the pressures from the Clinic to identify good training cases, together with the consultant's wish to help this appealing young man, contributed to an enactment revealing the conflict from which Mr. F. was suffering. In this case, as in some others, there was a sense of the consultant being not so much a 'ferryman' there to facilitate the patient's psychic passage into a desire to embark on psychoanalysis, but more as playing a shepherding role for the Clinic, 'rounding up' the patient to be brought into analysis as a training case for a candidate.

We saw other examples of how the interviewing analyst's role as Clinic consultant can interact with the patient's psychic functioning to influence the interview dynamics, in ways not immediately perceptible to the interviewer.

The Man Who Seemed Muddled

In the case of Mr. O., his presentation of what seemed to be rather confusing material led to the consultant asking a great number of questions, ending up taking a history to try to straighten out the confusion. It was as if the developing process prevented her from noting and discussing with Mr. O. the consultation process, so dominated as it was by his muddled and confusing account of himself. There was evidence that Mr. O. was an intelligent and talented man and it was very striking to the workshop how he was clearly almost completely uninterested in using his talents, or making any investment in exploring his mind, enacted by his lack of interest in paying for his consultation. Rather than talking to him about this and inviting him to observe how his mental functioning was being expressed in the meeting, the consultant became drawn into an enacted active response to Mr. O.'s vagueness and passivity. It seemed to the workshop that the consultant had become powerfully drawn into an enactment of the deadliness in the patient's psychic life, his presumably defensive lack of interest or reflection about himself, by herself not only trying actively to clarify things, but also by leaving long intervals between appointments and leaving it to the Clinic administration to attend to arranging meetings. Thus, this experienced consultant and the patient were at risk of becoming locked into an enactment and she did not at first manage to find a third position from which to observe what had been going on in the consultation. However, she was able to seek discussion of the case with colleagues and in this way, invite some triangulation, so that something more reflective in her could emerge and the material began to take on some form that could be understood. As there was no alternative for this patient but to have almost free treatment in the Clinic, and as his psychic functioning was judged to be very fragile, he was offered exploratory treatment in the form of psychoanalytic psychodrama, as if there was a strong sense that otherwise he would destroy himself. The hope was that within an institutional setting where he would be thought about by others, he may himself in due course become more self-reflective.

Such situations point to important questions for future research, regarding the relationships between process and technique. On the one hand, one could construe what took place in this consultation as an 'enactment' on the part of the consultant or a 'mutual enactment' by consultant and patient (see also Chapter 9), revealing something that is predominantly 'in' the patient. Then again, one could also think that the consultant's technique influenced the process and thus how this enactment was expressed. For example, according to Michel de M'Uzan (2015), the first key of an 'economic' strategy (see Box 8.3) respecting the patient's equilibrium is the analyst's *silence,*which is an opening of his/her qualification as a transferential object. The second key is the proposal made to the patient to *associate to his speech*, which is coupled with the interpretation of the defence and not of the content of the patient's discourse. Thus, Michel de M'Uzan would be very silent at the beginning of the interview and let the patient speak until the latter feels he cannot add anything. The analyst's intervention would then be: 'What can be said after everything has been said?' It is interesting that after this intervention, the analyst is often surprised to hear new associations, demonstrating a lifting of repression and revealing new links between unconscious representations and affects. However, this technical attitude would be more appropriate with neurotic organizations; with patients presenting either a borderline or psychotic functioning, such silence could provoke a psychic disorganization, which would necessitate from the consultant a more active attitude aiming at the restoration of the patient's narcissism and self-esteem.

This brings us to the next section in this chapter, on technique in the first meeting or psychoanalytic consultation.

Technique in first interviews

In discussion of all cases, the matter of interpretive technique in first meetings was inevitably present – to interpret the transference or not? The transference by the patient of basic elements of their psychic organization onto the person of the analyst and the whole situation is of course a *sine que non* of psychoanalytic understanding. But the extent to which it is possible to discern the transference and its manifestations in a first meeting will vary. Individual analysts themselves will be making observations of different things in different ways – to what the patient says, to how the patient behaves, to what the patient evokes in the analyst, to how these kinds of 'data' have already appeared before the meeting has even taken place (see Chapter 6). There will also be variation in the weight any individual analyst gives to such observations; both at the time of the meeting, 'in the heat of the moment', or while 'in the eye of the storm', and subsequently when reflecting on what has gone on, perhaps while writing it up (Pérez et al. 2015), perhaps in discussion with colleagues.

In considering consultations within an institutional setting, the technique adopted by any individual analyst may be influenced by the procedures and expectations of the institution. For example, the 'pre-transference' which will of course be ubiquitous, is likely to be particularly affected by the patient's fantasy about the Clinic which they have decided to contact, even before they have any idea of the particular individual who they will see for consultation: what they know of the Clinic e.g. if it is in the state health system, if it is known as being linked to a psychoanalytic training organization, what reputation it may have and so on. If there has been another professional involved in recommending or referring the patient to the institution, it is likely that the institutional dynamic with the patient will involve the referrer's pre-existing relationship with the Clinic (as seen in the case of Mr. L., *The Hopeful Man*).

The Clinic too is likely to have gathered information about the patient and to have been in communication with the patient, learning quite a bit about them, even before an appointment with an individual consultant is made, perhaps from a pre-consultation questionnaire completed by the patient, perhaps from a letter of referral or even a full report from a professional colleague. The consultant in an institutional setting is very much more likely than in private practice to have had the opportunity before the first meeting to form some hypotheses, and to develop some conscious and unconscious 'pre-counter-transference' fantasy about the patient. For example, if the Clinic has the function of providing training cases for psychoanalytic candidates, the consultant may be drawn from the material they see beforehand into the 'shepherding' role by seeing some evidence suggesting a potentially 'good training case' (see for example Mr. F., *The Wary Scientist*).

There are clearly differences amongst analysts in their consciously adopted technique in relation to the transference. Some analysts in a first interview, while making their own private observations of transference and counter-transference manifestations and allowing this to inform their thinking, will refrain from verbalizing this to the patient, or will do so only sparingly or in general and exploratory terms (see Mr. L., *The Hopeful Man*). Others may feel that an analytic meeting has not taken place unless they have verbalized in a direct way a transference interpretation to the patient. And of course in practice most analysts would adapt their interpretive technique in a first meeting, depending on what appears to be appropriate to the individual patient: to interpret directly in the transference with some may provoke excessive anxiety of a persecutory or even paranoid type, or may feel unhelpfully intrusive, and may provoke resistance; whereas with others to *avoid* a direct transference interpretation may leave the patient with the impression and uneasy anxiety that, for example, their destructiveness, or perhaps seductiveness, is something the analyst consultant cannot cope with and needs to avoid facing with the patient.

The object of the transference is another variable: in some cases, the *transference to the person of the analyst* seems to predominate (e.g. see below, Mr. P., *The Man Who Feared to Play*); in others, what seems more obvious is the *transference to the process* of the meeting and its purpose. In cases where the consultation is undertaken on behalf of an institution or Clinic, the presence of that 'third object' in the transference is inevitable and may be the element of the transference most immediately discernible. Argelander (1978) and Wegner (1992) have discussed in detail the 'opening scene' and its significance in understanding the meaning of what subsequently unfolds in a first meeting. The *mise-en-scène* created by the patient's perception of the institution and its processes, as well as the information transmitted to the consultant by the Clinic prior to the first interview, will have a major impact on the 'opening scene' and the generation of the transference and counter-transference (see for example, Ms. M., *A Mysterious Arrival*).

The 'setting', the 'frame' of the psychoanalytic process, including the fundamental rule of free association (Freud 1912), requires that the analyst should aim to facilitate the patient to speak of his/her wishes, thoughts and associations, rather than to act on them – the corollary to this being that the psychoanalyst ideally 'interprets' rather than 'enacts'. Though of course enactment, initiated by inducements to enact or by loss of analytic stance, is inevitable and frequently seen in one form or another as part of 'the emotional storm' (see Chapter 9), the capacity of the consultant in a first meeting to recognize the enactment and to recover the analytic stance and frame is essential if an analytic process is to be sustained. The psychoanalyst needs a 'third' to enable him/her to recover the stance – the setting is the third – this may be personified as the Clinic in an institutional consultation, or in a consultation where the intention has been to refer on.

In any setting, a first meeting can be seen predominantly as being 'seduction' by the person of the analyst, that is, where the patient feels that this analyst and perhaps *only* this analyst will be the one they can see. In such cases, it seems a narcissistic process takes place whereby the patient and analyst both fall into the belief that they are 'right' for each other, that they fulfil the needs of each other (e.g. in a concrete way, the analyst's need for a patient and the income that will be brought, or a less consciously determined perceived need for *this* patient; and the patient's *need* for 'this' analyst). However, if this process dominates unchallenged and unexamined, it will be acting as a resistance to or defence against the development of a psychoanalytic process (see Box 8.2).

Box 8.2 Seduction by the person and by the process

It may be helpful here to unpack the term 'seduction'. This word may cause some degree of confusion for some primarily English speakers, due to the almost exclusively negative connotation of how the term is used in English. In French, 'seduction' can have a positive, life-sustaining and object-related connotation, alongside the more familiar destructive connotation of perverse or narcissistic abuse.

Laplanche (1997) believes that the mother's unconscious desires inevitably influence her care of the child, 'seducing' with 'enigmatic messages' for which the child must find meaning and which help to structure the latter's psyche. Similarly, he describes the analytic situation as an inevitable and necessary seduction of the patient by the analyst (Laplanche 1992). Thus, in French psychoanalytic thought, the term 'seduction' can be used on the one hand to describe how, in the psychoanalytic process, the fantasy is evoked in the analysand (or in the analyst) of the possibility of a relationship where the other as a person can be seduced sexually or narcissistically, creating a resistance to the development of the analytical process. This 'seduction by the person' involves the issue of suggestion, both 'as a minimalist and discrete attempt, and therefore seductive and persuasive, to give rise to an idea or a wish in the other', as well as a possible 'totalitarian mastery, as shown in hypnotic subjection' (Donnet 1995).

However, in a more positive way, the idea of 'seduction by the method' in the French literature refers to the development in the psychoanalytic process through which the analysand is invited to speak of his/her wishes and not to act them, and discovers how useful and valuable this can be as a means towards self-discovery. The psychoanalytic method, involving specific conditions such as the setting and the fundamental rule that both patient and analyst need in order to work, is taken to be understood by the patient as part of a process they can respond to well. Therefore, 'seduction by the method' involves reference to the setting as a third party; in this way, the post-Oedipal superego is represented, favouring the development of the analytical process and of the self-reflective attitude. It also hints at the transformation of a symmetrical narcissistic relationship during the interview into an 'announced dissymmetry' inherent to the development of a triangulated psychoanalytic process (Baldacci and Bouchard 2012). From this perspective, 'seduction by the method' means that through his/her experience of a psychoanalytic consultation, a patient can be drawn into seeing how helpful this approach would be for him/her.

The general task for the analyst in any setting for a first meeting is to evaluate whether a patient can potentially benefit from an analytic process with an analyst in a psychoanalytic setting and not that he/she would be the 'right analyst' for the patient. Seen from the patient's perspective, the first would be seen as 'seduction by the method', the second as 'seduction by the person' (see Box 8.2, also the discussion of the case *The Mother's Son* in Chapter 5). The risk of confusing the two aspects, and getting carried away by the idea that 'you' are the right person for this patient is likely to be far better controlled in an institutional setting where discussion with colleagues is almost always built into the procedures, than it may be in a private setting.

However, the presence of a third does not by any means guarantee dissipation of a narcissistic seduction, as illustrated in the case of Mr. L. when the consultation was discussed in the WPIP Workshop.

In this case, *The Hopeful Man*, Mr. L. had clearly appreciated the consultant's efforts to understand him, saying to him that he has 'hit the nail on the head', and the idea of there being 'a good couple' at work here took hold in the discussion. But it was also clear from the material that the patient's underlying and chronic sense of terror at being close, his inability to feel at ease in a couple, does not get taken up in the transference by the consultant who is taking more of a receptive than an active role. Thus the anger and rage in the patient does not get into the consultation sufficiently to be metabolized there and it seemed to the WPIP research group that having been split off in the consultation process, it consequently penetrated into the Workshop discussion. The outrage expressed in the group that this '*Clinic*' that had arranged the consultation would not '*allow*' Mr. L. to continue in treatment with his consultant was striking. Mr. L.'s seeking out of an institutional setting in part at least to protect himself from an unknown, possibly dangerously intrusive object became transformed into the workshop's intense wish to protect him from this dangerous, bureaucratically insensitive Clinic and to leave him in the now known, but disarmed and idealized, consultation couple.

This case is also a good illustration of the role of the transference interpretation in consultations within an institutional context. The consultant is very clear in his own mind that he is seeing the patient on behalf of the Clinic and that he will not be taking this patient into treatment with him in the future. To that extent, the Clinic is a clear 'third' in the analyst's mind with which he identifies, and he operates in this way in the task of the consultation. This consultant does not as a rule in his usual work make use of interpretations about the transference to the person of the analyst as part of his consultation work, but in other ways conveys his wish to understand his containing stance through making links for the patient between his past and his current difficulties, which Mr. L. evidently found helpful, commenting in an appreciative way from time to time he 'had not thought of that before' or 'must think more about that', as well as conveying he was not wholly at ease in the consulting room or with the idea of the couch. But it seemed to the research group that something was being split off and put outside the meeting, perhaps so as to protect this now safe and idealized place, so the patient's unease could be described but was not linked to his experience of having a psychoanalytic consultation, of actually being in the room. Interpretations were not made about the transference to the *process* of the consultation, which could have been made, for example, in response to a dream the patient had about being served with the wrong sort of meal in a café, perhaps in order to not provoke what may have been sensed as a risky disturbance in the transference. The consultant described what seemed to the research group to confirm this when he mentioned there had been some material he now could not recall but which was followed by Mr. L. excusing himself because he 'needed to take a moment', a silent pause where he could recover himself. It was as if the consultant had himself registered that both he and the patient had needed to split something disturbing off. So, despite the links made and the thoughtfulness and reflective atmosphere in the consultation, it seemed to remain as a narcissistic seduction by the person of the analyst rather than a more triangulated process where the relationship to 'the couch', to the setting, and to the psychoanalytic approach could be explored, and put into words. The question of whether Mr. L. was 'seduced by the method' in the consultation remains equivocal, although he was in the end successfully referred for psychotherapy outside the Clinic.

The Man Who Feared to Play

In the case of Mr. P. a seductive transference was quickly revealed in a number of ways: the consultant and the patient each had different 'mother tongues' but both were also fluent in each other's language. The older woman consultant analyst felt impressed by this handsome younger man who could speak so well both her language and that of the country where they were meeting, and noted how she suppressed her impulse to offer him, seductively, the possibility of speaking in his native tongue. She then spontaneously responded to his emotional recounting of several early traumas with a maternally humorous calming statement, 'Ah, all the joys at once!', very much an 'in the transference' interpretation, to which Mr. P. reacted with material indicating considerable anxiety about an incestuous seduction. He spoke of three distinct childhood memories that seemed to show he was afraid to 'play' with the consultant: when his mother had been stung by a wasp, when he was shut into his bedroom, and when he refused to turn off the television and play with his mother, which had made her cry. He went on to speak of there later being numerous people in a new house but only one bedroom. It seemed her interpretation 'in' the transference rather than 'of' the transference at that early point in the first meeting was felt as seductive. A theme in relation to the father emerged later in the meeting and could be understood as being 'of' the transference in terms of the patient's current anxiety about whether he would or would not be 'chosen' by the Clinic to have analysis. The distinction between an interpretation 'in' the transference and one 'of' the transference is well illustrated here, where the patient's anxiety about being chosen because he has successfully seduced the consultant is aroused by an interpretation 'in' the transference relationship with the person of the analyst; whereas the interpretation 'of' the transference, in this case to the process, seems to rather lead him to feel his omnipotent fantasy has been identified and could be understood and tolerated by the institution.

So, in reply to the question posed at the beginning of this section – to interpret the transference or not in an initial interview – what we have seen in the WPIP cases is that in whatever setting the most convincing technique seems to be to interpret the patient's *transference to the process and setting*, whereas interpretations of *transference to the analyst* appear to be much more problematic. This seems to be something that is important to think about not just in institutional settings or where a referral on is going to be involved, but is also part of good technique in first interviews in any setting.

In general, some analysts prefer to be cautious in their interventions and not involve transferential issues in a first meeting, that is, to be working with an attitude based on an 'economic' model (see Box 8.3). Others are more in favour of a more 'topographical' model and will take the approach of involving the patient in the process though transferential interpretations (ibid.). As mentioned before, the anxiety with the one is that the impression may be created that the analyst is afraid to face the patient's destructive or seductive affects, and the anxiety with the other is that the patient may feel overly intruded upon or overly anxious about their effect on the analyst's state. But in practice, in first meetings in any setting, analysts are most likely to work to open up analytic space in a way that is compatible with the patient's mental equilibrium, with what the patient can cope with, rather than concentrating solely on bringing specific unconscious issues to consciousness.

The matter of interpreting the transference often raises particular concerns in relation to the process of referring a patient to have analytic treatment with someone else. The main concern is about how interpretation of the transference, or even the development of an observed transference, even if it is not interpreted, will mean that referral on to someone else is disturbing or unacceptably traumatic for the patient, perhaps presenting a serious obstacle to a successful referral and subsequently fruitful treatment.

Box 8.3 Technique and the use of the economic and topographic models

In his definition of metapsychology, Freud (1915b) described psychic processes from three points of view: the *dynamic* point of view, in which they are seen as the expression of the conflict between opposing psychic forces; the *topographic* point of view, where these forces are seen as taking place between, and structured by, differentiated psychic systems; and the *economic* point of view, which describes them in terms of the quantities of psychic energy involved. In French psychoanalytic thought, the 1915 topographic model with its systems Unconscious, Preconscious and Conscious is called the 'first topography'; the later structural model with the systems id, ego and superego (Freud 1923a) is the 'second topography'. Furthermore, considerable attention has been paid in French psychoanalysis to the economic point of view, with accent placed on the well-structured psyche's ability to bind energy through representation, whereas failures in representation by a less well-structured psychic apparatus can lead to discharge of the unbound energy through affective or somatic breakdown.

From this perspective, the *dynamics* of transference, if understood in terms of the patient's unconscious conflicts, calls for a *topographical* reorganization, i.e. 'making conscious what is unconscious', or 'where Id was, there Ego shall be' (Freud 1933). However, if understood in terms of the patient's capacity for representation, the transference also challenges the patient's psychical *economy* and requires a progressive reorganization of this economy, especially with less well-structured patients.

The perspective of purely topographical change can be thought of as calling for an interpretative *tactic*, i.e. well-timed focal interventions helping the patient to become conscious of something unconscious. In contrast, when the objective is to promote economic change, a long-term global *strategy* is required in which the analyst works to further the development of the patient's capacity to represent and limits his interventions to what the patient's psychic equilibrium can tolerate without becoming overwhelmed.

Many of the clinical cases in our study illustrate these issues, with regard to the aims and effects of the analyst's interpretative activity in the first interview.

There are some similarities between these contrasting 'topographic-tactical' and 'economic-strategic' models of psychoanalytic work, respectively, and Levine's (2010) 'archaeological' model based on uncovering pre-existing meanings, as opposed to his 'transformational' model in which the aim is to help the patient to create meaning. There are also some similarities with Enckell's (2010) 'model of archaeology' looking into something 'anterior', and his 'model of teleology', which is 'turned towards a world of possibilities'. These different models cannot be simply superposed, but they do seem to address convergent concerns.

Consultation outcome: recommendation decision and referral

In just about all Clinic or institutional cases studied, the consultation was carried out on the understanding that the consultant would not be in a position themselves to take the patient on for further treatment. The consultant usually acts on behalf of the institution which will take responsibility for making a referral or recommendation to the patient. In Clinics attached to Psychoanalytic Societies, the referral on may be to a candidate in training. Considerable feeling was stirred up in most of the WPIP Workshop groups in response to some of the cases where this was the situation. This was related to a debate about appropriate technique when seeing someone for a psychoanalytic consultation limited to just one or two meetings – centring around the question of interpreting the transference or not, as was well illustrated in the case of Mr. L. (*The Hopeful Man*).

As described above in the case of Mr. L., the ethics of the recommendation to be made to a patient at the end of a consultation can provoke strong feelings, and not just in the minds of the patient and the consultant. It is ethical to be interested in the patient and in what future direction may be taken with regard to further treatment, but there can be many pressures acting on the consultant at the point of making a recommendation or offer. As mentioned before, a consultant may be in danger of submitting to the 'super-ego' demand by the Clinic to provide a training case, or a case to fulfil a state-funding contract. Even technically there can sometimes be the ethical question of whether it is better to recommend the patient to confront things or whether to support his defences and not suggest analysis. When in private practice and making a referral, it is more possible to make a specific recommendation, to select the analyst with whom you feel this patient can most appropriately work. But in an institution, it is more likely that the patient would go onto a waiting list and be allocated to the next one who has a vacancy, leaving it to the Clinic to take care of any 'special' considerations that may need to be taken into account.

The concern raised in the WPIP workshops about how ethical it was to refer on to another analyst a patient with whom an analytic relationship has been formed was about how traumatic and ultimately destructive of future treatment this may be. Bolognini (2006) points out that it is also an issue for the consultant, because the subjectively charged nature of a psychoanalytic consultation:

> involves a highly concentrated and intense experience of meeting, contact and leaving. Often, in the second part of a deeply lived consultation, it is common to think along the lines: 'How can I send him on to a colleague? *I* would be the right analyst for this patient !!!'
>
> (Bolognini 2006)

Equally, it is not uncommon for analysts to whom referrals have been made by charismatic, senior psychoanalysts to feel in the course of an analysis that the senior colleague is brought into the analysis by the patient as an idealized object which is 'a hard act to follow' (Bolognini 2006, Klauber 1986). A successful referral on may help the patient 'to prepare for the future mourning of the object' (Donnet 2013). The first interview is therefore always linked to the *end* as well as to the *beginning* of an analytical treatment.

A central question here seems to be to do with whether the analytic relationship created in a good consultation is something that facilitates or something that threatens the formation of a future more long-standing analytic relationship. In institutional consultations, the transference very often appears to be a transference to 'the institution' and consultation process and this seems to help considerably with forming what Donnet has called the 'transferable transference' (2013), where the patient's investment in the analytic function of the consultant, rather than investment in him as a person, is carried forward into the subsequent analytic work.

Summary

The consultant, the patient and the 'other'

In our researches, we found the role of the 'third' is ubiquitous and in different respects is an invaluable way of understanding any consultation or first meeting. In an institutional setting, there is very obviously a third party involved in the consultation process, where appointments may be made by administrative staff, consultant analysts allocated to cases by a Director and so on, and in other and less tangible ways the Clinic takes on a symbolic role for the patient and for the consultant as 'the third'. The patient is very likely to allocate to the Clinic the role of a 'third' object, representative not only of the father in the Oedipal structure, but of any person or institution who may play a role, for example, in helping the individual not to be engulfed in a dual relationship (Green 1990, 2002). Of course, in any psychoanalytic encounter, there is also the 'observing' third, that part of the consultant's mind that is not only engaged in the room with the patient but is also 'observing' internally the process unfolding between them (Britton 1989). The meaning and prognostic value of attending to the vicissitudes of the third object in both consultant and patient are an essential part of the psychoanalytic process.

In comparison with the setting of an institutionally arranged first meeting, the setting in private practice is *virtual*, relying for the sense of the 'third' solely on the analyst's capacity to establish and sustain the analytic attitude, whereas in the context of, say, a Clinic, the 'third' is also given objective form. The latter can be particularly important for patients who are more borderline or psychotic than the neurotic patients for whom the *virtual* 'third' object is more likely to be sufficient (Gibeault 2012a). As described by Kestemberg (1981), the Clinic Director to whom the patient can refer as a third object in the course of his/her treatment, can also represent such a stabilizing third-person function. Finally, as seen in a number of our cases, the *objective* form of the third, as personified in an institutional staff group with the expectation of discussion of cases, has great value for the consultant encountering the unconscious 'emotional storm' inevitable in any first psychoanalytic meeting and working with the patient on opening up the analytic space.

9 COUNTERTRANSFERENCE AND ENACTMENT

Introduction

As we examined our research material, we were intrigued by the frequency of enactments on the part of both patient and analyst. There seemed to be considerable pressure to enact, and we came to think of this as an important aspect of the process of the first interview.

In some cases, the forces leading to enactment appeared to be particularly powerful, so that symbolization and representation were very difficult to achieve. However, even in such situations, the resulting turbulence in the analytic couple and in the patient's world was liable to create significant movements and could be seen to be part of the psychic work that was being done by the analytic couple.

Although the analytical method is based on representation, thought and meaningful words, we can also assume that the analyst's unconscious countertransference can drift into enactment or acting in when the situation doesn't allow sufficient elaboration of the analyst's own feelings and reactions before intervening. Vice versa, if the analyst can listen to his/her own countertransference responses to the vicissitudes of a first interview, she/he can give thought and meaning to the enactments and acting in that emerge within the couple at work.

Contemporary psychoanalysis assumes that countertransference involvement comes into play from the very first instant with a patient. If the analyst is in deep contact with the countertransference while listening to a potential analysand, this can provide useful clues about the person's ability to benefit from analysis. Correspondingly, when countertransferential phenomena cannot be sufficiently dealt with – for reasons to do with the patient, the analyst or, in this study, the context and dynamics of the first meeting – enactments or acting in on the part of the analyst can be the result. These issues may be especially important and frequent with patients who find it difficult to transform their impulses to enact into representations.

There is no unique conception in the psychoanalytic literature of enactment, acting out or acting in. Freud introduced the general concept as 'repetition', in his paper, 'Remembering, Repeating and Working-Through' (Freud 1914). In a passage in which he also refers to the beginning of treatment, he writes:

> The patient does not *remember* anything of what he has forgotten and repressed, but *acts* it out. He reproduces it not as a memory, but as an action; he *repeats* it, without, of course, knowing that he is repeating it. For instance, the patient does not say that he remembers that he used to be defiant and critical towards his parents' authority; instead, he behaves in that way to the doctor. . . . Above all, the patient will *begin* his treatment with a repetition of this kind. . . . As long as the patient is in the treatment he cannot escape from this compulsion to repeat; and in the end we understand that this is his way of remembering.
>
> (Freud 1914, p. 150)

Freud's clinical examples and discussion demonstrate that he referred to phenomena that can be subtle, are always related to the transference, and which bring the past into the present. They are not only a resistance to remembering and to 'intrapsychic experience' in general, but also a way of communicating it (Boesky 1982).

Laplanche and Pontalis (1967) suggested that Freud's use of the term 'Agieren' refers to a process of 'actualization', i.e. making real in the present, and proposed '*mise en acte*' ('putting into action') as a better translation. In English, Joseph Sandler proposed to translate this as 'enactment' (Sandler et al. 1973); he also described how patients actualize their object relationships with the analyst (Sandler 1976).

The choice of 'acting out' as a translation for 'Agieren' placed emphasis on the impulsive drive discharge aspect; this led to the use of 'acting out' to designate a wide range of impulsive behaviours of varying metapsychological and psychopathological status (Laplanche and Pontalis 1967, Sandler et al. 1973, Boesky 1982). 'Acting in' is a concept that parallels 'acting out', but takes place inside the session; it can be used to emphasize impulsive aspects of the session dynamics.

The two main contemporary positions can be summed up as 'enactment as a failure versus enactment as an inevitable part of the psychoanalytical process' (Bohleber et al. 2013).

Theodore Jacobs (1986, 2001), following Sandler (Sandler et al. 1973; Sandler 1976, 1993) introduced the concept of countertransference enactment in psychoanalysis and assumed that such enactment is inevitable. As early as 1958 Fairbairn had described how the patient 'press-gangs' the analyst into a repetition of his inner world (Fairbairn 1958). Later, several authors, especially from English-speaking regions, have studied this element in depth, proposing different features and nuances to explain how the analyst becomes involved in the actualization of the transference. Joseph (1989), for example, described how the patient can subtly 'nudge' the analyst to behave in correspondence to the patient's projections. According to Sandler (1976, 1993), the patient recruits the analyst through subtle cues, which are not exclusively related to projective identification. When projective identification *is* the main mechanism, it relies on verbal and nonverbal 'interpersonal pressure' to become effective (Gabbard 1995).

The analyst can monitor his/her involuntary 'role-responsiveness' (Sandler 1976) to such pressure in order to understand what is being actualized:

> I have suggested that the analyst has, within certain limits, a free-floating behavioural responsiveness in addition to his free-floating conscious attention. Within the limits set by the analytical situation he will, unless he becomes aware of it, tend to comply with the role demanded of him, to integrate it into his mode of responding and relating to the patient. Normally, of course, he can catch this counter-response in himself, particularly if it appears to be in the direction of being inappropriate. However, he may only become aware of it through observing his own behaviour, responses and attitudes, after these have been carried over into action.
>
> (Sandler 1976, p. 47)

These authors, including Jacobs, thus agree that enactment refers 'to subtle metacommunications, usually nonverbal in nature' (Hirsch 1998). These metacommunications create a pressure on the analyst, who is affected by them. Strong emotions and feelings, drives, regressive sensations, as well as projective counter-identifications can emerge with the result of a degree of collusion with the analysand through enactment and acting in.

The resulting phenomena, which we will subsume under the generic term 'enactment', can be understood from two complementary perspectives: as a form of impulsive 'acting in' and as a form of mental work. According to some authors, enactment as a form of mental work is connected both with the personality and the technique of the analyst, as well as the 'mutually unconscious influence' between analyst and patient, but it is not related to 'an actualization of an impulse' by the analyst during the session (Ponsi, quoted by Perelberg 2003). In contrast, we would talk about acting in by the analyst when 'action is replacing thought, outside the analyst's mentalization' (Ponsi 2012), perhaps stimulated by something happening during the session, but reflecting the analyst's own equilibrium and remaining basically disconnected from the relationship.

Other authors would not make this sharp distinction but would, like Bohleber et al. (2013) say in more general terms that 'countertransference enactment involves the occurrence of something unexpected', but 'if they are subjected to analysis afterwards, they may become a powerful means to reach inner depths dissociated from the self', so that 'what happens after the enactment will be decisive for the outcome – that is, whether or not the enactment is harmful'. From this point of view, enactment is unavoidable but needs to be elaborated by the analyst to become useful for the course of the therapeutic process, and can be a potentially powerful stimulus and aid to reflection.

On the other hand, as Bohleber et al. (2013) note, there is also the viewpoint which perceives enactment mostly as a failure of analytic work, implying that 'it can (and should) be avoided'. The main reasons for seeing enactments as a failure are that 'they are often the expression of the analyst's resistance to the analytic method and setting' (ibid.), and that they 'repeat old injuries' (Benjamin, in Bohleber et al. 2013). The implication here is that when there is a repetition, also on the side of the analyst, this means that the analyst wasn't able to reach a sufficient level of elaboration and meaningful thought.

An intermediate view would be that the analyst's enactments occur when 'a patient's behaviour or words stimulate an unconscious conflict in the analyst, leading to an interaction that has unconscious meaning to both' (ibid.). In such a living and dynamic view of the analytic process, enactment would be the normal result of the process itself, requiring further elaboration. Such a view is held by Tuckett (1997, 2011), who proposed the term 'mutual enactment' for these dynamics, which can lead to an impasse but can also open the way to deeper understanding and interpretation.

Several French-speaking authors hold the view that enactment is based on the action of words or behaviours, rather than on words as linked to a symbolization process (Green 2002, Donnet 2005, Gibeault 2010). Donnet (ibid.) and others point out that speech can be used not only to symbolize but also to act, in what is called an '*agir de parole*' ('action of speech'). Enactment is seen as a paradoxical process involving both repetition and transformation, in which action ('*mise en acte*') is also a way of 'staging' ('*mise en scène*') i.e. a representational activity reminiscent of Argelander's (1970) 'scenic function of the ego'.

The emerging consensus is that both role-responsiveness and countertransference, i.e. both enactment and acting in, are always involved as complementary aspects in a co-creation between patient and analyst (Gabbard 1995, Bohleber et al. 2013). This means, however, that the analyst must bear involvement, vulnerability, self-analysis and personal growth:

> When the analyst participates in an enactment, it is because she dissociates; and when she dissociates she finds herself in circumstances that make her vulnerable in a way she can manage, for the time being, only by dissociating . . . the patient cannot provoke such dissociation if the analyst is not vulnerable to it . . . the negotiation of an enactment requires growth from the analyst in just the way it requires growth from the patient. The analyst's role is not defined by invulnerability . . . but by a special (though inconsistent) willingness, and a practised (though imperfect) capacity to accept and deal forthrightly with her vulnerability.
>
> (Stern 2004, p. 216)

In light of these theoretical notes we will discuss a clinical case that illustrates vividly the passages between countertransference, acting in and enactment in the first encounter. The analyst had to accomplish difficult conscious and unconscious internal work in order to salvage the possibility of opening a psychoanalytic space with this patient.

The Unfortunate Lover

Opening scene: phone calls and messages

Before the analyst and Mr. Q. met, there was a long and rather unusual sequence of emails, text messages and phone calls to schedule the meeting. Cancellations, postponements and re-scheduled sessions signalled the ambivalence, the uncertainty, but also the control over the analyst's willingness to receive this patient. In the Clinical Workshop the analyst said:

> The young man called me on my cell phone in November. He asked me if I was C. (my first name), said he wasn't sure it would be exactly me, because the person who referred him to me had seen me many years ago. She is his colleague. He said he was looking for a psychotherapist, and asked her if she knew one, and she had said that in fact she did, and gave him my phone number.
>
> Then he asked me if I practised psychotherapy, if so what kind, and would it be possible to see me. There was some urgency in his voice. I said I had an hour for him next week, and he said he would come.

Then a text message was sent by Mr. Q.:

> Thanks . . . but this week I will need to pass . . . can't make it . . .

A series of email messages followed, with questions about available hours, and subsequent cancellations. To quote just a few:

> I have been travelling a lot . . . and soon will have to travel again, but I don't want to let more time go by.

> Hi C., haven't been able to call you . . . can we schedule a meeting?

> If you still remember me, I contacted you to initiate sessions. My time preference is after work, around 7 to 8 pm . . . but I am flexible. Hope to hear from you.

This period stretched up to three months.

Answering his last email message, the analyst wrote:

Hello, Mr. Q., for us it would be a good idea to meet at least once and decide how to proceed. This week I have free time on Wednesday (17:00) and on Friday (16:00). Please let me know if you can make it one of these days.

Mr. Q. answered at once, and a meeting was set.

In the Clinical Workshop and in the WPIP there was some discussion about why the analyst sent this last message to the patient. One idea was that perhaps 'the analyst foreclosed on the uncertainty of the patient's approach to her by deciding to settle it by writing to him'.

This sequence of events clearly shows that prior to the first interview there was already a hint of a relationship 'made up of expectations, of thoughts, feelings, beliefs, desires that each anticipate from the other' (Bohleber et al. 2013). All these expectations were enacted from both sides from the outset.

Green (2002) argues that the analyst is already the object of the patient's transferential feelings before the first interview, as is manifest in the opening scene. He uses the specific term 'pre-transference' for this element, which is already charged with affects, emotions and drives that can be ignited in the first encounter, or remain silent and hidden by resistances and defences. At the same time, the analyst also goes through early countertransferential configurations, leading to phantasies, expectations, pre-conceptions, defences, counter-resistances and hopes from the early hints given by the patient (his voice on the phone, who referred him, the way he speaks and so on). Pre-transference, and we can say pre-countertransference, may collude from the very first moment, that is, before the patient walks through the analyst's door. Both subjects are therefore involved at once in an emotional turbulence that is potentially already there before their encounter.

Preamble to the two sessions

The dynamics of the two sessions that follow can be understood as involving a repetition of the patient's fundamental conflict, which tends to be more enacted than elaborated in the sessions. Defence and enactment on both sides play an important role and threaten to leave little room for elaboration.

Mr. Q. asks for help because he is in serious trouble, both because his current girlfriend is going to have a baby and because he is affected by a diffuse and generalized state of anxiety. His anxiety can be linked to his tendency to compulsive acting out in his relationships with women, in an endless spiral whereby his anxiety provokes him to act out, and in which each new consequence of his acting out provokes more anxiety. In the first interview, Mr. Q. tells a long story with a detailed list of his love affairs and sexual relationships without making much reference to other aspects of his history. He fills the analyst with a profusion of material relating to his numerous love stories, some of which ended with abortions. Similarly, the second interview is taken up by the narration of a very long dream that rather impedes the creation of a vital space of communication between himself and the analyst.

First interview

Mr. Q. came ten minutes late, panting, with a panicked look on his face. He was perspiring and wiped his face with a handkerchief.

He took his coat off but held it tight, entered the analyst's office and sat down in the armchair, still holding his bag in one hand and pressing his coat to his chest with the other. They looked at each other. He said: 'I still need to catch my breath.'

An.: Of course, take your time.

He looked around, at the books, at the couch, and peered inquisitively into the analyst's face. Then he put his bag down on the floor but kept his coat on his lap. Mr. Q. was short, balding, but energetic, dressed casually, and rather like an adolescent; he sat like one, stretching his legs and reclining. After a while he said:

> Actually I have been in therapy once. In a different city where I worked. My therapist strongly advised me against taking a therapist in this town, she said I won't find anyone professional . . . But I am glad I did . . . For me, it is difficult to decide and to make a choice. What should I do now?

An.: Why don't you just tell me anything you think I should know. And then we shall see.

The patient mentioned only a few biographical facts, just enough to let the analyst understand that he was the last child from a big well-to-do Middle-Eastern family and was working in northern Europe as a journalist. He moved on to a very long list of his love affairs, which crossed each other during his life. He specified to the analyst in a very systematic way the beginning and ending year of each love affair (e.g. in 1995 I met S. until 1999).

After having mentioned his love affairs with S. and P., the patient described how he started a relationship with Y., with whom he fell in love, which led him to break up with P. But after one year he started a new love affair with W., and so he left Y.

He was very happy with W., but during a trip he met Y. once again. Mr. Q. said:

As a result of this encounter Y. got pregnant. I told W. about this. She was destroyed and I thought I had lost her forever. Anyway, time passed and W. and I started our relationship again. Meanwhile Y. had a miscarriage, and we never spoke again.

When I heard about Y.'s miscarriage I decided to leave everything and go for work reasons to another town, and W. was destroyed for a second time. I loved her but at the same time I wanted to get away from everything.

After some time, I met M. and we spent a night together. She was so magnificent, so unapproachable, I couldn't have imagined she could be interested in me. So, there was this night, and after a while she called me saying she was pregnant. After conflictual ups and downs about whether to keep the baby or not, she had an abortion. To support her, and because I felt really bad, I started living with her.

Mr. Q. fell silent. The analyst was also silent for a while, feeling dizzy after having listened to this detailed recital. While the analyst was thinking what to say, Mr. Q. continued: 'And so I am here.'

An.: This is a very perplexing story. What do you make of it yourself?

Mr. Q.: Well, many things are still difficult to see. I certainly know this. I have a strange sadness when I think about the future, and about the past as well; it is a deep feeling which often gets me very, very down. You won't believe it, but I think of my future with tears. And I don't want to grow. And I hate to lose possibilities.

He spoke of his doubts about whether to go to another town, and how to leave W., and of his anger that he had to renounce anything at all, even if it were for the love of his life. He wanted it all, and W. he already had, so the assignment in the other town had to be taken. Yet he was still in doubt if he should stay.

An.: What do you think your sadness is about?

Mr. Q.: Well, it's like something that I missed out on and will never be able to have again.

An.: These three things you said about yourself seem to be related. You refuse to make a choice because you imagine it kills any other possibility.

Mr. Q. seemed impressed – he sat straight, dropped his coat, and started to rub his palms on his knees. He opened his mouth to say something, then he reclined again, half-closed his eyes and started to breathe deeply. The analyst saw that he was trying to fight back tears.

Then he looked at the analyst and said: 'You know, even with these contraceptives, M. got pregnant again. I didn't believe this was possible. I thought she was letting me down.'

(continued)

(continued)

An.: And this time she decided to keep the baby.

Mr. Q.: Yes, and I also thought it would be dangerous to have this second abortion so soon. So we discussed it, and stayed together for a while, but I . . . I . . .

An.: You feel trapped.

Mr. Q.: Yes trapped and . . . and . . . M. is good and nice to me, but I don't trust her.

An.: So when do you expect?

Mr. Q.: In a week, but actually any day now.

It was now the analyst's turn to be impressed, and maybe it showed on her face. Mr. Q. sprang forward: 'My family is coming here in two weeks to see the baby. My mother is very enthusiastic. She is such a devoted mother. We are originally a Muslim family, and my mother is still very religious.'

An: She is happy about the baby?

Mr. Q.: She will be happy if she sees I am happy. If she thinks I am not, she will give M. a cold reception.

An.: You are very close to your mother.

Mr. Q.: I have always been my mother's boy. One of my brothers sometimes gets angry with her. But he feels bad lately, and takes antidepressants.

An.: Your complicated story with women – do you think it is somehow linked to your relationship with your mother?

Mr. Q. sprang up again: 'She is quite a character'. He goes on to tell the analyst of many instances when his mother was openly manipulative or, when that didn't work, used subversive methods to get what she wanted or insisted on.

It was time to stop, and the analyst announced that they would have to continue next time.

Some hypotheses about the session

What can we observe during this first interview in the patient, in the analyst and in their encounter?

Mr. Q. immediately brings the pressure of massive claustrophobic anxieties into the room. He styles himself as a Don Juan who can get women pregnant and make them have an abortion as he pleases, in a spiral of drives that destroy what he attempts to create because of a reiterated and acted out repetition compulsion. Nonetheless he acknowledges his wish to be his mother's baby, the royal baby, who would like to remain incorporated in the mother object, while on the other hand wanting to run away from it – indeed such escapes have continuously been acted out with women. It is as though the patient wishes to achieve a fusional dimension that becomes immediately intolerable.

There is a significant link between two major developments in the session. At first, through his long account of his love affairs, Mr. Q. implicitly describes how he considers himself the royal baby of all the women he meets. Then, after the analyst's question, 'What do you make of it . . . ?', he expresses his feeling of great sadness about the past and for the future. He is referring to his love for his lost childhood mother, and relates something of how he has been searching for an ideal mother whom he has probably never been able to find in women.

How does this aspect enter the relationship?

We can grasp it in the first lines of the session when the analyst describes the somatic expressions of the patient and the way in which he wants to impress her, styling himself as a Don Juan, including the analyst herself in his list of conquests when he says: 'And so I am here.' However this is the manifest, seductive, manipulative aspect.

The analyst reported to the Clinical Workshop that she had felt the patient to be very controlling, seductive and oppressive, and that his balding and sweaty appearance had made her feel annoyed and distanced. One can therefore think that the patient, who forcefully entered the room and the analyst's mind, at the same time created a condition of distance between himself and the analyst by trying to drag her, through his words and sensory channels, into a vortex alternating between seduction and rejection. In other words, he got himself inside the analyst, who simultaneously felt trapped by him. As a result, she let the patient alternately come close in some moments and become more distant in others.

The analyst, however, mostly maintained an analytical position, especially in her first explorative interventions, and tolerated being plunged into the flood of concrete elements and becoming a bit destabilized.

On the one hand, she let the bulk of the beta elements lead her, in order to contain them and give them back later after having worked them through. She did so by posing relevant and unsaturated questions until she reached an interpretation when she said: 'You refuse to make a choice because you imagine it kills any other possibility.'

This intervention changed the atmosphere in the session, provoking a turbulence that expanded in the relationship. It came across as a containing and holding intervention that allowed for a turning point. We notice this first in Mr. Q., who had a bodily reaction like dropping his coat; and soon after in the analyst, whose expression showed somatic turbulence when Mr. Q. reported that his girlfriend was about to have the baby. Such turbulence switched the emotional level, allowing Mr. Q. to come into contact with his maternal figure and with feelings such as nostalgia, sadness and the acknowledgement of his fear of growth.

This example supports our initial hypothesis of how the level of communication can switch, but it also shows how this work requires the analyst to function in a 'storm' of difficult transference and countertransference pressures.

At the same time, it can be seen how difficult it is to maintain an analytic position. At a certain point the analyst, after having listened to Mr. Q.'s long account of his love stories and after her first two comments, intervened a lot and seemed to enter concretely into the external reality of the patient, perhaps expressing her own intrusive response to Mr. Q.'s intrusiveness:

Mr. Q. said: 'You know, even with these contraceptives, M. got pregnant again.'

And the analyst replied: 'And this time she decided to keep the baby.'

Enactment and the analyst's transformative function

This interaction can be understood as an enactment determined by the fact that the analyst's mental space has been invaded to a degree that blocks the development of a narrative and dream register. The analyst has attempted to maintain her analytical attitude and listening, but she was being sorely tested by the pressure, the urgency and the unconscious provocation of Mr. Q.'s self-presentation. The outcome was more like a demonstration that she had guessed the patient's predicament. Although intended to show to Mr. Q. that she understood his anxiety, this communication came out as very close to an interpretative enactment (Steiner 2006) in which she reasserted her control of the situation in an omnipotent manner.

The analyst described her complex inner experiences in her discussion with the Clinical Workshop:

> 'I felt there was an urgency in the patient. I felt irritation and also sympathy. And when I saw him, and the feeling deepened over three meetings, I didn't like him.'
>
> After saying some more about her perceptions of Mr. Q., she said: 'Maybe you sense my unconscious reaction – he was emotional in how he spoke and he provoked a strong reaction in me.'

Such experiences show how difficult it is to differentiate between enactment as a failure, in the sense that 'the enactment represents a rupture in the analyst's conscious experience of himself/herself' (Bohleber et al. 2013), and enactment as a working process involving 'the analyst's experience within the relational field he established with the patient' (ibid.). In the latter perspective, enactment is a significant, ubiquitous factor in psychoanalysis, and even more so in first consultations, when patient and analyst meet for the first time.

Amongst other reasons, the ubiquitous dimension is due to the fact that, just as the patient can reveal his own emotional and affective states to the analyst through his posture, gestures, movements, manifest and imperceptible bodily reactions, so too the analyst responds with body movements, facial expressions and changes in her tone of voice. This point is well described in the analyst's account of this session. These manifestations are instances of what Jacobs defines as the 'wide spectrum of behaviours', through which enactments 'become shared experiences reacted to by both participants' (Jacobs 2001). They deserve to be thought about and analyzed because they are significant for the understanding of what happens during an interview.

When the analyst, towards the end of the session, says, 'You are very close to your mother' and the patient answers, 'I have always been my mother's boy', we have a movement from previous enactments on both sides to a deep expression of affect that can bring about further movements and transformations, giving some meaning to the initial turbulences created by the first impact of their meeting, beginning as early as their first emails and phone calls.

The patient had actually already entered forcefully the transference-countertransference dynamics and had told the analyst that despite all the defences – the contraceptives – he had made the analyst pregnant. However, we can also assume that the analyst's answer was that she, on her side, had decided to keep the baby-patient.

Thus, the analyst had received and contained the childlike parts of the patient. We notice an interesting switching of level when the patient referred to the maternal figure towards the end of the session and introduced it again in the beginning of the following session.

However, although the analyst thus fulfilled a maternal symbolic function, this response may also have had a defensive role. In the last exchanges of the session, the analyst concentrated on the patient's relationship to his mother. This may have been a defence against the patient's other reality – as an impulsive, energetic sexual man who rendered women pregnant – and who could, symbolically speaking, impregnate the analyst. Concentrating on the patient's mother may have been her way of taking on a somewhat more distant position in the face of the patient's seductiveness towards her and her own fear of colluding.

Our hypothesis is that this can happen, especially in a first interview, because what is being exchanged is not only the language of words, but also, as we pointed out above, the language of the senses. The indicators of malaise, but also of pleasure, go beyond words and enter into contact with the other person through movements and aspects of the body; like a faint blush, a stiffening of the posture, an imperceptible stammer, sweating, a smile; nuclei, threads, fragments of the unconscious polysemy that is short of representation, but can nevertheless lead to representation. The analyst's body shows itself as well, talking through shadowy, subtle, elusive and enigmatic cues, but also more open facial expressions, in feedbacks that can create a distance or on the contrary excessive closeness. It is therefore worthwhile to be aware of how much our body talks to an analysand whom we are meeting for the first time.

In this clinical case words and senses combine in an evocative way in the analytic couple, creating a movement in the patient's world.

Second interview

Dream: symbolic function and/or enactment?

Before coming to the next session, Mr. Q. sent three text messages: to check if he remembered the hour right, to check if he remembered the door code right, and to tell the analyst that he wouldn't be late.

In the second session, he left his bag in the lobby but took his coat with him. First he put it on his lap, then with some hesitation dropped it on the floor next to his armchair.

He gave the analyst half a smile and looked at her in a hopeful way. Then he said in a rather engaging and thoughtful manner: 'You know, maybe it was what you'd said about my mother, but I had a very long dream last night.'

He then told an endless, extremely detailed dream – reminiscent of a '*Tale of Scheherazade*' to use the evocative metaphor brought by a participant in the Clinical Workshop – of which we will only give a synopsis:

Mr. Q.: I am sleeping in my room at my parents' house. When I wake up in the morning all my friends are around my bed. At first, I am very happy, but then I feel very anxious, because I think my parents would not appreciate it. So I ask my friends to leave and wait for me in the garage where my cars are parked.

They leave, time passes, and I am extremely embarrassed because I can't get dressed until I find a blouse belonging to my sister, which I put on but which doesn't fit. Then I find my shirt. When at last I am about to go out, my mother grabs me by the arm and does not let me go. By the time I manage to get out, night has fallen, but my sister finds me and grabs me by the arm as well to take me home again, following my mother's orders.

I free myself and eventually reach the garage where I struggle to find the car keys. In the meanwhile, my friends are no longer there, nor is my best sports car that has been taken away by the garage hand to show it off to my friends. Then my friends and my car are there again, but in the meantime I have woken up with a feeling of anxiety and rage against the garage hand that had taken away my best car.

An.: An impressive dream. What do you think of it now when you are telling it?

Mr. Q.: Well . . . You know, as I said, my mother is very religious and very difficult sometimes. She is being especially difficult with my sister. My sister can't go out, and she can't bring friends home, and you know all this stuff about virginity, and proper behaviour, she never gets off her. I am not sure if my sister ever gets a life of her own, this poor castrated girl.

An.: You are talking of your sister, but it is you in the dream who gets out of the house very late, in the evening instead of in the morning, and feels very bad about it.

Mr. Q.: But I do get out, even if she grabbed me! I felt so proud I did! By the end, I did what I wanted. I was not like my sister.

An.: In your dream you triumphed over your mother, and now you are angry with me because I mention some anxious and hurtful moments too.

Mr. Q.: What hurtful moments?

An.: It seemed dangerous in your dream to keep your cars in the same space where your mother was.

Mr. Q.: Oh this! [He talks at length about his love for cars.] But I was anxious indeed when I couldn't find the keys, this sickening feeling when one's hands are sweaty and shaky.

After a pause, he continued: 'But my mother is very nosey. Nosey and suspicious. And she always mixes things up. I will give you an example.'

The example, which takes up the final part of the session, is long, detailed and confused. In abbreviated form, its gist is as follows:

> I have a small flat in my parents' city. My mother absolutely wanted to have my keys in order to check that nobody had stolen from the apartment. When she went there for the first time, she could not open the door. The reason she could not open it was that she had tried to open the door of the wrong flat, but afterwards she accused me of having tried to trick her by giving her the wrong set of keys.

All this was expressed with a lot of details, until their time seemed to be up. It only remained for the analyst to say: 'Unfortunately we don't have time to think of it together now. Shall we continue next time?'

Mr. Q. said 'OK', shook hands with the analyst and left. Walking out of her office, he gave her a wink.

Comment on the session

As a rule we tend to think that a patient bringing a dream, especially during the consultation stage, has good capacities for introspection and representation.

Naturally this dream, with its richness of expression, is suited to be read in all its unconscious complexity. It can be taken as the patient's way of talking freely of his mother and also, in the transference, of expressing in a rather clear way his ambivalence: whether or not to give the keys of the unconscious to the analyst; whether or not the analyst will find, or will be able to find, the psychic loci of the patient in an adequate and relevant way (the implicit assumption is that she will not); and whether or not the patient is going to use tricks of concealment and misunderstanding in order to protect himself.

In his dream, Mr. Q. was unconsciously identified with his sister. After the dream, the analyst responded to the patient's associations with a comment to this effect, but it was formulated in such a way that Mr. Q. heard it as though the analyst, like his mother, was remonstrating with him. We may surmise that he felt hurt by the analyst's remark, as if she were placing his sister and him on the same level, without taking the difference of sex into consideration.

He reacted in phallic protest, insisting that he was not at all like his sister and that, on the contrary, he overcame his mother and did what he wanted.

In response to this, the analyst offered a transference interpretation to suggest that his triumph over his mother was defensive: 'now you are angry with me because I mention some anxious and hurtful moments, too'. She answered Mr. Q.'s question, 'What hurtful moments?' with an allusion to his castration anxiety: 'It seemed dangerous in your dream to keep your cars in the same space where your mother was'.

Mr. Q. concurred that being unable to find his keys in the dream made him very anxious. He tried to justify this with a detailed story intended to demonstrate that his mother really was a very difficult person, but which can also be read as expressing his transference experience that the analyst was being too intrusive at this point and, furthermore, that she was not approaching him in a way he could be comfortable with; trying 'to open the door of the wrong flat', yet accusing him of having tried to 'trick her by giving her the wrong set of keys'.

As a result of the dream and other communications in the session, the analyst may indeed have been unconsciously identified with an intrusive maternal figure. Some colleagues in the Clinical Workshop pointed out that this long and detailed dream was the patient's attempt to create a space between him and the analyst: 'a way of making distance' and simultaneously expressing in the dream's content 'a fear of an intrusive object'. This was a very interesting comment, especially if we juxtapose it with the analyst's subjective experience that the patient was intrusive. Intrusiveness and anxiety about being intruded upon were themes that characterized the experience of both partners of the analytical couple and that created a difficult situation for the analyst.

The dream also had the appearance of a seductive bait for the analyst – 'look how much unconscious potential I am able to give you' – but above all the abundant dream material that filled much of the session seemed to be a way to keep the analyst at a distance, for fear that she could worm her way in and intrude into the dream, thus creating new psychic movements that the patient would then have to deal with.

If we put the night-time dream in sequence with the patient's story about the keys – also a sort of dream during the session – the trick seems to be not to give the analyst any chance to open up any space. The analyst is only allowed to listen to the patient's speech, but she must remain outside the door, perhaps peeping through the keyhole, as it were.

The analyst is not allowed to come in and for much of the time she does not come in; but when she does, in her first intervention after Mr. Q.'s associations to the dream, it comes forth in a way that can be experienced as intrusive and accusatory – thus doing to the patient what he, with the dream, had been doing to her. With his subsequent story about the apartment, Mr. Q. pointed out that this was what had happened.

At this juncture, after she has been backed into a corner, the analyst suddenly shuts the door, saying that there is no time left to think about it – thus again doing to the patient what he had done to her.

This development is understandable if the analyst were momentarily overwhelmed by the transference and countertransference dynamics, so that the only way in which she could save the situation was by ending the session in due time and saying that they would continue next time.

Although it *was* time to end the session, it was also as if, just before the analyst announced the end, the time for thinking had momentarily been wiped out. The sudden end of the session did not seem to be the result of an elaborated and metabolized response; it may also have been the analyst's reaction to her being invaded, or offended, by the patient's long and reproach-laden story about the keys. There was an aura of narcissistic, phallic competition to the patient's story, which undermined the analyst's attempts to introduce a more triangular, reflective perspective. Consequently, at this point the analyst's temporal function, like the psychoanalytic frame as a whole, was momentarily 'creaking' under pressure – as if there were too much weight on the floorboards of the analytic room, so to speak. It was a matter of urgency to empty the room, in obedience to an arbitrary sense of time; it was not possible at this point to plant the seeds of a more creative use of time – this prospect could only be salvaged by putting it off until another session.

Since both the triangular perspective and the sense of time are aspects of the oedipal process and the paternal function, it is striking to note how the father is missing in the session and in the dream.

Indeed, the patient's father is completely absent from the dream, as opposed to his mother and his sister, the latter intervening as the mother's emissary. There is no true masculine figure; the garage hand, who shows off the car to everyone, represents the patient's phallic position. The fact that he steals the patient's keys – the keys of power, but also of virility – suggests that the patient's phallic defence is vulnerable and breaking down. What is needed is not a narcissistic phallic defence, but a structuring paternal function.

Civitarese (2013) argues that the dream is a cognitive mental function, an alpha function tool that makes it possible to stage one's internal world. The patient opens a window into his inner world through his night-time dream and his dream–thoughts during the session. This can lead to a better knowledge of the patient (transformation in K), but it does not necessarily lead to an emotional transformation (transformation in O), that is to say, into something new and unprecedented which can occur in the encounter, and into which the analyst and the patient are mutually led by the movements of change originating from emotional turbulences.

We can assume that it was not only the dream and the in-session dream-thoughts, but also the way of telling them which functioned as a ploy or enactment used by the patient to keep at bay the world of turbulences and too close contacts. It was as if he felt the need to catch his breath and postpone to the next session the decision to continue, if ever, and how.

The analyst also felt the need to catch her breath, which she did through the abrupt closure of the session: a *conditio sine qua non* in order not to close off their dialogue once and for all, but to postpone it until a next session, as she explained it to the Clinical Workshop.

Towards the end of the discussion in the Clinical Workshop, the analyst revealed that they had three more sessions before starting a psychoanalytic psychotherapy at two sessions per week, face to face, which was later increased to three sessions a week.

This prolonged period of time was needed to create a bond, instead of a short and too turbulent time that would destroy any bond, as had up to then happened to the patient with all his women.

We can suppose that in abruptly ending the session, while at the same time offering the possibility of some more encounters before taking a decision about the frequency of the treatment, the analyst listened to her countertransference and her need to take time and to make space for an analytical link. This hypothesis would highlight the dual nature of enactment; as a failure of technique but also as an unavoidable phenomenon. The analyst listened to her inner disturbance and to the best of her abilities used it as a source of information, although she also temporarily felt overwhelmed by it.

In the Clinical Workshop, the analyst frequently underlined her experience of the patient as intrusive. When analysts describe such an experience, it may be a way of formulating their perception that their internal frame was under threat, and hence unable to hold the situation optimally. Although it is true that the patient tried to seduce the analyst, her sense that her internal frame was becoming overwhelmed may also have played a role in her need to become more distant with respect to this patient. On the other hand, despite these difficulties, she had unconsciously dealt with the situation in a way that allowed a treatment to begin.

Making space and giving time

In conclusion, this clinical material illustrates that we are dealing with a very complex mapping of the specific psychic features, not only of the patient, but also of the analyst. The analyst shows us, in a vivid way, some of her reactions that may have interfered with and disturbed the common ground shared by the couple at work, as well as how she dealt with these disturbances.

Psychoanalytic work makes a constant demand upon the analyst to differentiate between that which belongs to the analyst's psyche and that which belongs to the patient's psychic sphere. It is this effort to remain attentive to the borders (and border crossings) between two psyches that creates an analytic space for the patient, enabling a new freedom of expression and understanding. This work is constantly threatened by the inevitable and necessary tensions in the session, which tend to threaten and even disrupt boundaries. Remaining attentive to one's countertransference responses, to open maximally un-intruded time and space for the psychic life of the patient, is a never-ending task. The ability to hold and maintain this potential is very dependent on the analyst's personal psychoanalytic development, requiring constant maintenance in various forms; self-analysis, supervision, consultation with peers (and possibly further analysis). Such constant analytic self-maintenance is the analyst's central task.

The capacity to elaborate what is happening during a session therefore depends on the analyst's stewardship of their countertransference. Bollas (2012) argues that countertransference is a key element because of its implicit relationship with the 'professional autobiography of the analyst' (Ambrosiano 2005) inherent in his/her analytical identity. According to Bollas, the patient's encounter with the analyst is an encounter with analysis. More radically, Bollas writes that 'to be the analyst is to be in analysis' (2012). If this optimally desired state is true for the analyst, clearly a symmetrical situation cannot be assumed for the patient. The analyst may know that s/he and the patient are 'in analysis' from their first contact; but understandably a patient first needs to have the experience of a psychoanalytic moment or connection, in order to realize what psychoanalysis may offer. He/she may have an intuited 'unconscious knowledge of the analytical space' which leads to his/her 'unconsciously calling upon a transformative other that will relieve the self of suffering' (ibid.), but it is the psychoanalyst's task to attempt an initiation of a psychoanalytic possibility via such a transformative experience.

We think there are two interwoven, fundamental factors that may permit such a possibility: making space and giving time. This certainly happened in the clinical case the analyst presented.

Making space: In an evocative and effective way, Bolognini (2006) refers to the fact that we have to conceive of the first interview in terms of an 'aspirated vacuum'. It requires of the analyst a significant effort in maintaining a 'receptive and concave function' as against a more rejecting or defensive convex position (ibid.).

Giving time: In the interval between the first and the second session, the patient seemed able to think about the analyst's last intervention in the first session. He starts the second session saying 'maybe it was what you'd said about my mother but I had a very long dream last night'. We see here an example of a mind that can allow space to dream, perhaps born of a transformative experience, conceived during the first interview and growing during the interval.

We can suppose the patient accepted analytical treatment, after a prolonged series of consultations, because of such a transformative experience. One could think that this acceptance or consent to treatment was made at an unconscious level and not as a solely consciously based cognitive evaluation. This was acceptance based on successful transformation in a live, deepening connection between patient and analyst.

Enabling time and space for both minds, as facilitated by the analyst, allowed the analyst access to her own narrative thoughts regarding the patient – what she felt about him and what was happening in the relationship – in order to set in motion these elements of sensory experience and thinking, thus allowing movement and meaningful integration. This is a rigorous freedom; it combines creation of a secure psychoanalytic setting alongside the psychoanalyst's evenly suspended attention. This can be depicted also as including the analyst's 'progressive empathetic inner contact with the other's subjectivity' (Bolognini 2006). Empathy and triangulation can oscillate and resonate in the complex world of conscious, pre-conscious and unconscious experience.

The capacity to create such a space and rigorously maintained freedom may afford the analyst a particular gratification in observing a patient's deepening dialogue with and curiosity about the vast and unknown world of the unconscious – where suffering is frequently concealed and, although often punished, repressed or split off, pleasure often dwells as well. To reach this inner world, it is necessary to tap into an available source of 'libidinal–emotional psychoanalytic knowledge' (Racalbuto 2012) and an epistemophilic urge with which, optimally, every analyst should be equipped. Curiosity and the urge to know, however, should not be intrusive in a search for meaning at all cost. As Bollas (2012) says, 'our speech can never represent more than a fraction of the inner speech that underpins it'. This 'fraction of speech' is merely the expression of the fragment of a life built over a lifetime; consequently, it would be omnipotent and unrealistic to imagine offering complete and saturated answers in relation to a patient's request for help with problems during the first interview.

What we can do in the encounter is endeavour to create at least a possibility of passage from the external to the internal world, from everyday talk to an absolutely unique and peculiar type of psychoanalytic dialogue. This involves the creation of a psychoanalytic form of space and a time where a very unique experience of intimacy might begin to expand and evolve into new meanings for the potential analysand, and new freedom in the narration of personal history, memories, feelings, phantasies, dreams and associations. For those approaching the possibility of psychoanalytic treatment, this is often the implicitly sought alternative to remaining confined in an unthought and enacted world of (apparent) 'reality'.

10 WHERE ARE WE NOW?

Most certainly not where we thought we would be . . .

Our encounter with a large number and great variety of real first interviews was in many ways surprising. The research process also confronted us with unexpected observations. In order to make sense of our findings, we have been led to develop hypotheses about psychoanalytic work that will require further investigation.

In order to answer the questions: why are analytic couches often empty? how can we offer the valuable experience of psychoanalysis to more analytic patients? we set out to study initial interviews that resulted in the initiation of analysis with the expectation of finding identifiable, general processes – in the patient, in the analyst, in their dialogue – that could inform and perhaps guide practising analysts. As described in Chapter 3, we were interested to see:

- whether we could detect and describe any characteristic forms of conscious and/or unconscious dynamics taking place between analyst and patient in such interviews; and
- whether we could find relationships between such dynamics and the decision to begin an analysis, as well as the process of the ensuing analysis.

An a priori assumption drawn from experience and previous literature on initial interviews was that a psychoanalytic consultation would be something different from other clinical encounters, as well as from the different forms of diagnostic interviews. We formed the hypothesis that this difference must be connected to the task of giving the patient some sense of what psychoanalysis is about, and that the dialogue therefore should probably to some degree reach deeper levels of the patient's psyche. The term '*initiating psychoanalysis*' was used to underline that a process was begun, and the term '*switching the level*' to designate a component of the analyst's ability to bring communication to another level of exchange, where the analyst could help the patient look at his/her problem or life story in a novel and opening way. We looked for the specific characteristics of different kinds of interchange, and were prepared to see that this sort of interaction would produce an up-welling of affective and representational derivatives of unconscious conflicts, increasing the overall intensity of the interview, until a point was reached where the analyst might be able to pick up on something central which touched or surprised the patient.

As has been demonstrated from different perspectives through the chapters of the book, this turned out to be only one aspect of the process, and was not something that occurred in all initiations, nor all the time in interviews where 'switching the level' *did* take place. We have not seen *any* initial interviews where there was a smooth forward movement with deepening of contact from the beginning to the end. The reality of first interviews was shown to be much more chaotic, unpredictable and idiosyncratic even for interviews that resulted in analysis.

We discovered that behind these apparently disturbed and disturbing goings-on was what has become the core issue of our study: namely, that in all cases examined, the unconscious dynamics played out in the interviews were much more intense than we had expected and were powerfully present from the outset, even making a forceful appearance before the actual meeting. The patient entered with an '*unconscious storm*' of transference expectations and anxieties, in which both parties were immediately engaged. These unconscious dynamics could be 'blinding' because of their intensity, but also illuminating once it had been possible to take them in. From this perspective, the analyst's task therefore became more oriented towards finding ways *to cope with* this forceful projective activity and to *strive to* '*open psychoanalytic space*', rather than to lead the patient step by step towards unconscious material as in the idea of 'switching the level'.

We found that the patient–analyst couple found many different ways to deal with this intense transference and countertransference field. These ways could be more or less defensive, for example through denial of what seemed to be a core issue and/or idealization of psychoanalysis, and accordingly they were more or less open. The analyst's internal frame (see below) and capacity to think analytically about what was going on could be seen to help him/her to find or regain an analytic stance, but in all cases we saw various degrees of enactment, using this term in its broadest sense.

The reader, recognizing such phenomena in his or her own clinical experience, may have a feeling of, 'yes, that makes sense, but I already knew that'. However, the WPIP interest lay in studying numerous international examples of analytic work, and any confirmation of clinical experience found here results from evidence derived through the methodical scrutiny of this case material by hundreds of analysts.

The ubiquitous role of enactment was one of the lines of evidence leading the WPIP Team to discover the strength of the unconscious 'storm'. Through the investigative method it became increasingly clear that the dynamics of the initial interview resonated through all Stages of the investigative process: the case material presented by the analyst, the Workshop group's reactions, and the WPIP's group reaction and analysis of the material, were *all* shaped by the 'storm'. The unconscious interview dynamics impacted not only on patient and analyst, but also on all subsequent investigators who worked with them, and they were enacted in the presentation as well as in the groups' functioning. The successive Stages of experience and elaboration (in the analytic couple, the Clinical Workshops, and the Investigative Team) were often needed to progressively assimilate the dynamics and to understand them. This highlights the difficulty of first interviews, where the analytic couple doesn't yet have access to the later stages of elaboration made possible by the ensuing analysis.

Another, closely linked and outstanding observation was the omnipresence of poorly or differently symbolized phenomena that seemed to be at work in the communication and enactment of unconscious phantasy, such as 'scenic' communication and metaphor. Bronstein (2015) describes them as 'semiotic' communications in which primitive unconscious phantasies are 'lived out' in the analytic relationship in pre-symbolic, embodied forms. Embodied metaphor (Rizzuto 2001, 2009) is another area of current interest. We found that such phenomena could almost be seen as a third mode of thinking, interacting with primary process and secondary process thinking, or serving as a bridge between the two.

These experiences and findings have opened up new perspectives and questions about the nature of psychoanalytic work and psychoanalytic knowing. Although they arose in the context of our study of first interviews, they may have relevance for other aspects of psychoanalytic theory and practice.

The psychoanalyst's involvement in psychoanalytic work

One might wonder how the strength of the unconscious dynamics and their ability to break through could come as a surprise for psychoanalysts, whose main function is to hold on to the idea of the existence and workings of the unconscious and look out for its derivatives. But the discovery is most often a struggle. In clinical group-work among analysts, it frequently happens that analysts are uncomfortable when becoming aware of their own unconscious involvement. This is partly because it is part of our training to try to be aware of countertransference feelings and reactions, which can result in a tendency to idealize analytic neutrality and analytic functioning; and partly because it always involves a confrontation with something unknown and therefore potentially frightening.

Such factors can be expected to contribute to the analyst's countertransference anxiety about the welling-up of unconscious processes and their disturbing impact, with a fear of being overwhelmed by them, as well as of getting sucked in by them and caught up in enactments. At the same time, it is vital to emphasize that our discoveries in this study were possible exactly because we (the presenting analysts, the Clinical Workshop participants, and the WPIP Researchers) are all analysts trained not only in detecting the derivatives of the unconscious, but also in enduring not knowing. It is through this negative capability that we could ultimately become aware of and find meaning in the enacted dynamics. In this study it happened through the process of looking at both the clinical material and the Workshop proceedings from a distance, and furthermore from looking at our own group function. It is feasible to suggest that it is only as 'participant observers' that we were able to capture the deeper layers in communication, and that enactment was often a first step in metabolizing and transforming not-yet represented or representable psychic material.

Our first tendency – to be critical, thinking in terms of 'good technique' when trying to understand the presenting analysts' consultation technique in interviews that never followed a road that was smooth, progressing, deepening of meaning and contact, but were characterized by breaks, ruptures and detours – was replaced by a new understanding of what real first interviews look like, and what is at stake for analyst and patient in the attempt to open an analytic space. What we saw was psychoanalytic work far from an idealized picture of an analyst leading the patient step by step towards deeper understanding through a finely attuned analytic technique. It was more like an oscillation between understanding, misunderstanding and being at a loss; between solidity, fragmentation and retrieval of the analyst's analytic function. This could be thought of as a PS-D oscillation (Bion 1970, Britton 1998b), with rather a lot of paranoid-schizoid disintegration and relatively little depressive integration. The psychoanalyst's internal frame goes through the same oscillations; it is not a static structure but a dynamic function, which breaks down and is reconstructed. In a sense, it is created and recreated each time.

This picture of normal psychoanalytic work is not new, but very often forgotten. Mitchell (1988) refers to the following story when he describes how analysts inevitably and continually lose and regain their analytic attitude (ibid. p. 293):

> A wonderful story about the composer Stravinsky captures the importance of both dimensions of the dialectic between intent and actuality.
>
> He had written a new piece with a difficult violin passage. After it had been in rehearsal for several weeks, the solo violinist came to Stravinsky and said he was sorry, he had tried his best, the passage was too difficult; no violinist could play it. Stravinsky said, 'I understand that. What I am after is the sound of someone **trying** to play it.'
>
> (Powers 1984, p. 54)

And Mitchell continues (ibid.):

> Similarly, in characterizing the analyst's presence, two dimensions are crucial: what the analyst is trying to do and what he or she does while trying, the inevitable engagement in various configurations within the analysand's relational world. The relational conflict model places much greater importance on the content of the analyst's unintended forms of participation.

These dimensions of 'what the analyst is trying to do and what he or she does while trying' are well illustrated by the cases discussed in this book. It is worth insisting that 'the analyst's unintended forms of participation' are not only an inherent aspect of the psychoanalytic process, but also an essential source of information and understanding. One could think of them as a component of psychoanalytic work that we can be attentive to and integrate into our understanding of the process. Provided space and time are kept open for elaboration, this 'third', 'enactment' mode of thinking can interact with the 'free-associative' and 'reflective' modes, *finding* meaning in the latter, but also *giving* meaning *to* them.

As illustrated in diverse ways by the cases, 'the analyst's unintended forms of participation' can be closely linked to the analyst's personal needs, preoccupations, limitations and possibilities at the time of the interview, both conscious and unconscious. Furthermore, the analysts' involvement can be very physical in nature, eliciting their sensations and probably influencing their expressions, postures and movements. Psychoanalytic work is an embodied experience.

The analyst's 'internal frame' and the analyst's person

A closer look at our findings may help in understanding these considerations about the nature of psychoanalytic work and why we believe they may be of more general relevance for how we conceptualize the psychoanalyst's internal frame.

To some extent, but *only* to some extent, the analysts' work in the cases presented in our study seemed to be characterized by:

- maintaining a participant–observer position, in which the analyst allowed him/herself to be personally affected, but also mentally stepping to one side in order to observe and reflect on what was taking place between patient and analyst;
- tolerating anxiety and not understanding, a stance which involved trusting the interview process, as well as the analyst's spontaneous internal transformational work;
- using theory as an internal reference when needed, both to aid the analyst's elaboration of the unconscious dynamics and as a form of support to maintain his/her psychoanalytic stance, but without letting it take over; and
- intervening to further the process, both in terms of the patient's associative processes and his/her relationship to the psychoanalytic process and setting, but without intruding too much on the patient.

These qualities seemed to be more easily recognized as familiar and 'ego-syntonic' by the presenting analysts and their peers in the Clinical Workshops, as well as at first by the WPIP Investigative Team. They seemed to procure a form of analytic satisfaction, with a sense of insight into the unconscious dynamics and a feeling that it was well contained and elaborated. Conversely, when these characteristics seemed to be lacking, this could produce a sense of unease and the impression that something was being missed.

Whether or not such work led to the initiation of full psychoanalytic treatment was a more complex matter, as we saw in Chapter 7. Our tentative conclusion was that full psychoanalyses could also be started when the aforementioned characteristics were not present, although the work was then judged to be more difficult by the psychoanalytic peer groups. Conversely, work meeting these characteristics could also lead the interviewing analyst to recommend treatment modalities other than full psychoanalysis, in a psychoanalytic decision process which the peer groups experienced as satisfactory.

Moreover, other characteristics of psychoanalytic work could also be observed, both in interviews that led to full analysis and in those that had other outcomes. Usually they were present in the same interviews as the four characteristics outlined above, appearing in parallel or in alternation with them:

- The analyst could be not only *affected* internally by the unconscious dynamics, but also *effected*, in the sense of becoming involved in enactments. Sometimes the analyst became aware of these enactments during the interview and could use them to promote understanding, but at other times this was not possible. These enactments were not necessarily detrimental to the interview process.
- More generally, there could often be important aspects of the interview dynamics of which the analyst remained unaware, but without conscious discomfort, i.e. without necessarily having the sense of needing to tolerate something unknowable.
- In such situations, however, the analyst could still be seen to undertake psychoanalytic work that was not consciously thought through at the time, and so remained without conscious theoretical references, but which could nevertheless make sense as being psychoanalytically understandable by the Clinical Workshops and/or the WPIP Team.
- Some of the analysts' interventions departed from the ideal of unobtrusiveness, without necessarily being destructive for the interview process. The overall interview climate, including how such moments were dealt with, seemed to be more important.

Such observations depart from a psychoanalytic ideal, but are the result of a close study of real interviews. As described above, such forms of work could sometimes be experienced by the Clinical Workshops as problematic and accordingly criticized as un-analytic, but not always; their contribution to the interview process could also be recognized. At first the WPIP Team could feel similarly critical, but as the observations accumulated they forced us to rethink our global view of the interview process. We came to see them more as important and interesting phenomena that would merit further study.

In particular, there seem to be forms of psychoanalytic work that take place in nearly all interviews, but that do not correspond to a commonly described picture of the analyst as aware of what he or she is doing. Next to the work that becomes conscious during the interview, there also seems to be work that remains unconscious but which can nevertheless be qualified as real psychoanalytic work. Some of it seems to be more embodied than thought; or, as we have suggested, there may be embodied and enactment-based thought processes or proto-thought processes, different from the better-known primary and secondary thought processes. They might characterize any human relationship; alternatively, they might correspond to a form of implicit specialized knowledge developed by the psychoanalyst over years of experience.

We may describe this complex combination of internal processes, through which the psychoanalyst strives, consciously and unconsciously, to maintain and/or recover the psychoanalytic stance as the psychoanalyst's '*internal frame*' (Møller 2014, Reith 2012). This 'internal frame' seems to play a role in the analyst's ability to maintain what Bolognini (2006) calls the analyst's 'concave' function, an internal disposition, not only technical but also personal, which is necessary to make room for the patient and to allow meaning to emerge.

Our observations show that even during the work of mostly triangulated, creative psychoanalytic couples, the analyst's internal frame, and consequently the quality of psychoanalytic space, could be seen to be subjected to considerable tensions. Moreover, the internal work done by the analysts in our case studies was clearly not only conscious and reflective, but also unconscious, affective and sensorial. The internal frame is a living process, involving the analyst's entire person, an experience that the analyst may find difficult.

In a letter Breuer wrote to Auguste Forel answering a question about his share in *Studies on Hysteria* (Freud and Breuer 1895), he wrote:

> The main contribution that can be credited to me is that I recognized what an enormous instructive, scientifically important case chance had assigned to me for treatment, and I preserved an attentive and faithful observation and did not disturb the simple apprehension of the important facts with preconceived notions. In this way I at the time learned a great deal – much that was of scientific value, but also the important practical lesson that it is impossible for a 'general practitioner' to treat such a case without his activity and the conduct of his life thereby being completely ruined. I vowed at the time never again to subject myself to such an ordeal.
>
> (Grubrich-Simitis 1997, p. 27)

In this early description of an open, not-knowing attitude – a concave position and an attempt in the domain of negative capability – Breuer warned against doing this as just 'a general practitioner'. Seen from our present acknowledgement of what forceful dynamics a psychoanalyst in an open receptive position is engaging in, we must empathize with Breuer in his flight; he did not have the necessary psychoanalytic training to help him cope; he had had no possibility to develop the internal analytic frame that we now consider to be an integral part of analytic competence.

Psychoanalytic work as a live experience

It is not really surprising that the analyst should feel disturbed by such personal involvement, and it helps to understand unconscious resistance to analytic listening and the frequent reluctance to begin new analyses. One step towards overcoming this reluctance may be to find ways of understanding such inevitable involvement as a resource rather than an obstacle. In the course of our work, we have come to think of it as something creative and precious, which is necessary to both patient and analyst, and which contributes to psychoanalysis as a *live experience*. It is an important source of understanding, so long as it is also subjected to analytic investigation. If so, it should not be prevented, which is anyway impossible; but recognized, harnessed and channelled, for the purposes of understanding and change. We may then see it as an aspect of what is specific and precious about psychoanalysis.

In the psychoanalytic community, there can be a misunderstanding of 'neutrality' as meaning that 'the analyst is not there as a person'. This can go together with a superego defence against personal involvement, transforming the concept of neutrality into something standoffish and impersonal, rather than an unbiased interest in all aspects of the patient's personality and inner world, including how the latter *affect* and *effect* the analyst. Such superego prohibitions can contribute to undermining analysts' self-confidence when they discover that analytic work involves them as persons. Emphasizing instead the potential creativity inherent in the analyst's inner turbulence may help the analyst to feel more at ease about the challenges of beginning analyses.

From this perspective, it becomes particularly important to think about what supports or hampers the analyst in such personal work; what fosters and what threatens the analytic encounter.

The role of theory and technique

Being able to refer to a well-defined method and theory of technique is one important source of support. However, our cases show that one cannot make a complete distinction between 'person' and 'method'; the method is *embodied* in the analyst, who is personally involved in its application, and through whose presence the method is put in action. This is also how the patient experiences it; he or she encounters another person, the analyst, who has access to a theory and a technique; for the patient, the real proof of the theory and technique is how they are put into effect by the analyst. In consultation-for-referral settings (as in *any* setting), the difference between 'seduction by the person', where the patient is led to believe that only this particular analyst will be right for him/her, and 'seduction by the method', where the patient experiences a way of working that promises to be helpful (see Box 8.2 in Chapter 8), is not that in the latter, the analyst is absent as a person; it is rather that the analyst's way of working helps the patient to imagine that they could also find the same method embodied in *another* analyst.

Moreover, it would be a misunderstanding of psychoanalytic theory and technique to expect the method to protect the analyst from the inner turbulence that results from inevitable personal involvement. The real situation is more the other way around: it is the psychoanalytic method that produces disturbance in the analyst, and this is precisely what allows the method to work. It puts the analyst into contact with the patient as a real person on various conscious and unconscious levels, rather than with a theoretical 'case'. The aim of psychoanalytic theory and technique is rather to help the analyst to remain receptive to a real person, to recognize the resulting turbulence and to use it thoughtfully and creatively, within the psychoanalytic frame, and in the interests of the patient.

This is not necessarily only disturbing. Real pleasure can also be part of the experience and was conveyed by many of the case presenters during the Workshop discussions. Libidinal investment is an aspect of all object relationships – meaning that pleasure is involved as much as pain. This is also what the French concept of 'seduction' implies, in the life-sustaining sense of the term (see Box 8.2). The pleasure of the uniquely profound encounter with another person made possible by psychoanalysis, and the pleasure of working well with the psychoanalytic method, are inseparable and necessary aspects of psychoanalytic work.

Thus, we could describe psychoanalysis as an 'enlivening' experience as much as a 'live' one, for both the patient and the analyst. Thomas Ogden, in his book on *Reverie and Interpretation: Sensing Something Human* (Ogden 1997), describes psychoanalysis as an enlivening experience, as does Fred Busch in his paper 'Our Vital Profession' (Busch 2015). In fact, strict application of the psychoanalytic frame serves to enhance this vital aspect of psychoanalysis, not to diminish it. If 'objective' is taken to mean eliminating personal involvement through standardized procedures, then this is not the mode of action of psychoanalysis.

Triangulation and trust, from external to internal

Subjective involvement is essential in psychoanalysis, and 'objectivity' is achieved through triangulation, i.e. through a third-person perspective on one's first-person experience. This perspective opens a mental space in which it is possible to stay in touch with the immediacy of subjective experience, but to put it in context, with the extra degree of freedom needed to examine it and to symbolize it.

Triangulation for the analyst, however, cannot rely only on theory as a virtual third, however important it may be (Birksted-Breen 2008, Tuckett 2011), nor on the analytic setting to shore up the analyst's analytic stance. Although the analyst may find support in psychoanalysis as a good internal object (Wille 2008, 2012), given that analytic work can be disturbing before it becomes creative, it can also become a hated, and so temporarily persecuting, internal object. This is where other analysts can help as a third to restore trust in analysis (ibid.).

Consultation with other analysts, as for example in peer group consultation, can be a way to help to turn the live experience into a fruitful one. This view is based not only on what some of our presenting analysts said about their work, but also on our observation of the exploratory processes in the Clinical Workshops and the WPIP Team (described in Chapters 3 and 4). Other analysts can function as a containing and transforming third for the analyst. Psychoanalysts know from experience that this is how supervision and inter-vision work; based on our experiences with our study, one might describe them as a spontaneous form of psychoanalytic 'research', with beneficial effects. Rather than seeing psychoanalysis as something well-established which the analyst can hold on to by him/herself, one might think of it as a never-ending quest, which is best carried out with the help of colleagues.

Perspectives on psychoanalytic knowledge and research

These considerations force us to think about what we mean by psychoanalytic 'knowledge' and psychoanalytic 'research'.

There is a general theme running throughout our work and findings, which is that both the process of initiating psychoanalysis and our research process have to do with real relationships. It is within relationships that psychoanalytic knowledge arises – be it in the psychoanalytic setting proper or in consultation with colleagues. The same may be true for at least some forms of psychoanalytic research.

At the beginning of our study, we accepted as a working hypothesis that the presenting analyst possessed implicit knowledge about the unconscious dynamics of the interview, and that the task of the Clinical Workshops would be to help him/her to bring it out and render it explicit. Our actual findings, however, can also be taken to support a different view. The analysts whose work we studied could be seen to have been involved in what were to them *partially enigmatic experiences* with a patient. They had attempted to deal with this enigma as well as they could during the interviews, and in some ways were *still* dealing with it afterwards, during the presentation to the Clinical Workshop. When, in the Workshop, it was possible to look at how the analyst worked with the experience, including through examination of the analyst's implicit theories, this was not an application in the Workshop of a pre-existing body of knowledge in the usual sense of the term. It would be more exact to say that knowledge *arose* in the analyst through the very process of working with the patient, and later on through the process of presenting to the Workshop. In fact, it would be surprising if the analyst were able to understand and 'know' it all in the first interview. Coming to grips with unconscious dynamics takes time – the duration of the analysis and beyond.

Similarly, the investigative group work observed in the Clinical Workshops and the WPIP Team is compatible with a view of psychoanalytic knowing as a *process*; as the effect of the impact on the group of something enigmatic in the material. The group's inter-subjective exploration of the participants' subjective responses to the material, with associative chains coalescing in a 'selected fact' which helps to make sense of the enigma, suggest a process in which the group and its participants *are transformed by* the material as much as they transform it. This is an *experience* of knowledge as it arises, not the application of a defined body of knowledge to uncover and circumscribe ever more precisely some pre-existing state of affairs.

From this perspective, it could be misleading to think, as we have been tempted to do when studying some cases, that patient and analyst were to some extent unconsciously 'avoiding' the full impact of the 'storm'. It is probably more precise to say that they were as yet unable to come to grips with it in a way that could make sense to them. To think in terms of avoidance suggests organized defences against a perceived threat. This might sometimes be the case, especially in the sense of character defences that both patient and analyst can fall back on in their encounter with anything that is new and unfamiliar. But there may also be situations in which organized reactions are not yet a possibility, because the psyche doesn't yet 'know' what it is being required to deal with, so that intra- and inter-psychic processing is needed as a prerequisite to unconscious perception and defence. The analyst is confronted with raw data, such as beta elements, which cannot be contained and transformed all at once; it takes time to process and metabolize them into something understandable.

The two aspects – defences against something new and finding ways to process it – can coexist. Thus, our general observation that a mixture of elaboration, enactment and defence were present in all cases, could be completed by stating that in all cases we observed a mixture of elaboration, defence and enactment, *together with, and in the global context of, the analytic couple's striving to find a way to take in and process the dynamics of the meeting.*

In other words, whether in the psychoanalytic encounter or in psychoanalytic research, it may be mistaken to think in terms of our finding access to, and accumulating knowledge about, a pre-set unconscious reality. Instead, it may be more exact to say that what we *can* be certain of is that there *is* a dynamic reality, which we don't have voluntary access to, but which most definitely *has access to us*. If so, the best we can hope to do is to try to receive it and understand it as well as we can by living within it psychoanalytically. In other words, it is *experience-embedded* knowledge.

We described in Chapter 4 how the group investigative processes seemed similar in some respects to the mental work required of the interviewing psychoanalyst. In particular, and as we said in the introduction to this chapter, tolerating not knowing in order to let understanding emerge seemed to be as important an ability in the investigative group process as in the interview process. The same is true, of course, in all research. We might add that it is likely to be an important capacity to maintain in our psychoanalytic culture as a whole. 'Don't disturb my way of experiencing and perceiving the world!' is a tempting retreat, and something that can lie behind the analyst's reluctance to do analysis (Parsons 2006), and, parallel to this, his/her reluctance to conduct *research* on analysis. Accepting and understanding such phenomena, and their relationship to psychoanalytic knowing as a live process, may help to enrich our perspectives on research in psychoanalysis.

To whom, then, should we recommend analysis?

In this study we have found no demonstrable straightforward relationship between the kind of meeting and the subsequent outcome. Concerning the characteristics of the patient, this is in accordance with now well-established research findings that there are no identifiable patient characteristics pointing towards analysis (Caligor et al. 2009). Concerning the dynamics of the interviews, we have, contrary to our expectations, not found specific indicators either as to what kind of specific dynamics lead to initiation of psychoanalysis.

What we have seen instead is that beginnings are highly individual and in a way idiosyncratic to both participants. Each beginning is a creation of each analytic couple. Only one factor seems to stand out: that is the importance of the analyst's ability to maintain his/her analytic functioning and striving to open psychoanalytic space. In practice, however, this is done in a variety of ways, depending on the analyst, the patient and the dynamics that arise between them.

We therefore suggest that recommendation for psychoanalysis should be thought of in terms of a specific, creative, but unpredictable match between patient, analyst and setting, while insisting that this kind of transformational process has value in its own right (Kantrowitz 2002). The dynamics leading to this match are so individual that it is not surprising that they can't be captured by standardized methods.

This corresponds to what Rothstein (1998a) and Levine (2010) called 'creating patients instead of finding patients' (Levine 2010), by which they meant that it is the analyst's task to find a way to make analysis accessible to a patient for whom this could be the treatment of choice. It also corresponds to what Crick (2014) refers to as initiating an analytic process instead of selecting patients. The culture of diagnosing, selecting and excluding can be understood as a historical detour (presumably necessary), but we may now be led back to something rather similar to Freud's recommendation of 'trial analysis' as the only basis for recommending analysis (Freud 1913). By this we mean that what is needed, in a consultation that can lead to recommendation of analysis, is to start an analytic dialogue as a form of trial analysis. The interviewing analyst is thus functioning as psychoanalyst, although the consultation is not an analytic session in an ongoing analysis. The way the analyst listens and metabolizes the experience in a few consultations can be essential. This kind of listening involves non-focused, open receptivity and an expectation that new meaning can arise and that unconscious messages under the manifest material can eventually be heard. It takes a psychoanalytic presence to initiate psychoanalysis.

The possibility of this kind of psychoanalytic presence, creating an analytic dialogue, is not exclusively determined by patient factors related to an assessment of analyzability or other aspects of the patient's psychopathological structure. The most important precondition for the initiation of analysis is whether an analyst representing analytic functioning is available; an analyst who is safe and competent enough to embark on the project with individual patients and who is able to engage the patient in analytic work as of the first contact.

Psychoanalysis is thus a highly adaptable approach which transcends the different psychopathological syndromes. Seen from this perspective, it might be the treatment of choice in many more instances than usually thought, if – it must be stressed – analysis is what both patient and analyst find relevant and beneficial. This line of thought is quite different from approaches designed to provide specific treatments for specific symptoms. Psychoanalysis is perhaps best understood as an individualized treatment offer that provides a valuable alternative to shorter, more focused therapy forms. Because of its highly individualized approach to treatment and to treatment indication, it is a potential treatment for a very broad group of psychic disturbances. This leads us to argue for the necessity to hold on to the possibility of psychoanalysis. The availability of analysts in the treatment culture is a necessary competence to keep alive, which can help to secure an individualized evaluation and indication process and sometimes initiate the profound developmental process which psychoanalysis allows.

APPENDIX 1
Facts and Figures

The 28 cases, which are the source of the ideas developed in this book, are a subset of a total of 38 cases of first interviews studied by the WPIP over the course of its activity. Of the 38 cases, three were used to test and refine the methods for Phase 1 of the study, while five were used for this purpose in Phase 2. Two of the remaining 30 Workshop cases intended for the study proper had to be rejected, one in each Phase, because it turned out that they did not meet the inclusion criteria (one was seen when the analyst was still unqualified and the other concerned the first sessions of an analysis that had already been decided).

Seven more Workshops were held for their experiential value as a public service at conferences, but were not planned to be included in the complete study procedure because of the WPIP Team's limited capacities. Our informal experiences with these Workshops may have had indirect effects, influencing and/or reinforcing our global impression of initial interviews. Counting these, the total number of cases examined would amount to 45.

Of the 28 cases that we were able to examine in detail, nine were from 'consultation for referral' settings and 19 from 'private' settings as defined above. Although we were of course aware of the differing theoretical and technical approaches to consultation, as well as their adaptation to the patient's needs (Reith et al. 2012), we knew that the limited number but great variety of cases would make it difficult to discern more than broad patterns relevant to our overall study, and that it would be difficult to describe very clear differences in terms of interview settings and outcome. We believe that there are some clear differences between the processes arising in the two kinds of settings, mainly related to the impact of their frame, but that the similarities in terms of fundamental dynamics are more significant: this is examined in Chapter 8.

The outcomes of the 28 cases in terms of treatment choice were: 19 psychoanalyses (three to five sessions per week on the couch); eight psychoanalytic psychotherapies (one to three sessions per week face to face, and one case of two weekly sessions on the couch); and one other psychoanalytic treatment (psychoanalytic psychodrama). The later evolution of the psychoanalyses ranged from long treatments (most cases) to an interruption after six months, with processes of varying difficulty.

Here, too, the design of our study, together with the small number and great variety of cases, did not permit any firm observations or conclusions about possible relationships between the kinds of psychoanalytic process that develop in first interviews and their outcome in terms of treatment choice and later evolution of the treatment. On the basis of what we have, our tentative conclusion is that there are no discernible relationships between the kind of process and the treatment choice. We discuss this in Chapters 3 and 7.

All 28 analysts whose work is represented in this book were experienced, qualified IPA psychoanalysts, seven men and 21 women. The 28 patients included 12 men and 16 women; six patients were under 30-years-old; fifteen were aged 30–39; and seven were 40-years-old and over.

APPENDIX 2
Explicit group procedures

In addition to those described in Chapter 3, our prescribed group procedures for the Clinical Workshops included the following:

1. Before the Workshops, the participating analysts received an introductory document, which they were asked to read. This described the aims and methods of the study, explained the Workshop procedures and introduced the pre-determined 'discussion questions' (see point 5 below).
2. The moderator introduced each Workshop with a summary of the aims and procedures, insisting on confidentiality and including an explicit reminder that the purpose was to undertake psychoanalytic exploration, not supervision.
3. As part of these instructions, Workshop participants were asked to link their contributions (observations, personal impressions, associations, reflections, hypotheses, questions to the presenting analyst, and answers to the discussion questions) to specific illustrative passages in the written material, and to check back to these if relevant in the course of the ensuing discussion.
4. In contrast to some psychoanalytic group procedures, we allowed the participants to actively exchange with one another and with the presenting analyst. We wanted to enable them to respond freely to each other's contributions, for example by bringing up similar or different associations to the same sequence in the material. Questions to the presenting analyst were permitted, for example to clarify a meaning or to ask about conscious countertransference responses.
5. During the second session, the Workshops were asked to respond to a short set of specific, pre-determined 'discussion questions' as part of their task. These were designed to stimulate their reflection on the dynamics in the material and on their own understanding of it. Devising and adapting these 'discussion questions' was an important part of the WPIP's task, as we describe in Appendix 3.

The moderator's tasks also included:

1. promoting a free flow of discussion, encouraging people to engage with each other and not only with the presenting analyst and moderator, and ensuring that all participants have an opportunity to speak;
2. asking participants to clarify difficult-to-understand statements, where needed;
3. when appropriate, pointing to emergent themes in the discussion or, on the contrary, aspects of the case material that the group might be avoiding.

All these procedures were applied analogically to the WPIP's own investigative meetings on the cases.

The reasons behind our choice of procedures were as follows:

- As in all working party approaches, we wanted to provide a containing environment that could help to minimise the obstructive or destructive group dynamics that are prone to appear in situations where clinical material is discussed. We chose a minimally research-oriented environment for this, rather than a purely group-associative environment.
- We sought to promote a critical investigative spirit. Some form of frame was required to remind the working group to look back on itself, to consider its work, to examine its prejudices and to ensure that it was really in contact with the object of investigation. Asking the groups to refer to actual instances in the material and to answer some pre-set discussion questions was thought to be one way of carrying out these explorations in an investigative spirit and not in a 'supervising' one.
- We expected the presenting analysts to have implicit knowledge about the interview dynamics, which could be brought out and rendered more explicit by the peer-group work if the groups could help the presenters to become aware of it, express it and find meaning for it.
- We also hoped that such exchanges would stimulate both the participants and the presenting analyst to reflect upon their personal reading of the material and perhaps to become aware of how this was influenced by explicit or implicit theoretical preferences. We were particularly interested to see how the analyst's implicit theories (Sandler 1983) might influence the interview process, and we thought that reflective discussion might help to highlight some of these.
- From a research point of view, we needed some minimum structure to allow us to compare the findings across the many different cases explored by the different Workshop groups. Without some minimally structured way to record the findings, comparison between cases would

be nearly impossible. At the same time, the Workshop procedures needed to be flexible enough to promote psychoanalytically meaningful work by each freshly composed Workshop on each unique case. We hoped that the Workshop answers to the 'discussion questions' would be one way of bringing together and recording the results of the groups' more primary process work and so would provide one preliminary basis for comparison.

- We also hoped that asking the participants to refer to specific instances in the material would help us to understand more precisely, during our later data analysis, what it was that they were responding to.

APPENDIX 3

Devising, testing and applying the discussion questions

Realizing that we were introducing novel procedures, we began by testing them in our first three Trial WPIP Workshops held at the EPF conference in 2005. We asked the Trial Workshops to use a first, tentative set of discussion questions, which we had developed on the basis of our preliminary hypotheses about 'switching the level', as described in Chapter 3. The Workshops were followed by a plenary panel, in which we hoped to get instructive feedback from the participants.

The questions were:

Trial Phase 1 questions

1. How do patient and analyst work together to reflect together about the patient?
2. How do patient and analyst work together to increase the overall intensity of the interview?
3. How do patient and analyst arrive together at a meaningful common formulation?
4. How do patient and analyst reach a novel perspective on what seems to be the problem?
5. How do patient and analyst relate the findings of the interview to the patient's expectations about analysis?

The hoped-for recursive process was successful, in that the feedback demonstrated that the questions were too oriented towards one specific hypothesis, and therefore inadequate to describe much of the interview material. They were also too cognitive and behavioural, so that the Workshop participants felt that they couldn't use them psychoanalytically.

Their suggestions, together with our re-examination of the Trial cases and the Workshop proceedings in the WPIP Team, allowed us to formulate a new set of four questions, which we hoped would be pointed enough to stimulate exploration of the interview material and yet open enough to allow the Workshops the necessary leeway to describe whatever struck them from their point of view as psychoanalysts:

Phase 1 discussion questions

1. What kind of meeting took place between the patient and the analyst in these interviews?
2. What is there in this material that indicates to the interviewing analyst that this patient would benefit from psychoanalysis?
3. What does this material indicate about how this particular analyst works with this particular patient to make the project of an analysis possible?
4. What do we find in this material that gives an indication as to what leads this patient to want to begin an analysis after this interview?

Although these questions may seem simple, they proved very effective in helping the Workshops to examine the interview material. They were applied successfully in the 15 Phase 1 Workshops held at the EPF conferences in 2006 and 2007 as well as at the IPA conference in 2007.

It is worth noting that although these new questions did not give up the hypothesis of 'switching the level', they no longer promoted it as a theme for the Workshops to concentrate on. Instead, the greater freedom to explore the material led the Workshops to describe a wider range of phenomena as relevant to the interview dynamics. This, in turn, meant that the WPIP Team were required to do more work to detect the common denominators behind these phenomena. The results were the concepts of the unconscious 'storm', 'weathering the storm' and 'opening analytic space'.

When we introduced Phase 2 of the study, in which the Workshops and WPIP Team did not have sure knowledge of the outcome of the interview before they had finished exploring them (see Chapter 3), we needed yet more open questions, which were not based on the hypothesis that the interviews would lead to psychoanalysis. At first, we did not give enough thought to how we wanted to formulate our discussion questions for this new phase, anticipating that basically the same questions as those deployed for Phase 1 would do the job. We thus came up with a cumbersome adaptation of our Phase 1 questions for the Trial Phase 2 Workshops in 2008:

Trial Phase 2 questions

A. Your prediction:

What do you think that this patient and/or this interviewing analyst decided that it would be worthwhile for the patient to do, as a result of this (these) preliminary interview(s)? What do you think lies behind their decision(s), and how can you justify this on the basis of what you can see in the interview dynamics?

B. Your supporting observations:

1. What kind of meeting took place between the patient and the analyst in these interviews?
2. What is there in this material that indicates to the interviewing analyst that this patient would benefit from psychoanalysis, or from some other kind of treatment, or no treatment at all?
3. What does this material indicate about how this particular analyst works with this particular patient to make possible the treatment project that seems most likely to be beneficial for the patient, be it an analysis, or another kind of treatment, or no treatment at all?
4. What do we find in this material that gives an indication as to what leads this patient to want to begin an analysis, or another kind of treatment, or no treatment at all, after this interview?

In retrospect, it should have been obvious that these questions wouldn't work: they were much too complex and ambiguous, and the Workshops didn't like them. The Workshops also seemed disorganised, unable to get a handle on the material, which could be due to their confrontation with a new kind of material with uncertain outcomes, but which could also be a result of the maladapted discussion questions.

Work by the WPIP Team on the case material and Workshop proceedings of the five Phase 2 Trial cases allowed us to develop a much better set of Phase 2 discussion questions:

Phase 2 discussion questions

1. What are the central unconscious dynamics at work in this encounter?
2. How do we see the analyst working with these dynamics?
3. How do we see the patient responding to how the analyst works?
4. What will be the outcome of this process?

These apparently (and even deceptively) simple questions were applied successfully in the 15 Phase 2 Workshops held in 2009 to 2012. Although they still left much freedom, they were slightly more oriented than the Phase 1 questions, asking the investigators to concentrate on the unconscious interview dynamics and on how the analyst worked with them; themes that were central to the WPIP's preoccupations by this time. As a result, the responses helped to refine our thinking on these issues. This work also led to the tentative conclusion that there are no clear differences in the unconscious dynamics between interviews leading to psychoanalysis or not (see Chapters 3 and 7).

REFERENCES

Ambrosiano, L. (2005). The Analyst: His Professional Novel. *International Journal of Psychoanalysis 86*: 1611–1626.

Anzieu, D. (1999). *Le groupe et l'inconscient: l'imaginaire groupal*, Third edition. Paris: Dunod.

Argelander, H. (1970). The Scenic Function of the Ego and Its Role in Symptom and Character Formation. *International Journal of Psychoanalysis 94*: 337–354, 2013. [Original German: Die szenische Funktion des Ichs und ihr Anteil an des Symptom - und Charakterbildung. *Psyche – Z Psychoanal 21*: 325–345.]

Argelander, H. (1978). The psychoanalytic initial interview and its method. A postscript to Freud's case 'Katharina'. In: B. Reith, S. Lagerlöf, P. Crick, M. Møller, E. Skale (Eds.) *Initiating Psychoanalysis: Perspectives*, The New Library of Psychoanalysis Teaching Series (pp. 26–34). London: Routledge, 2012. [Original German: Das psychoanalytische Erstinterview und seine Methode. Ein Nachtrag zu Freud's Fall 'Katharina'. *Psyche 32*: 1089–1098.]

Bachrach, H.M., & Leaff, L.A. (1978). 'Analyzability': A Systematic Review of the Clinical and Quantitative Literature. *Journal of the American Psychoanalytic Association 26*: 881–920.

Bachrach, H.M., Galatzer-Levy, R., Skolnikoff, A. (1991). On the Efficacy of Psychoanalysis. *Journal of the American Psychoanalytic Association 39*: 871–916.

Baldacci, J.L., & Bouchard, C. (2012). The analytic encounter: the historical and process-oriented perspective. In: B. Reith, S. Lagerlöf, P. Crick, M. Møller, E. Skale (Eds.) *Initiating Psychoanalysis: Perspectives*, The New Library of Psychoanalysis Teaching Series (pp. 108–119). London: Routledge, 2012.

Baranger, M., & Baranger, W. (2008). The Analytic Situation as a Dynamic Field. *International Journal of Psychoanalysis 89*: 795–826.

Basile, R., Birksted Breen, D., Bonard, O., Denis, P., Diercks, M., Ferro, A., Hebbrecht, M., Hinze, E., Jackson, D.J., Mariotti, P., Mauss Hanke, A., Tuckett, D. (2010). How Do Psychoanalysts Work? The Work of the EPF Working Party on Comparative Clinical Methods 2003–2009. *Psychoanalysis in Europe: Bulletin of the European Psychoanalytical Federation 64 (Supplement)*: 5–32.

Berger, B., & Newman, S. (2012). *Money Talks in Therapy, Society, and Life*. New York: Routledge.

Bernardi, R. (2003). What kind of evidence makes the analyst change his or her theoretical and technical ideas? In: M. Leuzinger-Bohleber, A.U. Dreher, J. Canestri (Eds.) *Pluralism and Unity? Methods of Research in Psychoanalysis* (pp. 125–136). London: International Psychoanalytic Association.

Bion, W.R. (1957). Differentiation of the psychotic from the non-psychotic personalities. In: *Second Thoughts*. London: Karnac, 1967.

Bion, W.R. (1959). Attacks on linking. In: *Second Thoughts*. London: Karnac, 1967.

Bion, W.R. (1961). *Experiences in Groups*. London: Tavistock.
Bion, W.R. (1962). *Learning from Experience*. London: Karnac.
Bion, W.R. (1965). *Transformations*. London: Karnac.
Bion, W.R. (1967). *Second Thoughts*. London: Karnac.
Bion, W.R. (1970). *Attention and Interpretation*. London: Tavistock.
Bion, W.R. (1979). Making the best of a bad job. In: W.R. Bion, F. Bion (Eds.) *Clinical Seminars and Four Papers* (pp. 247–257). Abingdon, UK: Fleetwood Press, 1987.
Bion, W.R. (1997). *Taming Wild Thoughts*. London: Karnac.
Birksted-Breen, D. (1996). Phallus, Penis and Mental Space. *International Journal of Psychoanalysis 61*: 39–52.
Birksted-Breen, D. (2008). Introductory foreword. In: D. Tuckett, R. Basile, D. Birksted-Breen, T. Böhm, P. Denis, A. Ferro, H. Hinz, A. Jemstedt, P. Mariotti, J. Schubert (Eds.) *Psychoanalysis Comparable and Incomparable. The Evolution of a Method to Describe and Compare Psychoanalytic Approaches*. The New Library of Psychoanalysis. London: Routledge, 2008.
Birksted-Breen, D. (2016). *The Work of Psychoanalysis: Sexuality, Time and the Psychoanalytic Mind*. The New Library of Psychoanalysis. London: Routledge.
Boesky, D. (1982). Acting Out: A Reconsideration of the Concept. *International Journal of Psychoanalysis 63*: 39–55.
Bohleber, W., Fonagy, P., Jeménez, J.P., Scarfone, D., Varvin, S., Zysman, S. (2013). Towards a Better Use of Psychoanalytic Concepts: A Model Illustrated Using the Concept of Enactment. *International Journal of Psychoanalysis 94*: 501–530.
Bollas, C. (1979). The Transformational Object. *International Journal of Psychoanalysis 60*: 97–107.
Bollas, C. (1987). *The Shadow of the Object: Psychoanalysis of the Unthought Known*. London: Free Association Books.
Bollas, C. (2012). The Psychoanalytic Passage. *Psychoanalysis in Europe Bulletin 66*: 75–85.
Bolognini, S. (2006). The Profession of Ferryman. *International Journal of Psychoanalysis*, *87*: 25–42. Reprinted in: B. Reith, S. Lagerlöf, P. Crick, M. Møller, E. Skale (Eds.) *Initiating Psychoanalysis: Perspectives*, The New Library of Psychoanalysis Teaching Series (pp. 310–327). London: Routledge, 2012.
Bolognini, S. (2011). *Secret Passages: The Theory and Technique of Interpsychic Relations*. The New Library of Psychoanalysis. London: Routledge.
Botella, C., & Botella, S. (2001). De la recherche en psychanalyse. *Revue Française Psychanalyse 65 (Hors Série)*: 355–372.
Bouhsira, J. (2013). La consultation au Centre de consultation et de traitement psychanalytique. Aperçu historique in *La consultation psychanalytique* (pp. 89–105). Paris: Presses Universitaires de France.
Britton, R. (1989). The missing link: parental sexuality in the Oedipus complex. In: R. Britton, M. Feldman, E. O'Shaughnessy (Eds.) *The Oedipus Complex Today* (pp. 83–101). London: Karnac.
Britton, R. (1998a). Subjectivity, objectivity and triangular space. In: R. Britton (Ed.) *Belief and Imagination: Explorations in Psychoanalysis* (pp. 41–58). London: Routledge.
Britton, R. (1998b). Before and after the depressive position: Ps(n)→D(n)→Ps(n+1). In: R. Britton (Ed.) *Belief and Imagination: Explorations in Psychoanalysis* (pp. 69–81). London: Routledge.
Britton, R. (1999). Getting in on the Act: The Hysterical Solution. *International Journal of Psychoanalysis 80 (1)*: 1–14.
Britton, R. (2003). Narcissistic problems in sharing space. In: R. Britton (Ed.) *Sex, Death and the Superego: Experiences in Psychoanalysis* (pp. 165–178). London: Karnac.

Britton, R., & Steiner, J. (1994). Interpretation: Selected Fact or Overvalued Idea? *International Journal of Psychoanalysis 75*: 1069–1078.
Bronstein, C. (2015). Finding Unconscious Phantasy in the Session: Recognizing Form. *International Journal of Psychoanalysis 96*: 925–944.
Brown, G.W. (1973). Some Thoughts on Grounded Theory. *Sociology 7/1*: 1–16.
Bryant, A., & Charmaz, K. (2007). Grounded theory in historical perspective: an epistemological account. In: A. Bryant, K. Charmaz (Eds.) *The Sage Handbook of Grounded Theory* (pp. 31–57). London: Sage.
Busch, F. (2015). Our Vital Profession. *International Journal of Psychoanalysis 96*: 553–568.
Caligor, E., Stern, B.L., Hamilton, M., MacCormack, V., Winiger, L., Sneed, J., Roose, S.P. (2009). Why We Recommend Analytic Treatment for Some Patients and not for Others. *Journal of the American Psychoanalytic Association 57*: 677–694.
Campbell, D. (2015). Interpretation and the Development of the Patient's Self-Analysis. Paper given at the Interpretation Today Conference, UCL, London, December 5, 2015.
Caper, R. (1997). A Mind of One's Own. *International Journal of Psychoanalysis 78*: 265–278.
Cartwright, D. (2010). *Containing States of Mind. Exploring Bion's 'Container Model' in Psychoanalytic Psychotherapy*. London: Routledge.
Charmaz, K. (2006). *Constructing Grounded Theory: A Practical Guide through Qualitative Analysis*. London: Sage.
Charmaz, K., & Bryant, A. (2011). Grounded theory and credibility. In: D. Silverman (Ed.) *Qualitative Research: Issues of Theory, Methods and Practice*, Third edition (pp. 291–309). London: Sage.
Civitarese, G. (Ed.) (2013). *Il sogno necessario*. Milano: Franco Angeli.
Crick, P. (2013). Thinking and Judgement in Psychoanalytic Assessment and Consultation. *Psychoanalytic Psychotherapy 27*: 199–214.
Crick, P. (2014). Selecting a Patient or Initiating a Psychoanalytic Process. *International Journal of Psychoanalysis 95*: 465–484.
Dantlgraber, J. (1982). Observations on the subjective indication for psychoanalysis. In: B. Reith, S. Lagerlöf, P. Crick, M. Møller, E. Skale (Eds.) *Initiating Psychoanalysis: Perspectives*, The New Library of Psychoanalysis Teaching Series (pp. 194–222). London: Routledge, 2012. [Original German: Bemerkungen zur subjektiven Indikation für Psychoanalyse. *Psyche 36*: 193–225.]
Danto, E.A. (2005). *Freud's Free Clinics: Psychoanalysis and Social Justice, 1918–1938*. New York: Columbia University Press.
Devereux, G. (1967). *From Anxiety to Method in the Behavioural Sciences*. The Hague: Mouton.
Diercks, C. (2002). The Vienna Psychoanalytic Polyclinic ('Ambulatorium'). *Psychoanalysis and History 4*: 67–84.
Doehrman, M. (1976). Parallel Processes in Supervision and in Psychotherapy. *Bulletin Menninger Clinic 40*: 9–104.
Donnet, J.L. (1995). *Le divan bien tempéré*. Paris: Presses Universitaires de France.
Donnet, J.L. (2005). *La situation analysante*. Paris: Presses Universitaires de France.
Donnet, J.L. (2013). La rencontre consultative. In: *La consultation psychanalytique* (pp. 29–49). Paris: Presses Universitaires de France.
Donnet J.L., & M'Uzan, M. de. (1998). The analytical encounter. In: B. Reith, S. Lagerlöf, P. Crick, M. Møller, E. Skale (Eds.) *Initiating Psychoanalysis: Perspectives*, The New Library of Psychoanalysis Teaching Series (pp. 123–145). London: Routledge, 2012. [Original French: La rencontre analytique. *Revue Française de Psychanalyse 62*: 189–208.]
Ehrlich, L.T. (2004). The Analyst's Reluctance to Begin a New Analysis. *Journal of the American Psychoanalytic Association, 52*: 1075–1093. Reprinted in: B. Reith, S. Lagerlöf, P. Crick, M. Møller, E. Skale (Eds.) *Initiating Psychoanalysis: Perspectives*, The New Library of Psychoanalysis Teaching Series (pp. 330–344). London: Routledge, 2012.

Ehrlich, L.T. (2013). Analysis Begins in the Analyst's Mind: Conceptual and Technical Considerations on Recommending Analysis. *Journal of the American Psychoanalytic Association 61*: 107.

Elzer, M., & Gerlach. A. (Eds.) (2014). *Psychoanalytic Psychotherapy: A Handbook*. London: Karnac.

Emde, R.N. (1990). Mobilizing Fundamental Modes of Development: Empathic Availability and Therapeutic Action. *Journal of the American Psychoanalytic Association 38*: 881–913.

Enckell, H. (2010). Reflections in Psychoanalysis: On Symbols and Metaphors. *International Journal of Psychoanalysis 91*: 1093–1114.

Erlich-Ginor, M. (2013). The Working Party on Education. Psychoanalysis in Europe. *Bulletin of the European Psychoanalytical Federation 64 (Supplement)*: 33–56.

Faimberg, H. (1996). Listening to Listening. *International Journal of Psychoanalysis 77*: 667–677.

Faimberg, H. (2005). *The Telescoping of Generations: Listening to the Narcissistic Links between Generations*. The New Library of Psychoanalysis. London: Routledge.

Fairbairn, W.R.D. (1958). On the Nature and Aim of Psychoanalytic Treatment. *International Journal of Psychoanalysis 39 (5)*: 374–385.

Ferro, A. (2012). Consultation, reverie and story-telling. In: B. Reith, S. Lagerlöf, P. Crick, M. Møller, E. Skale (Eds.) *Initiating Psychoanalysis: Perspectives*, The New Library of Psychoanalysis Teaching Series (pp. 261–271). London: Routledge, 2012.

Finch, H., Lewis, J., Turley, C. (2014). Focus Groups. In: J. Ritchie, J. Lewis, C. McNaughton Nicholls, R. Ormston (Eds.) *Qualitative Research Practice: A Guide for Social Science Students and Researchers*, Second edition (pp. 211–242). London: Sage.

Freud, S. (1893). Katharina. In: *Studies on Hysteria, Part II, Case Histories, S.E. 2*: 125–134. [Reprinted in: B. Reith, S. Lagerlöf, P. Crick, M. Møller, E. Skale (Eds.) *Initiating Psychoanalysis: Perspectives*, The New Library of Psychoanalysis Teaching Series (pp. 16–23). London: Routledge, 2012.]

Freud, S. (1912). Recommendations to Physicians Practising Psycho-Analysis. *S.E. 12*: 109–120.

Freud, S. (1913). On Beginning the Treatment (Further Recommendations in the Technique of Psychoanalysis I). *S.E. 12*: 121–144.

Freud, S. (1914). Remembering, Repeating and Working-Through. *S.E. 12*: 145–156.

Freud, S. (1915a). Observations on Transference Love (Further Recommendations in the Technique of Psychoanalysis III). *S.E. 12*: 157–171.

Freud, S. (1915b). The Unconscious. *S.E. 14*: 159–204.

Freud, S. (1919a). Lines of Advance in Psycho-Analytic Therapy. *S.E. 17*: 157–168.

Freud, S. (1919b). A Child Is Being Beaten. *S.E. 17*: 175–204.

Freud, S. (1919c). The Uncanny. *S.E. 17*: 217–252.

Freud, S. (1923a). The Ego and the Id. *S.E. 19*: 1–66.

Freud, S. (1923b). Preface to Max Eitingon's Report on the Berlin Psycho-Analytical Policlinic (March 1920 to June 1922). *S.E. 19*: 285.

Freud S. (1933). New Introductory Lectures on Psycho-Analysis. *S.E. 22*: 5–182.

Freud, S., & Breuer, J. (1895). Studies on Hysteria. *S.E. 2*.

Frisch, S., Bleger, L., Séchaud, E. (2010). The Specificity of Psychoanalytic Treatment Today (WPSPTT). *Psychoanalysis in Europe: Bulletin of the European Psychoanalytical Federation 64 (Supplement)*: 81–110.

Gabbard, G.O. (1995). Countertransference: The Emerging Common Ground. *International Journal of Psychoanalysis 76*: 475–485.

Gabbard, G.O. (2000). Disguise or Consent: Problems and Recommendations Concerning the Publication and Presentation of Clinical Material. *International Journal of Psychoanalysis 81*: 1071–1086.

Gediman, H., & Wolkenfield, F. (1980). The Parallelism Phenomenon in Psychoanalysis and Supervision: Its Reconsideration as a Triadic System. *Psychoanalytic Quarterly 49*: 234–255.

Gibeault, A. (1986). La symbolique de l'argent. In: *Chemins de la symbolisation* (pp. 111–143). Paris: Presses Universitaires de France, 2010.
Gibeault, A. (2010). *Chemins de la symbolisation*. Paris: Presses Universitaires de France.
Gibeault, A. (2012a). Commentary to: E. Kestemberg, Well, then, anything new? What the first interview can teach us. In: B. Reith, S. Lagerlöf, P. Crick, M. Møller, E. Skale (Eds.) *Initiating Psychoanalysis: Perspectives*, The New Library of Psychoanalysis Teaching Series (pp. 48–50). London: Routledge, 2012.
Gibeault, A. (2012b). Commentary to: The Analytic Encounter by Jean-Luc Donnet and Michel de M'Uzan. In: B. Reith, S. Lagerlöf, P. Crick, M. Møller, E. Skale (Eds.) *Initiating Psychoanalysis: Perspectives*, The New Library of Psychoanalysis Teaching Series (pp. 120–122). London: Routledge.
Glaser, B., & Strauss, A.L. (1967). *The Discovery of Grounded Theory: Strategies for Qualitative Research*. New York: Aldine de Gruyter.
Green, A. (1975). The Analyst, Symbolisation and Absence in the Analytic Setting (On Changes in Analytic Practice and Analytic Experience). *International Journal of Psychoanalysis 56*: 1–22.
Green, A. (1990). On thirdness. In: *Psychoanalysis: A Paradigm for Clinical Thinking* (pp. 233–277). London: Free Association Books, 2002.
Green, A. (2002). *Key Ideas for a Contemporary Psychoanalysis*. London and New York: Routledge, 2005. [Original French: *Idées directrices pour une psychanalyse contemporaine*. Paris: Presses Universitaires de France.]
Grubrich-Simitis, I. (1997). *Early and Late Freud: Reading Anew. Studies on Hysteria and Moses and Monotheism*. London: Routledge.
Habermas, J. (1984). *The Theory of Communicative Action*, Vol. *1*, T. McCarthy (Trans.), Cambridge: Polity Press.
Harper, D., & Thompson, A. (Eds.) (2012). *Qualitative Research Methods in Mental Health and Psychotherapy: An Introduction for Students and Practitioners*. Chichester, UK: Wiley-Blackwell.
Herron, W.G., & Rouslin Welt, S.R. (1992). *Money Matters*. New York: The Guilford Press.
Hinshelwood, R.D. (2013). *Research on the Couch: Single-Case Studies, Subjectivity and Psychoanalytic Knowledge*. East Sussex: Routledge.
Hinze, E. (2015). What Do We Learn in Psychoanalytic Training? *International Journal of Psychoanalysis 96*: 755–771.
Hirsch, I. (1998). The Concept of Enactment and Theoretical Convergence. *Psychoanalytic Quarterly 67*: 78–101.
Jacobs, T. (1986). On Countertransference Enactments. *Journal of the American Psychoanalytic Association 34*: 289–307.
Jacobs, T. (2001). On Unconscious Communications and Covert Enactments: Some Reflections on Their Role in the Analytic Situation. *Psychoanalytic Inquiry 21*: 4–21.
Joseph, B. (1989). *Psychic Equilibrium and Psychic Change. Selected Papers of Betty Joseph*, Eds. E.B. Spillius & M. Feldman. New Library of Psychoanalysis. London: Routledge.
Junkers, G., Tuckett, D., Zacharisson, A. (2008). To Be or Not to Be a Psychoanalyst: How Do We Know a Candidate is Ready to Qualify? Difficulties and Controversies in Evaluating Psychoanalytic Competence. *Psychoanalytic Inquiry 28*: 288–308.
Kaës, R. (2005). *La parole et le lien: Processus associatifs et travail psychique dans les groupes*, Second edition. Paris: Dunod.
Kahn, L. (2004). La clause d'irréalité. In: *Cures d'enfance* (pp. 71–99). Paris: Gallimard.
Kantrowitz, J.L. (1986). The Role of the Patient–Analyst 'Match' in the Outcome of Psychoanalysis. *Annual of Psychoanalysis 14*: 273–297.

Kantrowitz, J.L. (1993). The Uniqueness of the Patient–Analyst Pair: Approaches for Elucidating the Analyst's Role in the Outcome of Psychoanalysis. *International Journal of Psychoanalysis 74*: 893–904.
Kantrowitz, J.L. (1996). *The Patient's Impact on the Analyst*. Hillsdale, NJ: The Analytic Press.
Kantrowitz, J.L. (2002). The External Observer and the Lens of the Patient Analyst Match. *International Journal of Psychoanalysis 83*: 339–350.
Kestemberg, E. (1981). Le personnage tiers: sa nature, sa fonction. In: *La psychose froide* (pp. 145–177). Paris: Presses Universitaires de France, 2001.
Kestemberg, E. (1985). L'argent dans la cure. In: *Les Cahiers du Centre de Psychanalyse et de Psychothérapie* (pp. 1–29). Association de Santé Mentale de Paris 13th edition, number 11.
Klauber, J. (1972). Personal attitudes to psychoanalytic consultation. In: *Difficulties in the Analytic Encounter* (Chapter 9). London: Free Association Books, Maresfield Library. Reprinted in: B. Reith, S. Lagerlöf, P. Crick, M. Møller, E. Skale (Eds.) *Initiating Psychoanalysis: Perspectives*, The New Library of Psychoanalysis Teaching Series (pp. 63–74). London: Routledge, 2012.
Klauber, J. (1986). Personal attitudes to psychoanalytic consultation. In: *Difficulties in the Analytic Encounter*. London: Free Association Books, Maresfield Library, 1986. Reprinted in: B. Reith, S. Lagerlöf, P. Crick, M. Møller, E. Skale (Eds.) *Initiating Psychoanalysis: Perspectives*, The New Library of Psychoanalysis Teaching Series (pp. 63–74). London: Routledge, 2012.
Klebanow, S., & Lowenkopf, E.L. (1991). *Money and Mind*. New York: Plenum.
Klein, M. (1926). The psychological principles of early analysis. In: *Love, Guilt and Reparation and Other Works (Writings, Vol. 1*, Chap. 6). London: Hogarth, 1975.
Klein, M. (1930). The importance of symbol-formation in the development of the ego. In: *Love, Guilt and Reparation and Other Works (Writings, Vol. 1*, Chap. 12). London: Hogarth, 1975.
Krueger, D.W. (1986). *The Last Taboo: Money as Symbol and Reality in Psychotherapy and Psychoanalysis*. New York: Brunner/ Mazel.
Lagerlöf, S., & Sigrell, B. (1999). A Discussion of Models for the Selection of Patients for Supervised Psychoanalysis. *Journal of Clinical Psychoanalysis 8*: 149–172.
Lagerlöf, S., & Skale, E. (2012). 'Are you a doctor, Sir?': Introduction. In: B. Reith, S. Lagerlöf, P. Crick, M. Møller, E. Skale (Eds.) *Initiating Psychoanalysis: Perspectives*, The New Library of Psychoanalysis Teaching Series (pp. 12–15). London: Routledge, 2012.
Laplanche, J. (1992). Transference: its provocation by the analyst. In: D. Birksted-Breen, S. Flanders, A. Gibeault (Eds.) *Reading French Psychoanalysis*, The New Library of Psychoanalysis Teaching Series (pp. 233–250). Abingdon, UK: Routledge, 2010.
Laplanche, J. (1997). The Theory of Seduction and the Problem of the Other. *International Journal of Psychoanalysis 78*: 663–682.
Laplanche, J., & Pontalis, J.B. (1967). *Vocabulaire de la psychanalyse*. Paris: Presses Universitaires de France.
Leuzinger-Bohleber, M., & Bürgin, D. (2003). Pluralism and unity in psychoanalytic research: some introductory remarks. In: M. Leuzinger-Bohleber, A.U. Dreher, J. Canestri (Eds.) *Pluralism and Unity? Methods of Research in Psychoanalysis* (pp. 1–25). London: International Psychoanalytic Association.
Levine, H.B. (2010). Creating Analysts, Creating Analytic Patients. *International Journal of Psychoanalysis 91*: 1385–1404.
Loewald, H.W. (1960). On the Therapeutic Action of Psycho-analysis. *International Journal of Psychoanalysis 41*: 16–33.
Milner, M. (1952). Aspects of Symbolism in Comprehension of the Not-Self. *International Journal of Psychoanalysis 33*: 181–194.

Mitchell, S.A. (1988). *Relational Concepts in Psychoanalysis: An Integration*. Cambridge, MA: Harvard University Press.
Møller, M. (2014). The Analyst's Anxieties in the First Interview: Barriers Against Analytic Presence. *International Journal of Psychoanalysis 95*: 485–503.
Murdin, L. (2012). *How Money Talks*. London: Karnac.
M'Uzan, M. de (2015). Introduction à la théorie de l'entretien préliminaire. In: *L'inquiétude permanente* (pp. 77–82). Paris: Gallimard.
Norman, J., & Salomonsson, B. (2005). 'Weaving Thoughts': A Method for Presenting and Commenting on Psychoanalytic Case Material in a Group. *International Journal of Psychoanalysis 86*: 1281–1298.
Ogden, T.H. (1986). *The Matrix of the Mind*. Northvale, NJ: Aronson/London: Karnac.
Ogden, T.H. (1989). *The Primitive Edge of Experience*. Northvale, NJ: Aronson/London: Karnac.
Ogden, T.H. (1992). Comments on Transference and Countertransference in the Initial Analytic Meeting. *Psychoanalytic Inquiry 12*: 225–247. Reprinted in: B. Reith, S. Lagerlöf, P. Crick, M. Møller, E. Skale (Eds.) *Initiating Psychoanalysis: Perspectives*, The New Library of Psychoanalysis Teaching Series (pp. 173–188). London: Routledge, 2012.
Ogden, T.H. (1994a). The Analytic Third: Working with Intersubjective Clinical Facts. *International Journal of Psychoanalysis 75*: 3–19.
Ogden, T.H. (1994b). *Subjects of Analysis*. Northvale, NJ: Aronson/London: Karnac.
Ogden, T.H. (1997). *Reverie and Interpretation: Sensing Something Human*. New York: Aronson.
Parsons, M. (2006). The Analyst's Countertransference to the Psychoanalytic Process. *International Journal of Psychoanalysis 87*: 1183–1198.
Parsons, M. (2014). *Living Psychoanalysis: From Theory to Experience*. London: Routledge.
Perelberg, R. (2003). Panel on Acting Out and/or Enactment. *International Journal of Psychoanalysis 84*: 151–155.
Pérez, A., Crick, P., Lawrence, S. (2015). Delving into the 'Emotional Storms': A Thematic Analysis of Psychoanalysts' Initial Consultation Reports. *International Journal of Psychoanalysis 96*: 659–680.
Pérez-Sánchez, A. (2012). *Interview and Indicators in Psychoanalysis and Psychotherapy*. London: Karnac.
Ponsi, M. (2012). Evoluzione del pensiero psicoanalitico. Acting out, agire, enactment. *Rivista di Psicoanalisi 58* (3): 653–670.
Powers, T. (1984). What's It About? *Atlantic Monthly*. January.
Quinodoz, D. (2001). The Psychoanalyst of the Future: Wise Enough to Dare to be Mad at Times. *International Journal of Psychoanalysis 82*: 235–248. Reprinted in: B. Reith, S. Lagerlöf, P. Crick, M. Møller, E. Skale (Eds.) *Initiating Psychoanalysis: Perspectives*, The New Library of Psychoanalysis Teaching Series (pp. 310–327). London: Routledge, 2012.
Quinodoz, D. (2003). *Words That Touch: A Psychoanalyst Learns to Speak*. London and New York: Karnac. [Originally published in French: *Les mots qui touchent: Une psychanalyste apprend à parler*. Paris: Presses Universitaires de France, 2002.]
Racabulto, A. (2012). The Consultation in Psychoanalysis and Its 'Location': Working on the Frontier. Paper presented at *L'assetto mentale dello psicoanalista nella consultazione* [The analyst's mental attitude in consultation], Milan, October 2004. Reprinted in: B. Reith, S. Lagerlöf, P. Crick, M. Møller, E. Skale (Eds.) Initiating Psychoanalysis: Perspectives, The New Library of Psychoanalysis Teaching Series (pp. 245–258). London: Routledge, 2012.
Racker, H. (1968). *Transference and Countertransference*. Madison, CT: International Universities Press.
Reith, B. (2011a). The First Interview: Anxieties and Research about Initiating Psychoanalysis. Paper given to the English Psychoanalytic Society, December 2011.

Reith, B. (2011b). The WPIP Investigative Process: From the Anxiety of the Analytic Couple to That of the Research Team. *Psychoanalysis in Europe: Bulletin of the European Psychoanalytical Federation 65*: 57–60.
Reith, B. (2012). What Interpsychic Conditions Lead to Full Analysis? Some Findings from the Working Party on Initiating Psychoanalysis. Part 1: The Analyst's Internal Frame. *Psychoanalysis in Europe: Bulletin of the European Psychoanalytical Federation 66*: 94–102.
Reith, B. (2013). Complementary models of the mind in Freud's *The Unconscious*? In: S. Akhtar, M.K. O'Neil (Eds.) *Freud's 'The Unconscious'. Contemporary Freud: Turning Points and Critical Issues* (pp. 179–202). London: Karnac.
Reith, B. (2015). The First Interview: Anxieties and Research on Initiating Psychoanalysis. *International Journal of Psychoanalysis 96*: 637–657.
Reith, B. (2016). Discussion of 'Listening and Interacting through Different Filters: Sessions with Nina'. *International Journal of Psychoanalysis 97*: 155–166.
Reith, B., Boots, J., Crick, P., Gibeault, A., Jaffè, R., Lagerlöf, S., Møller, M., Skale, E., Vermote, R., Wegner, P. (2010). The Specific Dynamics of Initial Interviews: Switching the Level, or Opening up a Meaning Space? Report on Phase 1 of the WPIP Study of Initial Interviews. *Psychoanalysis in Europe: Bulletin of the European Psychoanalytical Federation 64 (Supplement)*: 57–80.
Reith, B., Lagerlöf, S., Crick, P., Møller, M., Skale, E. (Eds.) (2012). *Initiating Psychoanalysis: Perspectives*, The New Library of Psychoanalysis Teaching Series. London: Routledge.
Ritchie, J., Lewis, J., McNaughton Nicholls, C., Ormston, R. (Eds.) (2014). *Qualitative Research Practice: A Guide for Social Science Students and Researchers*, Second edition. London: Sage.
Rizzuto, A. (2001). Metaphors of a Bodily Mind. *Journal of the American Psychoanalytic Association 49*: 535–568.
Rizzuto, A. (2009). Metaphoric Process and Metaphor: The Dialectics of Shared Analytic Experience. *Psychoanalytic Inquiry 29*: 18–29.
Rothstein, A. (1994). A Perspective on Doing a Consultation and Making the Recommendation of Analysis to a Prospective Analysand. *Psychoanalytic Quarterly 63*: 680–695. Reprinted in: B. Reith, S. Lagerlöf, P. Crick, M. Møller, E. Skale (Eds.) *Initiating Psychoanalysis: Perspectives*, The New Library of Psychoanalysis Teaching Series (pp. 281–291). London: Routledge, 2012.
Rothstein, A. (1998a). *Psychoanalytic Technique and the Creation of Analytic Patients*. Madison, CT: International Universities Press.
Rothstein, A. (1998b). On analyst's evaluating, diagnosing, and prognosticating. In: *Psychoanalytic Technique and the Creation of Analytic Patients* (pp. 59–75). Madison, CT: International Universities Press.
Rothstein, A. (2002). Reflections on Creative Aspects of Psychoanalytic Diagnosing. *Psychoanalytic Quarterly 71*: 301–326.
Roussillon, R. (2006). Pluralité de l'appropriation subjective. In: F. Richard, S. Wainrib (Eds.) *La subjectivation* (pp. 59–80). Paris: Dunod.
Salomonsson, B. (2012). Psychoanalytic Case Presentations in a Weaving Thoughts Group: On Countertransference and Group Dynamics. *International Journal of Psychoanalysis 93*: 917–937.
Sandler, J. (1976). Countertransference and Role-Responsiveness. *International Review of Psycho-Analysis 3*: 43–47.
Sandler, J. (1983). Reflections on Some Relations between Psychoanalytic Concepts and Psychoanalytic Practice. *International Journal of Psychoanalysis 64*: 35–45.
Sandler, J. (1993). On Communication from Patient to Analyst: Not Everything Is Projective Identification. *International Journal of Psychoanalysis 74*: 1097–1107.

Sandler, J., Dare, C., Holder, A. (1973). *The Patient and the Analyst: The Basis of the Psychoanalytic Process*. London: Allen & Unwin.
Schachter, J. (2012). The Beginning and the End of the Beginning. Psychoanalysis in Europe. *Bulletin of the European Psychoanalytical Federation 66*: 148–155.
Searles, H.F. (1955). The informational value of the supervisor's emotional experiences. In: *Collected Papers on Schizophrenia and Related Subjects* (pp. 157–177). New York: International University Press.
Segal, H. (1997). The uses and abuses of countertransference. In: J. Steiner (Ed.) *Psychoanalysis, Literature and War. Papers 1972–1995*, The New Library of Psychoanalysis (pp. 111–119). London: Routledge.
Silverman, D. (Ed.) (2011). *Qualitative Research: Issues of Theory, Methods and Practice*, Third edition. London: Sage.
Skale, E. (2012). Commentary on: Argelander, H. (1978). The psychoanalytic initial interview and its method. A postscript to Freud's case 'Katharina'. In: B. Reith, S. Lagerlöf, P. Crick, M. Møller, E. Skale (Eds.) *Initiating Psychoanalysis: Perspectives*, The New Library of Psychoanalysis Teaching Series (pp. 24–25). London: Routledge, 2012.
Steiner, J. (2006). Interpretative Enactments and the Analytic Setting. *International Journal of Psychoanalysis 87*: 315–320.
Stern, D. (2004). The Eye Sees Itself: Dissociation, Enactment, and the Achievement of Conflict. *Contemporary Psychoanalysis 40*: 197–237.
Stolorow, R.D. (1990). Converting Psychotherapy to Psychoanalysis: A Critique of the Underlying Assumptions. *Psychoanalytic Inquiry 10*: 119–130.
Sullivan, H.S. (1954). *The Psychiatric Interview*. New York: Norton.
Symington, N. (1990). The Possibility of Human Freedom and Its Transmission (with Particular Reference to the Thought of Bion). *International Journal of Psychoanalysis 71*: 95–106.
Tuckett, D. (1994). Developing a Grounded Hypothesis to Understand a Clinical Process: The Role of Conceptualisation in Validation. *International Journal of Psychoanalysis 75*: 1159–1180.
Tuckett, D. (1997). Mutual enactment in the psychoanalytic situation. In: J. Ahumada, et al. (Eds.) *The Perverse Transference and Other Matters: Essays in Honor of R. Horacio Etchegoyen* (pp. 203–216). New York, London: Aronson.
Tuckett, D. (2002). Presidential Address: The New Style Conference and Developing a Peer Culture in European Psychoanalysis. *European Psychoanalytical Federation Bulletin 56*: 32–46.
Tuckett, D. (2003). Presidential Address: A Ten Year European Scientific Initiative. *European Psychoanalytical Federation Bulletin 57*: 7–22.
Tuckett, D. (2004). Presidential Address: Building a Psychoanalysis Based on Confidence in What We Do. *European Psychoanalytical Federation Bulletin 58*: 5–20.
Tuckett, D. (2005). Does Anything Go? *International Journal of Psychoanalysis 86*: 31–49.
Tuckett, D. (2011). Inside and Outside the Window: Some Fundamental Elements in the Theory of Psychoanalytic Technique. *International Journal of Psychoanalysis 92*: 1367–1390.
Tuckett, D. (2016). 2000–2004: The new scientific policy and the ten year scientific initiative. In: S. Frisc, L. Bleger, U. Burkert, A.M. Janssen, E. Schmid-Gloor, F. Ylander (Eds.) *50 Years of the European Psychoanalytical Federation*. Giessen: Psychosozial-Verlag.
Tuckett, D., Basile, R., Birksted-Breen, D., Böhm, T., Denis, P., Ferro, A., Hinz, H., Jemstedt, A., Mariotti, P., Schubert, J. (2008). *Psychoanalysis Comparable and Incomparable. The Evolution of a Method to Describe and Compare Psychoanalytic Approaches*. The New Library of Psychoanalysis. London: Routledge.
Tuckman, B., & Jenson, M. (1977). Stages of Small Group Development Revisited. *Group and Organisational Studies 2* (4): 419–427.

Tweed, A., & Charmaz, K. (2012). Grounded theory methods for mental health practitioners. In: D. Harper, A. Thompson (Eds.) *Qualitative Research Methods in Mental Health and Psychotherapy: An Introduction for Students and Practitioners* (pp. 131–146). Chichester, UK: Wiley-Blackwell.
Varvin, S. (2003). Psychotherapy with a victim of extreme violence: clinical case report and quantitative analysis. In: M. Leuzinger-Bohleber, A.U. Dreher, J. Canestri (Eds.) *Pluralism and Unity? Methods of Research in Psychoanalysis* (pp. 168–183). London: IPA.
Vermote, R. (2012). Paper given at a panel of the Working Party on Initiating Psychoanalysis, EPF Conference, Paris, 2012. Published as Vermote, R. (2012). What Interpsychic Conditions Lead to Full Analysis? Some Findings from the Working Party on Initiating Psychoanalysis. Part 2: Preliminary Sessions: The Resistance of the Patient is the Resistance of the Analyst. *Psychoanalysis in Europe: Bulletin of the European Psychoanalytical Federation 66*: 103–106.
Viderman, S. (1970). *La construction de l'espace analytique*. Paris: Denoël.
Viderman, S. (1979). The Analytic Space: Meaning and Problems. *Psychoanalytic Quarterly 4*: 257–291.
Wainrib, S. (2012). Is Psychoanalysis a Matter of Subjectivation? *International Journal of Psychoanalysis 93*: 1115–1135.
Wallerstein, R.S. (1990). Psychoanalysis: The Common Ground. *International Journal of Psychoanalysis 71*: 3–20
Wallerstein, R.S. (1994). Psychotherapy Research and Its Implications for a Theory of Therapeutic Change: A Forty-year Overview. *The Psychoanalytic Study of the Child 49*: 120–141.
Wallerstein, R.S. (2009). What Kind of Research in Psychoanalytic Science? *International Journal of Psychoanalysis 90*: 109–133.
Wegner, P. (1992). The opening scene and the importance of the countertransference in the initial psychoanalytic interview. In: B. Reith, S. Lagerlöf, P. Crick, M. Møller, E. Skale (Eds.) *Initiating Psychoanalysis: Perspectives*, The New Library of Psychoanalysis Teaching Series (pp. 225–242). London: Routledge, 2012. [Original German: Zur Bedeutung der Gegenübertragung im psychoanalytischen Erstinterview. *Psyche 46*: 286–307.]
Wilkinson, S. (2011). Analysing focus group data. In: D. Silverman (Ed.) *Qualitative Research: Issues of Theory, Methods and Practice*, Third edition (pp. 168–184). London: Sage.
Wille, R. (2008). Psychoanalytic Identity: Psychoanalysis as an Internal Object. *The Psychoanalytic Quarterly 77*: 1193–1229.
Wille, R. (2012). The Analyst's Trust in Psychoanalysis and the Communication of That Trust in Initial Interviews. *Psychoanalytic Quarterly 81* (4): 875–904.
Winnicott, D.W. (1971a). *Playing and Reality*. London: Tavistock.
Winnicott, D.W. (1971b). *Therapeutic Consultations in Child Psychiatry*. The International Psycho-Analytical Library *87*: 1–398. London: The Hogarth Press and the Psychoanalytic Institute.

CASE INDEX

Case Vignette	**Initials**	**Pages**
A Mysterious Arrival	Ms. M.	129–132, 141
Looking for the Right Place	Ms. N.	132–133
The Elegant Woman	Mrs. H.	112–115
The Handsome Man on Crutches	Mr. A.	10–21, 44, 62, 63, 71, 72, 74, 82, 83, 123
The Hopeful Man	Mr. L.	129, 133, 140, 141, 143–144, 147
The Maiden Challenged	Ms. E.	97–102
The Man in the Middle	Mr. J.	118–120
The Man with a Grievance	Mr. K.	120–123, 124, 134, 137
The Man Who Feared to Play	Mr. P.	141, 145
The Man Who Seemed Muddled	Mr. O.	139
The Mother's Son	Mr. C.	62, 64–70, 71, 72, 73–74, 80, 81–82, 84, 85, 86–87, 143
The Promising Patient	Ms. I.	116–118, 124
The Self-Assured Academic	Ms. B.	48–58, 62, 69, 71, 72, 73, 74, 80, 84
The Unfortunate Lover	Mr. Q.	154–168
The Wary Scientist	Mr. F.	106–108, 138, 141
The Weaver Unravelled	Ms. G.	108–112, 124
The Woman Who Planned	Ms. D.	91–97

GENERAL INDEX

abandonment 52, 53, 110–111, 119
abuse 11–12, 19, 130, 142
acting in 70, 150, 151, 152, 153
acting out 70, 90, 151, 155–156
actualization 151, 152
analytic couple 2, 4, 21, 171, 181; dialogue 8; enactments 46, 150; *The Handsome Man on Crutches* 20; psychoanalytic space 77, 79; *The Self-Assured Academic* 54; 'switching the level' 28; unconscious dynamics 36, 70; unconscious storm 87; vicissitudes of the 14, 76, 87
analytic relationship 20, 28, 53, 73; consultation 148; 'internal frame' 15; interpreting the transference 84; 'opening scene' 103
analytic third 78, 79
analyzability 2, 38, 56, 123, 182
anger: *The Hopeful Man* 143–144; *The Man in the Middle* 119; *The Mother's Son* 68, 74; *The Self-Assured Academic* 51, 54
anxiety: ability to tolerate 82, 174; containment by the analyst 72, 74; countertransference 172; *The Elegant Woman* 113; *The Handsome Man on Crutches* 18–19, 20; interpreting the transference 84, 141, 145–146; *The Man Who Feared to Play* 145; *The Man with a Grievance* 121; *The Mother's Son* 64, 68; *A Mysterious Arrival* 130–131; *The Promising Patient* 116–117, 118; *The Self-Assured Academic* 52, 58; unconscious dynamics 81; *The Unfortunate Lover* 155–156, 162–163, 164; of the unknown 91; *The Wary Scientist* 106, 107–108; *The Woman Who Planned* 93
Argelander, H. 9, 21, 47, 90, 141, 153
assessment 4, 27, 28, 122, 135

Basile, R. 81
bi-personal field 79–80, 85
Bion, W.R. 14, 36, 75–76, 77, 88
Birksted-Breen, D. 78
Bohleber, W. 151, 152–153, 155, 160
Bollas, C. 103, 167, 168
Bolognini, S. 78, 127, 136, 148, 167, 168, 176
Botella, Sara and César 59
Breuer, J. 176–177
Britton, R. 78, 114–115
Bronstein, C. 172
Busch, Fred 178

case reviews 34, 35, 40
castration anxiety 164
Civitarese, G. 166
Clinical Workshops 3, 5, 23–24, 33, 80–81, 183; aim of 26; analysts' qualities 174; discussion questions 188–191; *The Elegant Woman* 113; enactments 175; envious reactions 115; exploratory processes 179; group processes 40–44, 46, 47, 60–61; *The Handsome Man on Crutches* 16–18, 20; *The Hopeful Man* 144; *The Maiden Challenged* 100, 101; *The Man in the Middle* 119; *The Man with a Grievance* 120, 137; procedures 29–32, 185–187; psychoanalytic knowledge 179–180; *The Self-Assured Academic* 53–55, 57–58; three-stage model 6, 59; unconscious dynamics 71, 171–172; *The Unfortunate Lover* 155, 164, 166; *The Wary Scientist* 107

Clinics 127–149; Clinic as third 128, 129, 142, 144, 148–149
collusion 112, 115, 125, 152; collusive or narcissistic dynamics 105; *The Elegant Woman* 113; *The Man in the Middle* 119; *The Promising Patient* 116, 117; *The Unfortunate Lover* 161
'common ground' 26–27
communication 68, 72, 173; analytic dialogue 124; scenic communication 172; semiotic communication 172; 'switching the level' 160, 170; unconscious storm 76
'concave' and 'convex' stances 86–87, 136, 137, 167–168, 176
constructivist grounded theory 26
consultation 5, 104–105, 124–125, 170; aim of 135; 'consultation for referral' settings 29, 30, 32, 85, 125, 177–178, 183; enactments 160; institutional settings 128, 135–149; *Looking for the Right Place* 133; *The Man in the Middle* 118–119; with peers 15, 167, 179; *The Promising Patient* 116; technique 173; 'trial analysis' 182; *The Wary Scientist* 106–107, 108
containment 46, 58, 72, 74–75, 77; institutional 132–133; *The Woman Who Planned* 95, 96
countertransference 2, 7, 167; awareness of 172; containment by the analyst 74; enactments 46, 70, 150–154; Freud 9; *The Handsome Man on Crutches* 13, 14; *Looking for the Right Place* 132; *The Maiden Challenged* 98; *The Man in the Middle* 119, 120; *The Man with a Grievance* 122; *The Mother's Son* 64–65; mutual idealization 105; 'opening scene' 91; 'pre-countertransference' 141, 155; psychoanalytic space 77, 78; reflexive perspective 26; 'storm' of countertransference pressures 160; unconscious dynamics 36, 48, 62, 75; *The Unfortunate Lover* 161, 165, 166
Crick, P. 136–137, 181–182

Dantlgraber, J. 78
data analysis 33–35
defences 20–21, 115, 180; *The Handsome Man on Crutches* 13; *The Man in the Middle* 119; narcissistic 55; phallic 45, 56, 57, 58, 164, 165–166; 'pre-transference' 155; *The Promising Patient* 118; *The Self-Assured Academic* 58; superego 18, 19; *The Weaver Unravelled* 111
defensive group functions 45, 46
denial 36, 76, 171
dependencies 65, 66, 67
dialogue 7, 8, 23, 124, 169; *The Elegant Woman* 114, 115; *The Promising Patient* 116; 'trial analysis' 182; *The Wary Scientist* 108
'diffraction' 41, 43
Donnet, J.L. 143, 148, 153
dreams 169; *The Handsome Man on Crutches* 12, 17; *The Maiden Challenged* 99, 100, 101; *The Man with a Grievance* 121, 134; *The Promising Patient* 116; *The Self-Assured Academic* 52–53, 57; *The Unfortunate Lover* 156, 162–166, 168; *The Wary Scientist* 106; *The Weaver Unravelled* 110–111
drives 19
drug use 65, 106

eating disorders 97, 98, 101
'economic' model 145, 146–147
ego 47, 86, 146, 153
Elzer, M. 90
emotional resonance 41, 95–96
emotional storm 75–76, 88, 104, 124, 142, 149
emotions 152
empathy 168
enactment 7, 15, 36–37, 59, 81, 126, 142, 171, 173, 180; collusive 105; countertransference 70, 150–154, 172; 'enactment' mode of thinking 174; group processes 40, 45–47; *The Handsome Man on Crutches* 13, 18–19, 20–21; *The Man Who Seemed Muddled* 139; *The Man with a Grievance* 122, 123; *The Mother's Son* 65–66, 68–69, 74; mutual 70, 72, 74, 76, 89, 102, 111–112, 118, 139, 153; 'opening scene' 91, 102–103; phallic 56; *The Promising Patient* 118; proto-representations 70; unconscious dynamics 87, 175; *The Unfortunate Lover* 155, 160–161, 166; *The Wary Scientist* 138; *The Weaver Unravelled* 109–110, 111–112; *The Woman Who Planned* 92, 93, 96, 97
Enckell, H. 147

ethical issues 147
European Psychoanalytical Federation (EPF) 1, 3, 4, 22–23, 24, 30, 39
European Scientific Initiative 3, 4, 22–23, 31
expressive group functions 45, 46

Faimberg, H. 83
Fairbairn, W.R.D. 102, 151
fantasies: analyst's 81; group processes 41, 45; interpreting the transference 84; 'opening scene' 89, 90–91, 97; 'pre-countertransference' 141; *The Woman Who Planned* 93, 94–95; *see also* phantasies
fathers: *The Handsome Man on Crutches* 10–11; *The Maiden Challenged* 98, 99, 101; *The Mother's Son* 68, 69, 74; *The Self-Assured Academic* 51–52, 54, 55, 56; *The Unfortunate Lover* 165; *The Wary Scientist* 106, 107–108
Ferro, Antonino 75
fields 7, 79
financial issues 37, 133–134
Forel, Auguste 176
free association 24, 31, 35, 41–42, 47, 59, 142, 174
Freud, Sigmund 9, 12, 13, 21, 62, 88–89; enactment 150–151; 'Free Clinics' 127; psychoanalytic space 77; 'topographical' model 146; 'trial analysis' 182; 'uncanny' experiences 80

Gerlach, A. 90
Green, A. 78, 155
grounded theory 26
group processes 15, 18, 31, 40–47, 60–61, 101, 107

homosexuality 11
hypotheses 25, 26, 29, 38

id 146
idealization 36, 105, 144, 148, 171; *The Elegant Woman* 112, 113, 114, 115; mutual 105, 112, 116, 117
identity confusion 76
identity of experience 82
implicit theories 16, 23, 31, 43, 83, 179–180, 186
indication 2, 8, 182
individualized approach 182
initiating psychoanalysis 1, 5, 28, 35–36, 87, 170, 181–182; consultation 104–105, 125; *The Elegant Woman* 114; institutional settings 7, 128; 'opening scene' 7
institutional settings 7, 29, 37–38, 127–149
inter-psychic dynamics 115
inter-psychic field 46, 79, 80
inter-psychic perspective 5
inter-psychic processing 180
inter-psychic reality 9
'internal frame' 15, 36, 123, 166, 174–177; analytic stance 171; *The Handsome Man on Crutches* 19; *The Man in the Middle* 120; oscillations 173; unconscious storm 124
internal objects 45, 69, 70, 72, 82, 179
intersubjectivity 76, 78, 79, 180
intra-psychic conflict 50
intra-psychic processing 180
intra-psychic reality 9
intrusion: *The Handsome Man on Crutches* 16, 17–18, 19, 20, 44, 63; *The Maiden Challenged* 101; *The Mother's Son* 69; *A Mysterious Arrival* 130; patient's anxiety 146; *The Self-Assured Academic* 54, 57; *The Unfortunate Lover* 164, 165, 166; *The Wary Scientist* 107–108

Jacobs, Theodore 151, 161
Joseph, B. 151–152

Kantrowitz, Judy 2
Katharina 9, 13, 21
Kestemberg E. 149
Klein, M. 77
knowledge 179–181, 186

Laplanche, J. 142, 151
Levine, H.B. 86, 147, 181
live experience 177
Loewald, H.W. 82
low-fee option 107, 120, 121, 122, 133–134

meaning 77, 79, 104, 172–173, 174
'meaningful common formulations' 28, 36, 37, 63, 73
'medical model' 136
merging 95
meta-perspective 23

metacommunications 152
metaphor 7, 28, 50, 75, 78, 88–89, 97, 103, 172
Mitchell, Stephen 173
mothers: *The Elegant Woman* 113, 114; *The Maiden Challenged* 98, 100; *The Man in the Middle* 119; *The Mother's Son* 67–68, 69, 74; *The Promising Patient* 116, 117; *The Self-Assured Academic* 49, 51, 52, 55, 56–57; *The Unfortunate Lover* 158–159, 161, 162–164; *The Wary Scientist* 107–108
M'Uzan, Michel de 139–140

narcissism 21, 125, 140, 142; *The Elegant Woman* 112, 113, 114; *The Man in the Middle* 119, 120; *The Man with a Grievance* 134; seduction 143, 144; *The Self-Assured Academic* 55; *The Unfortunate Lover* 165
negative capability 172–173
neutrality 172, 177

object relations 45, 56–57, 71, 89, 91, 94, 102
'observing' third 149
oedipal conflicts 72
oedipal interaction 112
oedipal phantasies 18, 19
oedipal process 165
Ogden, Thomas 75, 77–78, 79, 89, 178
'opening scene' 7, 71, 88–103, 130, 141, 154–155
'otherness' 81

panic attacks 67
parallel process 18, 46–47, 48, 58
paranoid tendencies 131
participant-observer position 83, 173, 174
patient characteristics 2, 5, 8, 27, 104, 135, 181, 182
Pérez, A. 137–138
Pérez-Sánchez, Antonio 2
persecutory projections 130, 131–132
phallic defences 45, 56, 57, 58, 164, 165–166
phantasies 36, 45, 71, 169; communication of 72, 172; *The Handsome Man on Crutches* 13, 18, 19; *The Mother's Son* 69, 85; 'opening scene' 91; 'pre-transference' 155; 'seduction by the person' 85; *The Self-Assured Academic* 53, 54, 56, 80; 'switching the level' 63; 'uncanny' experiences 80; *see also* fantasies
'phoric' function 45
physical distance 65
play 77
pleasure 178
Ponsi, M. 152
Pontalis, J.B. 151
pre-analytic scene 64
'pre-countertransference' 141, 155
'pre-transference' 12, 90–91, 92, 140, 155
preconscious dynamics 6, 59, 60
primary process 31, 42, 44, 172, 176
'private' settings 29, 30, 32, 85, 127, 147–148, 149, 183
processes 27, 176, 180; *see also* group processes
projective identification 82, 87, 152; *The Handsome Man on Crutches* 18; *The Maiden Challenged* 100, 101; *The Mother's Son* 68–69, 72; unconscious storm 76; *The Woman Who Planned* 96
pseudo-analysis 55, 58
psycho-drama 59, 139
psychoanalytic method 7, 8, 178; *see also* technique
psychoanalytic space 6, 15, 36–37, 61, 76–80, 87, 181; analyst's internal frame 176; borders 167; discussion questions 189; institutional settings 149; making space 167–168, 169; *The Mother's Son* 69; 'seduction by the method' 85; third-person perspective 83; unconscious storm 86, 171
psychoanalytic subcultures 3, 5, 22–23, 105, 123, 124, 125
psychosexual levels 19
psychotherapy 122, 123, 183

qualitative research 3, 6, 25–26
quantitative research 24, 25

Racalbuto, Agostino 75, 137, 168
reality-testing 42
referrals 4, 23, 125–126; 'consultation for referral' settings 29, 30, 32, 85, 125, 177–178, 183; institutional settings 7, 128, 147–148; interpreting the transference 146; *The Maiden Challenged* 97, 98, 101–102
reflective processes 42–43, 47, 59, 174

reflexive perspective 26, 165
rejection 54, 110, 111, 159
relational conflict 173
repetition 89, 102, 150–151, 153, 155, 158; *see also* enactment
representation 70, 86, 87, 103, 150; dreams 163; enactments 150, 153; language of the senses 161; psychoanalytic space 79; 'topographical' model 146
research: psychoanalytic 3, 25–26, 58–60, 179–181; qualitative 3, 6, 25–26; three-stage model 6, 48, 58–60, 90, 93
resistance 2, 74, 124, 142, 177
reverie 41, 75, 77, 79, 82, 95–96
role-responsiveness 70, 72, 76, 87, 152, 153
Rothstein, Arthur 2, 115, 137, 181

sadomasochism 118–119, 120
Sandler, Joseph 151, 152
'scenic function' 47
secondary process 31, 42, 44, 172, 176
seduction: *The Handsome Man on Crutches* 16, 17; *The Man Who Feared to Play* 145; meaning of 142; *The Mother's Son* 64, 66, 68–69; *A Mysterious Arrival* 131; narcissistic 143, 144; by 'the person' and by 'the method' 85, 133, 142–143, 144, 178; *The Unfortunate Lover* 159, 161, 164; *The Weaver Unravelled* 110; *The Woman Who Planned* 93
Segal, H. 78
self-analysis 78, 153, 167
self-destructiveness 16, 17, 68
self-knowledge 73
self-observation 82–83
senses, language of the 161–162
sexuality 12, 17, 19
Shakespeare, William 88
silence 139–140
sociocultural issues 37
space, making 167–168, 169; *see also* psychoanalytic space
splitting 72
spontaneous elaboration 82
'staging' 47
Stern, D. 102, 153
Stolorow, R.D. 125
'storming' 44
subcultures, psychoanalytic 5, 123, 124, 125
subjective experience 78, 79–80, 138, 164, 178–179
suicide 50, 54, 55, 56, 94, 121
superego 18, 19, 20, 143, 146, 177
supervision 167, 179
'switching the level' 14–15, 28–29, 35–37, 63, 72–73, 104, 170–172; analytic dialogue 124; discussion questions 189; initiating psychoanalysis 87; *The Mother's Son* 69, 74; opening psychoanalytic space 77; *The Self-Assured Academic* 50; unconscious storm 86; *The Unfortunate Lover* 160; *The Wary Scientist* 107–108; *The Woman Who Planned* 96
symbolization 59, 70, 73, 79, 150; enactments 153; proto-symbolization 47; unconscious conflicts 62; *The Woman Who Planned* 96

technique 21, 80–81, 140–146, 173, 177–178; *see also* psychoanalytic method
theory 83, 104, 137, 174, 177–178
third: analytic 78, 79, 179; Clinic as 128, 129, 142, 144, 148–149; concrete or symbolic 36; *The Elegant Woman* 114; 'observing' 149; 'third object' 141, 149; 'third position' 83, 105, 108, 111, 124, 139; virtual 7, 149
third-person perspective 42–43, 78, 82–83, 178–179
three-stage model 48, 58–60, 90, 93
time, giving 167–168, 169
'topographical' model 145, 146–147
training cases 136, 137, 138, 141, 147
transference: *The Elegant Woman* 114; enactments 46; Fairbairn 102; Freud 9, 89; *The Handsome Man on Crutches* 11, 13, 14, 19; institutional settings 145, 148; interpretation of 84–85, 140, 141, 145–146; *The Man in the Middle* 119; *The Man Who Feared to Play* 145; *The Man with a Grievance* 121, 122; *The Mother's Son* 66, 69, 85; mutual idealization 105; 'opening scene' 7; 'pre-transference' 12, 90–91, 92, 140, 155; psychoanalytic space 77, 78; reflexive perspective 26; *The Self-Assured Academic* 50–51, 53, 54, 56–57, 84; 'storm' of transference pressures 160; 'topographical' model 146; 'transferable'

148; unconscious dynamics 36, 48, 62, 75, 171; *The Unfortunate Lover* 161, 164, 165; *The Weaver Unravelled* 109; Winnicott 126; *The Woman Who Planned* 92, 94
transitional space 77, 92
transpsychic dynamics 80
trauma 20
treatment recommendation 27, 37–38, 125–126, 181–182, 183; analyst's characteristics 105, 175; *The Elegant Woman* 115; institutional settings 147–148; *The Man with a Grievance* 120
'trial analysis' 182
triangulation 21, 42–43, 83, 105, 138, 178–179; *The Elegant Woman* 114; empathy and 168; envious reactions 115; institutional settings 132, 133; *The Man Who Seemed Muddled* 139; *The Mother's Son* 74; *The Self-Assured Academic* 53, 57; triangular space 78; *The Unfortunate Lover* 165
Tuckett, David 3, 112, 153
'two-track' perspective 86

unconscious conflicts 28, 36, 62, 70, 71–72, 170–171; analyst's enactments 153; 'opening scene' 7; 'topographical' model 146
unconscious dynamics 5, 21, 27, 36–37, 63–70, 87, 170, 171–172; analytic dialogue 124; awareness and elaboration 72–74; containment by the analyst 74–75; discussion questions 190–191; *The Elegant Woman* 113; enactments 175; group processes 18, 40, 46, 47; implicit knowledge 179–180; institutional settings 149; mode of expression 72; onset 71; 'opening scene' 91; origin and content 71–72; *The Self-Assured Academic* 56; as source of anxiety 81; three-stage model 6, 48, 58–59, 60; use of the term 62; *The Wary Scientist* 106, 107–108; *The Weaver Unravelled* 111
unconscious reality 9, 14, 15
unconscious storm 14–15, 17–18, 36–39, 87, 104, 171; analytic dialogue 124; Clinic consultations 137; concept of 75–76; discussion questions 189; exploratory process 61; *The Maiden Challenged* 101; transference and countertransference pressures 160; 'weathering' the storm 15, 82, 86, 95, 132, 189; *The Weaver Unravelled* 111; *The Woman Who Planned* 93–94, 95, 96
unthought known 80, 103
unthought unknown 20

Vermote, R. 124
vicissitudes of the analytic couple 14, 76, 87
Viderman, S. 77, 79
violence: *The Handsome Man on Crutches* 10–11, 12, 14, 15, 16, 17; *The Maiden Challenged* 99, 100, 101; *The Self-Assured Academic* 54
virtual third 7, 149

'weaving thoughts' method 24
Wegner, P. 78, 82, 141
Winnicott, D.W. 77, 126
Working Party on Initiating Psychoanalysis (WPIP) 1–6, 24–25, 27, 81, 104, 183; analysts' qualities 174; data analysis 33–35; discussion questions 188–191; *The Elegant Woman* 113, 114; enactments 175; envious reactions 115; exploratory processes 179; group processes 40–45, 47, 60–61; *The Handsome Man on Crutches* 18–20; *The Hopeful Man* 143–144; hypothesis testing 38; institutional settings 128, 147, 148; *The Man in the Middle* 119, 120; *The Man with a Grievance* 120, 122, 123, 137; metaphor 88; 'opening scene' 90, 91; procedures 29–32, 185–186; psychoanalytic knowledge 180; *The Self-Assured Academic* 55–58; study phases 32–33; three-stage model 6, 59–60; unconscious dynamics 71, 171–172; *The Unfortunate Lover* 155; *The Wary Scientist* 107